Copyright © 2022 Tim Marczenko

All Rights Reserved. No part of this publication may be reproduced, stored in a retrieval system, or transmitted, in any form or in any means – by electronic, mechanical, photocopying, recording or otherwise – without prior written permission from author.

Although the author has made every effort to ensure the accuracy and completeness of the information contained in this book, we assume no responsibility for errors, inaccuracies, omissions or any other inconsistency herein. Any slights of persons, places, companies or organization are unintentional.

GONE COLD: DEATH AND DISAPPEARANCES IN THE NORTHWOODS

Library and Archives of Canada
ISBN 978-1-7781004-0-6

Non-fiction

Developmental editing by Jennifer Marczenko
Copy editing by Britanie Wilson

If you enjoyed this book, please leave a review.

GONE COLD

Death and Disappearances
in the Northwoods

TIM MARCZENKO

You live only as long as the last person
who remembers you.
— Unknown

To the people in this book:

May history age you well,
May your footprints never fade,
As you wander in infinity.

Contents

Acknowledgements i
Foreword by The Honourable Gloria J. Epstein 1
Introduction: Awaken into Darkness 3

Chapter 1. The Missing Person Problem 7
Chapter 2. So Others May Live 14
Chapter 3. The Freedom of Information Fabrication 28
Chapter 4. Vital Vachon 45
Chapter 5. Sander Lingman 54
Chapter 6. Geraldine Huggan 77
Chapter 7. Pierre Michaud 112
Chapter 8. George Weeden and Merle Newcombe 117
Chapter 9. Agnes May Appleyard 134
Chapter 10. When No One Is Looking 154
Chapter 11. Who Do You Think We Are? 162
Chapter 12. Forbidden Theory 178
Chapter 13. Leaving No Trace 196

Afterword 209
Appendix A 214
Appendix B 218
Appendix C 222
Endnotes 225
Bibliography 230

ACKNOWLEDGEMENTS

Like many young people, I was enamoured with the TV series *Unsolved Mysteries*. Every week I would look forward to Robert Stack creeping out of the fog to share a true story that would almost certainly stick with me days after. To this day, his words still echo in my head, and I sometimes repeat them aloud: "Perhaps, even you could solve a mystery." I never really believed that I could. Most of the stories were from American cities that I never have any connection to, yet each week I kept coming back. Years later, here I am, trying to solve those mysteries that have lingered since childhood.

The key to many mysteries is locked in the past, and I was fortunate enough to connect and converse with many who have access to such time capsules. The information comes in tiny pieces that slowly build into a fragmented story of what happened. These tidbits are found anywhere from archives to attics. The following libraries and museums were integral in preserving some of these pieces.

The Archives of Ontario was a terrific resource and allowed me the use of police journals, court records and photographs to retell some lost history with great accuracy.

Thank you to Michael deJong, Trevor and the staff at the Thunder Bay Museum, and to Sara Janes of Lakehead University, for kindly digging up and scanning old newspaper articles that helped to piece together a disappearance from 1960. Likewise, assistance from the Brodie Resource Library, Greater Sudbury Public Library and the Timmins Public Library were very appreciated. Bonnie has been open and helpful during the process and has turned out to be quite the genealogy detective.

Special credit goes to the University of Manitoba Archives and Special Collections for use of the *The Winnipeg Tribune* and priceless photographs. The *Winnipeg Free Press* for their cooperation and for capturing a grim history. Harry Goodwin for providing a local perspective.

A special thank you to Darren and the beautiful people of Winnipeg who helped me find something equivalent to closure during one of these investigations. I had many Winnipeggers happily willing to walk through a cemetery for me, but eventually Darren was chosen to do it. I am grateful to Dorothy Kennedy and Deb Cantrell, daughter and granddaughter of Harry Hawes, who were incredibly kind to me and shared not only photographs, but Harry's incredible letter. I am forever thankful to the Hawes family for their generosity in allowing me to share this letter, and for understanding the importance of it after all these years. It is a piece of the puzzle that many of us were looking for and they have graciously provided it. I'm grateful for the use of the Johnson poem, reprinted with permission from *Lögberg-Heimskringla*.

If it weren't for Bill McLeod, I don't think I would have been able to write Chapter 8. Bill did some considerable digging into the story for one of his books, and after reading it we quickly became fast friends. Bill was helpful and kind and encouraged me to write the story. Unfortunately, Bill passed away in June of 2021 and probably took some of his secrets with him. Perhaps now he knows what really happened to Weeden and Newcombe.

I must acknowledge Teresa for trusting me and helping me spotlight her loved one's story. Thank you to Gary, Arline and anyone else I may have missed.

A special thank-you to the family members of the missing and deceased who were willing to speak with me and share their stories. Without you, this book would not be possible.

To the families I was not able to track down, I hope I have done your loved ones justice and perhaps offered some exposure to their cases, which have since run cold.

I am forever indebted to The Honourable Gloria Epstein for her endorsement of this book. Her review and support of the material means more than I can put into words.

Real heroes exist in the form of search and rescue workers. Kevin Gill, VP of the Ontario Search and Rescue Volunteer Association was generous with his time and cared enough to explain things to me. OSARVA is entirely made up of volunteers that get no financial support from the government. They are responsible for raising funds and getting word out in the community. All funding goes into their operational budget and towards purchasing rescue gear to improve their chances of success in finding our lost or injured loved ones. If you're looking for a cause to donate to, please consider your local SAR group. Their liability insurance alone is a major expense they deal with. I am grateful for the time and effort put forth by K-9 handler Kim Cooper of the OVSARDA Team. We need more people like you. Elizabeth Doyle, PhD, coroner, anthropologist and assistant professor of Department of Anthropology, was able to clarify and correct many of the scientific aspects of this book.

A good deal of "Thank-yous" are owed to my loving wife, who heard every victory and frustration (mostly frustration) during the research scourge of this book. Thanks for listening to the struggle and I hope you can understand why I needed this book to exist. Thank you for destroying all my earlier drafts so I could put them back together.

Thank you to my loving parents, who supported me through this process and always asked for updates. They were responsible for buying me *Scrivener*, the program I used to complete this book, which has been extremely helpful in keeping a tangled mess of files organized. I hope I continue to make them proud.

Thank you to all these people who have helped in my attempt to achieve the impossible task I was inspired to do those many years ago — solve mysteries. With any luck, and perhaps with help from you, reader, the fog will clear, and the answers will emerge.

Foreword

In Gone Cold, Tim Marczenko has found a creative and impactful way to help explain many fundamental issues surrounding the annual disappearance in Canada of thousands of individuals. He begins his compelling exploration of these issues with particular focus on the myriad of complex challenges associated with the proximate and extended search for the missing.

Against this background, Marczenko then brings the importance of these challenges to life. It is here where the author, in a powerful manner, impresses the reader with the complexity and significance of the issues surrounding searching for those who disappear. He does this by relating, in remarkable detail, the story of seven individuals who disappeared in Northern Ontario. These accounts allow the reader to get to know, to the extent possible in the light of the difficulties surrounding obtaining relevant evidence, the person who disappeared and those affected by his or her disappearance. It is the lives involved, not only of the missing but also of those affected by their disappearance that are at the heart of this powerful book.

The book is well worth reading for several reasons. Significantly, it encourages discussions about the importance of issues surrounding the missing, discussions that may prompt more research and resources that should be applied to the challenging issues surrounding the many thousands of individuals who annually disappear in this country. And, significantly, the author creates a lasting memorial to the seven missing souls who are featured in the book. For both reasons, as I finished the read, I found myself wishing more had been done and hoping more will be done in the future.

The Honourable Gloria J. Epstein Q. C.
Former Justice of the Superior Court
Head of the Independent Civilian Review into Missing Person Investigations
April 2022

Gone Cold

Introduction
Awaken into Darkness

A nightmare would be a welcome treat from the torture I have been facing over the past few years. I say nightmare because it often comes to me once the sun goes down. I'm sure we've all experienced wakefulness, where as soon as we hit the pillow, our brains go into overdrive and we are overwhelmed with ideas, to-dos, and the mysteries of the universe. A few years ago, my 10-month-old son had woken me up. This would be a common occurrence over the next five-or-so years, so much so that I dreaded climbing the stairs to bed.

It wasn't the discomfort of being jarred awake by my son that bothered me, it was knowing what came next. My mind did not flood with the mundane, like failing to take something out of the freezer for dinner or forgetting to turn on the dishwasher. I was aware of several incidents where ordinary people, like me, had vanished into thin air in my home province. Given the slightest opportunity, my mind raced to the deepest corners of northern Ontario, which was the birthplace of these enduring mysteries. I would go over these people's stories in my head and imagine the circumstances and surroundings of their disappearances.

For decades, unsuspecting people literally blinked out of existence like they never, well… existed. Over the past few years, I was haunted by their lives and untimely ends — if they ever really did end…. Once I learned about some of the specifics of these instances, it was as if I carried a curse with me and could never forget them, despite knowing little about them. Now gripped by these true campfire stories, I knew it would be near impossible for me to get back to sleep.

There was a missing person phenomenon that had been going on for longer than anyone could know. I wasn't the only one who noticed this either. These supernatural-like vanishings started off as rumours until the 1800s, when they began to appear in newspapers and could be scrutinized more widely. Since then, other writers have gone gumshoe and tried to figure out what's going on. Well over one hundred years later, we've gotten basically nowhere.

One night, a handful of these names kept popping into the foreground of my mind. It was those cases that I was imagining over and over as I lay there in the dark. The winding bushwhacked paths, the lonely surroundings and where their footprints ended would all flash before my eyes like some psychic vision.

I imagined standing alone in some far-off corner of a remote forest. I had the clear image of a pale slick of moonlight rippling on the lake's surface, beneath the swaying tops of monster pines. I saw myself sitting on the shore, marooned with the chainsaw-like buzz of insects whisking around me. It was peaceful at first, being alone in untouched beauty, but soon, accompanied with the night breeze, a feeling of unease washed over me. I missed my family and shared what I interpreted as what the lost must have felt. It was like hidden eyes gazing upon me, like I was a portrait trapped in time, being studied from the tree line.

Being alone and forgotten in the dead of night was all I could think about. It was a gut-sucking feeling of utter despair and sadness that is hard to describe otherwise, and it would prevent me from sleeping for the rest of the night and many nights long after. All this brought on a question as I laid there between these two worlds: how often do we put ourselves in the shoes of these lost souls?

It is not just the missing that leave us with a mystery, though. There are many cases of bizarre, unexplained deaths and long-lost bones that are recovered in wild places and remain unnamed. Many human skeletons still weather and rot in far-flung nooks of our wilderness, pleading to be discovered and brought home to their families.

My first book, *Disembodied Voices: True Accounts of Hidden Beings*, acted as a bridge to get me here. The research was addictive, painstaking, and exhilarating. Nothing was more rewarding than hours of digging, reading and interviewing manifesting into one juicy morsel of a sentence I had been looking for. Moreover, it gave me a chance to include the subject of disappearances, which I had been interested in for years. Although it was highly possible that a voice could be responsible for some of the disappearances, speculation wasn't doing much to help the problem. I realized that a lot of the stories I was citing were often forgotten about, and therein lied the real problem of unresolved cases. I had dug up some information during the production of my first book and had quite a collection of history that I did not know what to do with. This extra material was the catalyst that spilled over into a second book, where I would again continue to research such cases. I have no connection to the names here, and I have no obligation to them. This is my attempt at telling those stories as accurately as possible with the aid of written record and people that survived. I have tried to be fair to all those involved. Though I may come off as a bit harsh towards law enforcement agencies at times, the writing here is based on actual data and experience, in which I have removed all bias and opinion.

I began compiling information for this book in 2019. After a busy day at the library, archives or speaking with people about such cases, it really took a toll. Once night fell, my mind would race me back to a heavily wooded section of the province, a place off-trail where an unnamed hiker had come across a human skull. It was positioned among the naturally mulched leaves of April, under the maple trees, as stark and smooth as a shell.

The skull remained unnamed, and his story left incomplete. Thinking about his last moments left me frustrated. We didn't know anything about this man, where he came from or why he was there. So often I badly wanted to go to these places. I simply wanted to be out in the woods and just stand there with them or where they were last seen. Then, even if these cases went forever unresolved, at least for a brief period this lost member of society would not feel so alone. I wanted to be surrounded by what surrounded them and see if I could feel their energy still lingering.

While I knew it would be impossible to visit all these places, I thought maybe if I dug a little deeper, I could tell a fuller, more complete version of their story. In most cases, we only know the person's name — nothing more. But as we all can relate from brief introductions and meetings, names are easily forgotten. In fact, often, when it comes to meeting people, the first thing we forget is their name. *There must be a way to preserve the memory of these vanishing victims*, I thought. Of course, these were just nighttime ramblings of the brain, an overflow of thought that only came when the kids were in bed and the TV was switched off.

Months of insomnia continued. No matter how many pieces of the missing puzzle I put together, I still could not get these individuals out of my head. Once again, I awoke in the darkness, only this time I was not in my bed. I was in my sleeping bag, over 300 kilometres from my home, on a backcountry lake all by myself. Water slapped against the rocks, not 10 feet from my head. The wind thrashed my tarp like a sail in a tsunami and I prayed my knots would hold. Rain sprinkled the site, bouncing up from the pine needles like grasshoppers. A foreboding growl of thunder in the distance ensured I was in for a long, tense night. I was uncomfortable and positively isolated from other human beings, hoping, perhaps foolishly, to get a sense of what it was like to be one of these missing people. I laid as still as possible, obsessing over every sound, envisioning man-eating bears, weakened tree limbs, monsters of folklore or other nightmares that my imagination chose to throw at me.

I was experiencing what it was like to be vulnerable and helpless — a coldness that runs deep — and it made me shrink down in my sleeping bag. I felt I had to do something. I hoped this new perspective would help me tell their stories as accurately as possible. That is why I pitched my tent on the shore of this lake in the middle of nowhere.

T. Marczenko, 2021

Gone Cold

1

The Missing Person Problem

*"…Doesn't that seem strange to you?
Someone disappears and no one gives a damn?"
— Rutu Modan*

No one starts their day thinking they are about to inexplicably vanish. Hundreds of ordinary people wake up just as you do… and then simply don't come home. It remains one of the world's most baffling mysteries — people are vanishing. If they are not swiftly found, then the chance of a case resolution quickly diminishes. These individuals are not well-known amongst the general public. Their names ring no bells. What's worse is the older a case gets, the more our memory of them fades and new, time sensitive distractions compete for our attention. Soon, it is as if they never existed at all. Many of them have never been headline news, taken up billboard space or received any media coverage.

These people's lives disintegrate with time, as if time were an acid, actively eating away at them. Their cases are always the most frustrating because they lack information and new leads. At the time of their disappearance, somehow they left no footprints or in some cases, no clues at all. Perhaps a small handful of people will recall a name or two from the early days of their disappearance, but outside of the family members and friends, the people in this book have all been forgotten.

The later chapters contain strange cases of people who have mysteriously gone missing, been the object of a frustrating search or have perished under bizarre circumstances. Body parts and bones have been found, but mostly there is no trace of them whatsoever. They are the "there one minute, gone the next" type of cases that have always chilled me to the bone, and have been a driving force in my life as a researcher and writer. It's a depressing and thankless job to go digging up these heartbreaking old stories that have little to no information, and where proper investigations have yet to begin. But these are human beings, and their stories must be told, if not to solve their disappearances, then because of the painful reality that these people are teetering on the very edge of oblivion.

The absence of fellow humans is unsettling, but outside of the revolving news bulletins about missing people, how much do we really know about them? The truth is that we only know what we are told. In fact, we know very little about these people, who they were and the circumstances surrounding their disappearance. As consumers of the media, without an official police connection, we are only given a snippet of the full story — like reading a book of 300 pages, when 285 of those pages have gone missing… or been torn out.

Famous stories of vanishing people have always captivated. There are many cases that would make almost anyone shift uncomfortably in their seat. For instance, the historically famous story of Benjamin Bathurst, who disappeared on a street in front of his carriage, or the 1880 vanishing of David Lang, who took steps into an open field in Gallatin, Tennessee and vanished in front of five witnesses. Dennis Martin disappeared under the watchful eye of his father in the Smoky Mountains, and Oliver Larch of Indiana whose footprints vanished in fresh snow after walking 50 feet to fetch water. Even the disappearance of Ambrose Small, who seemingly evaporated in downtown Toronto, remains unsettling and unsolved. Then there are the haunting final words of pilots and captains as they sailed their vessels out of sight and into oblivion.

All these stories have similar criteria to the kinds of missing persons cases I was interested in. They disappeared in the blink of an eye, either witnessed by others or within close proximity to them.

Over the years, you'd often find such stories in hokey compilations where the same blurb was repeated over and over, like a story passed around the campfire. More recently, these stories have garnered scrutiny due to lack of data. No matter how they are perceived, I believe that mysterious disappearances are real and that they could happen to anyone. No one seems to be safe, including me.

The criteria I used to vet cases for this book should be understood before delving any deeper. A mysterious disappearance is different from any other because there is no one theory that is stronger than the next. I am more interested in the cases classified as "long-term". This designation refers to cases that are at least 6 months old, with no new leads. Essentially, we are talking about cold cases that are non-criminal in nature. Cold cases of homicide are frequently discussed and circulated, but missing person cold cases have yet to catch on. The cases described here are very cold, some 50 years or older, where no evidence of the victim was found, even though tracking dogs and seasoned searchers may have been used to look for them. Incidents from the 30s, 40s, 50s, 60s, and 70s rarely make it into the spotlight, and are given little exposure.

Cases of obvious misadventure or that involve runaways, animal attacks, homicide or suicide are unfortunate, but not mysterious. I have also excluded cases in populated city centres. You will find most of these stories have a wilderness theme, which is intentional.

The theory of an animal attack is one that always surfaces in wilderness missing persons cases. Funny enough, this fear is commonly pushed by members of the public that are not regular bush-goers, but instead project their fear of this frightening end upon the case. Yes, moose, black bears, wolves and cougars can be very dangerous animals and do attack humans in rare instances. The black bear spends more than 20 hours a day in the late fall foraging for food in preparation of its winter sleep. Competing for food or surprising a bear could lead to a fatal interaction. Moose are in the peak of the rutting season in October, which sees a spike in their testosterone levels, making them twice as aggressive and emboldened. Even when not in the rut, the moose can be a fierce animal in the wild. They are known to stand their ground in an altercation and aren't afraid to charge through even the densest bush towards an apparent threat, be it human or animal. They have even been known to take on cars and trains. Wolves too can be dangerous, but attacks are rare. The cougar is a stealthy predator that surprises prey from behind, killing it and dragging it away. But the one problem with the theory of an animal attack is that the cases covered here show no evidence of a struggle. There would have been some mess, some sign of a scuffle, some blood and clothing. Even a bear would not be able to devour an entire human in one feeding. With no kill scene and the absence of remains, this theory seems impossible.

Most runaways leave home for a short period of time and are usually in contact with friends. Adult runaways will still use their bank accounts, credit cards and vehicles.

How many people are reported missing every year? That number fluctuates greatly.

The following fact sheets provided by police agencies are enough to make your jaw drop. Keep in mind, I am only reporting on cases said to be non-criminal in nature. I have excluded abduction (parental or otherwise), human trafficking and runaways.
    As of March 2022, in Canada, there were 26,456 adults reported missing — 5,992 of these in Ontario, and 7,663 children were reported missing, 1,742 from Ontario. These numbers are skewed due to the heavy quarantine measures and closures put in place during the Covid-19 Pandemic. These restrictions meant that there were less opportunities for people to go missing. If we compare the data from the previous years, we see a 20% decrease in reporting because of these measures. The statistics for Ontario show a 2% decrease in adults reported missing and a 7% decrease in the number of children reported missing.

    But the reported numbers don't take into account all of the missing people, in fact many are not included in the data because of poor reporting and improper record-taking or keeping. Two hundred and seven missing adults were not included in the data as there was no probable cause entered on the report and 21 individuals were excluded because their sex was marked as "Other" on the report. Twenty-eight missing children were not included as there was no probable cause entered. Thirty-two missing children were not included because their sex was "Other."

This imprecision of data is not a fluke, in fact it occurs annually. In 2019, four missing adult males were not included because the province on the police report was classified as "Other," meaning they could have been from another country or unknown to the officer. When it comes to children, three females were not included in the numbers because their province was classified under "Other."

An additional 196 missing adults were not included in the statistics because there was no probable cause entered on the police report. An additional 24 missing adults were not included because their sex was unknown or listed as "Other." An additional 59 missing children were not included because there was no probable cause entered in the report, and 70 missing children were not included just because their sex was marked as "Unknown" or "Other."

The data reveals a startling admission: we do not know how many people we are missing.

And it gets worse.... There is yet another problem with these numbers. The data used for these fact sheets is gathered from information uploaded to the Canadian Police Information Centre (CPIC). The CPIC is not a flawless system and is subject to human error. Data for every missing person may not be uploaded or could contain typos. But then it gets more confusing — 89% of missing adults and 92% of missing children were removed from the total number (which includes criminal cases) within a week. The literature does not state the updated figures and from which category they were removed. Due to poor data, we do not know how many people are missing and how many have been found.

With these discrepancies looming in the background, we cannot accurately decide on a number. Instead, we can only speak in approximations and generalities. As stated by the Royal Canadian Mounted Police (RCMP), "Generally, out of those people reported missing in a given year, approximately 500 remain missing after one year."[1]

There are approximately 270 cold cases (or long-term) missing persons added annually, and the number increases with time.[2]

The initial numbers I stated might be safe, but it's clear that no one really knows. Not even the police can say for sure — believe me, I've asked. It's a frightening realization when you learn that no one can confidently tell you how many human lives have disintegrated into nothingness over the years. We only know that it's a lot.

To compound this haunting truth, between 50 and 100 sets of human remains are found in Canada every year and are left unclaimed.[3] Right now, more than 720 unknown bodies are in the database, and the number is growing.

Often the public will only see the same frustrating blurb about the missing person, which pops up in news reports, police websites, social media and other forums. The blurbs are updated annually by official sources if any new information bubbles to the surface, which unfortunately is rare. Updating profiles is the responsibility of the investigating officer. However, some of these cases aren't even assigned to a detective until a tip or a lead comes in. The saddest thing about these blurbs is that they almost never change over time — they act as a brief biography and are literally all that is known about the individual. Sometimes no more than two sentences sum up the person's life, which is hardly a complete picture of a human being or their story. How satisfied would you be if only a single sentence summed up your existence? It's an injustice to any human being, no matter the age of the person. Surely we are more valuable and complex than that. After all, these are our fellow men, women and children who have been swallowed up into darkness. They have been taken prematurely from their families and friends and robbed of the chance to finish out their lives.

Other than these blurbs, the names of the vanished appear in print less than a dozen times, and in some cases are spelled wrong. Often, the errors run rampant in these types of cases — birthdates, ages, dates of disappearances, even the ethnicity is either incorrect or not known when revealed to the public. Over the years, these errors have not been corrected, but instead are continually repeated on forums and websites. Can we ever really know the answer to the mystery if we don't fully understand what we're looking for?

To make matters worse, the police refuse to share information about these cases, so assistance can never come from other agencies or the public unless they are researched independently. The cases are considered "open" but that does not mean they are being investigated. This is a separate issue that can also result in more cases going cold.

The *Missing Person Problem* is a composite of many factors that work independently of one another to create a perfect storm: poor data collection, failed or ill-advised search protocols, inconsistent investigative practices, and a lack of transparency, cooperation and resources.

The *Missing Person Phenomenon* is the undeniable fact in which any person can vanish off the face of the earth, in the presence of others, or in an impossibly small window of time, leaving little or no trace.

Make no mistake, until we can explain every bizarre incident, it is a phenomenon. The missing person phenomenon can act independently or in conjunction with the missing person problem, which creates a much more complex and seemingly unsolvable mystery.

All the factors that make up the missing person equation can be contributed by any number of agencies, media sources or members of the public, and no one of them is singlehandedly at fault. It is this missing person problem that is turning hot cases cold and preventing decades-old cases from being solved.

Incidents of mysterious disappearances have wide gaps and unknowns that make it impossible to relay a concise story. Every effort was made here to present a full and fair picture, which includes family, police and local perspectives whenever possible. Read on knowing that I took no liberties with the truth. What evidence has been unearthed will act as anchors to these stories that my investigation was based on. The blanks I tried to fill came from process of elimination and the most likely scenarios based on the individual and location. I have considered all that I have learned about the areas and the individuals, nevertheless some of the "Hows" and "Whys" may still be unclear.

In most long-term cases, family members have passed on and so there is no one left to mourn them, and therefore no one left to look. If remaining family haven't passed on, they may have moved on, a long drawn-out investigation being too painful for them, or more likely, they cannot afford the price tag associated with media releases, billboards and other exposure that is needed in such cases. To put ourselves in the shoes of the dead, the lost and the ones left behind who still suffer may be the only way we can see progress in these cold cases. Gaining the perspective of just one of these victims gives us the strength we need to continue searching for them.

The sad fact is that most of these historical cases can never be solved. Many links to the truth have been erased. It is difficult to accurately tell these people's stories when many things have changed. Names of the original locations have been replaced, town lines have shifted and blurred. Houses have been built, land has been exchanged as often as the changing seasons and most of the people involved have died. Through no fault of their own, these people have gone missing, but it is a system failure and our collective short-term memory that is really the end for these people. It isn't long before they are totally erased from existence.

One way of preventing this from happening would be to make sure that they age well. To do this, a more detailed profile must be made of the individuals. So, I began digging deeper, past the headlines and the repetitive blurbs. I began collecting addresses, cross streets and lot numbers of where the individuals were last seen. I jotted down any links that might remain from others involved, to places of employment to relatives, and on and on.

Sadly, good record-keeping is not something that most people care about until it's too late, so the information comes in shrapnel pieces, flung this way and that. Because of this fact, my conclusions have been kept short and fragmented, and this is the way I will present the investigation— in fragments. At least then we will learn a little more about the people, the environments and the investigation into their cases. Maybe, with a new perspective on the missing person problem, we can learn from past mistakes and prevent ourselves from becoming future ones. It could happen. Before you know it, your existence could be summed up in two vague sentences.

Someone out there may know something or provide a vital clue that could put these cases to rest. It's important we share and cooperate on such mysteries. Our information should be distributed in the way we found it, flung far and wide. Somewhere out there in our wilderness areas, is the final resting place of the lost. They lie under log and thicket, or are snagged and submerged in cold, deep water. Maybe if we all start looking, we can bring them home.

2

So Others May Live

"Here many miles from human habitation, prayer for the first time is offered by "white men" to "The Great Spirit"; the missing ones are not forgotten, and earnest supplication is made that God would direct their steps."
—Thomas McMurray

The missing person problem cannot be discussed in full without delving into the world of those that search. There are many moving parts and associations involved, all of which have different protocols for resolving such cases. From the public's perspective, we only see a small percentage of what really goes into these investigations. Due to certain protections, gated information and the brief, filtered media spots, members of the public and sometimes even relatives of the missing are kept out of the loop, and yet we all play a role in bringing lost loved ones home.

When speaking specifically about long-term cases, there are a handful of organizations responsible for either searching for the missing, identifying remains or keeping records of them. Those organizations include the Ontario Provincial Police (OPP), the Royal Canadian Mounted Police (RCMP), local police forces, National Centre for Missing Persons and Unidentified Human Remains (NCMPUR), Office of the Chief Coroner and volunteer emergency response teams.

What is expected of law enforcement, search and rescue teams, the media and the public once someone goes missing? The same question can be posed for unidentified human remains and unexplained death, both of which are not as publicized as missing people. Each group faces a different set of obstacles when they receive a call to action. The police must deal with expansive, hard-to-reach areas and resource-draining investigations, not to mention other pressing criminal activities within their jurisdictions. Volunteer search teams are under intense pressure to comb an area quickly and remain at the mercy of police and jurisdictional protocols. The public and the media have their hands tied when it comes to providing any kind of assistance to an investigation. Privacy laws and insufficient resources make progress almost non-existent. Personal privacy, information gatekeeping and physical search efforts are not only related to one another but are often intertwined by way of the police report. When a member of society goes missing, however, there are responsibilities and requirements for all those involved, many of which are not public knowledge.

These stories nearly always play out in the same sequential order. When a loved one fails to return home, the police are the first to be notified.

The OPP certainly have their work cut out for them. They are responsible for patrolling one million square kilometres of land and waterways, including isolated communities to the north that are walled in by untouched nature. Some of these areas have never seen human foot traffic. Thousands of lakes, islands, bays, bogs and mountains remain nameless, making it even more challenging to coordinate search efforts. The spongy forests of the north, permeated with muskeg and swamps, can never be developed into habitable land or infrastructure, and yet as long as they are charted to our maps, must be included in their search jurisdiction. Ontario is larger than France and Spain combined, spanning two time zones and is made up of 70 million hectares of woodland. That translates to 70% of the province being shrouded in forest. To those who feel more comfortable in the southern reaches, or who have yet to appreciate its vastness, 90% of Ontario sits above the city of Sudbury. Provincial and regional police are sympathized with in this regard, as the territory they must cover is enormous. Even if someone is reported missing in a timely manner, it may take many hours just to get to the location of where they were last seen.

These statistics may startle even some lifelong residents. When you look at Ontario on a map, you can see just how difficult the landmass is to navigate. The highways, like its lakes and rivers, seem endless. Some towns and rest stops are hundreds of kilometres apart, bringing on a stir of anxiety for road-trippers who constantly keep an eye on their gas gauges.

In an interview with the OPP, they conveyed just how much of a burdensome task lay before them:

> We have had instances where hikers go missing and it takes a combined effort of aviation, canine and speciality units to locate the missing persons. Additionally, a person can be missing for weeks, and sometimes months, before investigators are made aware that they have gone missing. Other difficulties lie where limited information is provided to the police, which then limits the information available to the public for support.[4]

Therein lies another reality of the problem that we will delve into later.

At the first sign of trouble, all manner of vehicles and resources are used by police to help locate missing people. To reach far out places in the province, boats, jet skis, snowmobiles, canoes, kayaks, helicopters and airplanes are deployed, depending on the budget and availability at the time. In the past, it was not uncommon to recruit Indigenous trackers if they were more familiar with the land or active in the area. The best trackers who had success in past searches were often sought out. Mountain bikes, ATVs and air boats have been used in the past and can be deployed quickly into areas that larger vehicles cannot penetrate.

Unless there is reason to believe otherwise, all searches begin with the expectation of finding the person alive. It is this thought that makes it so important to deploy resources as quickly as possible. If available, police dogs may be the first to perform an initial grid search before ground crews can be deployed. However, no matter what the jurisdiction, there always seems to be a lack of police presence and resources on these scenes, and therefore additional help is requested in the form of volunteer search and rescue (SAR).

Volunteer search groups have popped up all around the province to aid police in assembling grid searches as quickly as possible. Some are of their own initiative, and many operate under the Ontario Search and Rescue Volunteer Association (or OSARVA) and are broken down into teams based on six geographical regions designated by the OPP. These are the hardworking men and women who literally beat the bushes and poke through snow drifts looking for any trace of a missing individual. They give up vacation time to train and leave their jobs at a moment's notice to aid wherever needed.

Search and rescue teams are trained to deal with a variety of situations. They are skilled in land navigation, communication and clue locating. It takes a special kind of person to participate in volunteer search and rescue. OSARVA has a memorandum of understanding (MOU) with the OPP. This MOU is what closely binds volunteer searchers to police, both provincial and municipal. After police conduct a small, initial search they will send a call out to regional search teams. A search and rescue team cannot self-deploy and will always be called in by the authority bearing jurisdiction over the area in question.

The police are also responsible for calling off the search. Because SAR groups are only there for support, they can only remain in the field until the active police force tells them differently. Even with a multitude of factions involved, it is still the police who call the shots.

In the initial launch of a lost person investigation, search groups will sometimes create a Lost Person Questionnaire (LPQ) with the help of the police. The document contains a basic description as well as all pertinent information about the missing person, such as their wilderness experience, medical issues, gear they took with them and their planned destination, if any. All information is provided by police and is only pertinent to locating the missing individual. As they arrive on scene, searchers are briefed by the police, and again at the end of each operational period.

To get a better understanding of their goals and the difficulties they come across, I spoke with Kevin Gill, Vice President of OSARVA. OSARVA (and its regional teams) will continue the search for as long as the authorities deem necessary. This can either be a few days or a few weeks, depending on the location and likelihood of finding the subject. However, in past cases I have learned of situations where searches are run entirely by the volunteers if there is not enough police presence in the area. Often the responsibilities are shared between an officer and a SAR manager, together leading the charge. While they may have more personnel, volunteer organizations have a scaled down version of the resources available to police.

As time goes on, technology and more skilled efforts have been put into searches for the lost. Searchers can cover even more hidden ground with the aid of scuba divers and submarines. Night vision, FLIR (forward looking infrared), artificial intelligence and drones are just some of the advancements that searchers can use to aid them. Drones, for example, have been beneficial in the way that they are inexpensive, can be deployed quickly and can access areas that would be too difficult or dangerous for searchers to enter. Members are trained in High Angle Rope Rescue, which is used when significant heights are a factor; this could include cliffs, buildings and mineshafts.

There are also unconventional ways to locate people, which SAR and police have used in the past. Psychics and remote viewers have been recruited for a more mystical approach. To my knowledge, they have never been able to bring searchers to a body, but they have intrigued many with visions of their last moments. In special cases, call blasting has been used. I have even heard of cases where thousands of leaflets have been dropped from the sky to reach a missing child.

Dogs are the one constant means of searching that has been used since the beginning of time. Even with technological advancements, search teams still rely on man's best friend to wag and sniff their way towards their target. Search dogs, sometimes called K-9 units, are a great asset to a human team. They can both smell and hear things over expanse distances that humans cannot. If the missing person is believed to be deceased, then cadaver dogs that specifically search for dead bodies are brought into the area. When dealing with cold cases, the cadaver dog may be our best shot at bringing the missing home. Search dogs exist on two Ontario SAR teams, both of which are OPP certified (OPP will only use dogs certified by them).

Their cadaver dogs are certified in the United States under the North American Police Working Dog Association (NAPWDA), which is where many Canadian police dogs are sent.

There is a startling scientific reason behind why dogs are always used (and sometimes prioritized) before ground teams can enter an area. A dog's sense of smell is 10,000 times more acute than a human on the low end of the spectrum and 100,000 times as acute on the higher end, depending on the breed. Alexandra Horowitz makes a jaw-dropping visual comparison in her book *Inside of a Dog*, saying a dog could detect a teaspoon of sugar in a million gallons of water, or in two Olympic-sized swimming pools. I have covered the science behind the powerful sense of smell possessed by our four-legged friends in a previous book, but since it is relevant, I will mention it again here.

> More than 400 odours come off the decomposition of human remains, and dogs are shockingly good at detecting these smells. The scent of human death is specifically unique to humans, and dogs would be able to tell the difference between human remains, animal remains and other organic material. Cadaver dogs can track down human remains in any form and possible situation, ranging from ashes to shards to wet or submerged bones, and can even pinpoint them down to a single drop of blood. Amazingly, if a human corpse was buried deep enough in the earth but was still touching the root of a tree, a cadaver dog would still be able to detect that scent through the tree trunk! In addition to visiting staged body sites for their training, dogs are sometimes brought to historical cemeteries where they are still able to detect remains of a corpse that have been in the ground for well over 100 years. Canines are thoroughly trained to sharpen those already instinctual needs to search and retrieve.[5]

Search dogs are trained for both on-and off-leash deployment, during which they sniff back and forth across a designated search zone under the direction of the handler. The dog is trained to indicate all related scent items along the way, including discarded clothing and foreign items that have the potential to belong to the target (e.g. cigarette butts). When the dog detects the scent of its human target they will signal to their handler by barking, sitting near the site or jumping on the handler.

Kim Cooper of the Ottawa Valley Search and Rescue Dog Association (OVSARDA) shares data that emphasizes how valuable dogs are, as well as the confidence held by their handlers. Cooper sites specific data gathered from years of her own deployment in the field.

Dogs used by OVSARDA are undeterred by even the harshest environments, including muskeg, swamps, taiga or large bodies of water. They will access these areas by helicopter, boat, from shore, or by swimming — basically anyway they can get their paws dirty and whatever it takes to enter the search zone. The depth of the water does not appear to pose a problem for properly trained dogs. Cooper's dogs have detected the odour of human remains 218 feet underwater.

When Vinnie Yeo's canoe capsized in Elliot Lake, Ontario in 1999, dive teams searched for 12 days without success. OVSARDA deployed a canine to the last known location to assist and was able to detect Yeo's scent in just 15 minutes.[6] Vinnie Yeo's body was found in the area where the dogs had indicated, 96 feet below the water's surface.

Age is of no consequence to cadaver dogs either. Dogs do well at detecting odour from old graves with the help of specialized training. They are drawn to the actual odour of the decomposition and not the grave itself. This could mean that a dog could get a "hit" off a nearby tree instead of an actual grave marker. Dog handlers have had success with locating 1,000-year-old human bones in training environments "without hiccup."[7]

There is evidence that cadaver dogs may be able to assist in locating remains much older than that. Archaeologist Vedrana Glavas breaks down how dogs had success in locating ancient burial sites from a paper published in the *Journal of Archaeological Method and Theory* in 2018.

> Our research was conducted at the burial site of the prehistoric hillfort of Drvišica (Croatia), located on the littoral slope of the Velebit Mountains. A total of four HRD (human remains detection) dogs were used in both a blinded and double-blinded search. Those locations where an HRD dog produced an indication were subjected to both visual inspection and archaeological excavation. This research has resulted in the discovery of five new prehistoric tombs, as well as HRD dogs detecting previously excavated tombs.[8]

These facts are extremely important to keep in mind when reviewing the missing persons and unexplained death cases in the chapters to come. Dogs prove again and again to be an invaluable part of a recovery team.

Weather plays a pivotal role in search and rescue operations and will greatly affect the outcome of the search. Snow, hail and storms in general can obliterate tracks and pathways and erase any scent for a dog to follow. Most dog handlers will tell you that they would prefer to walk their K-9s through a search zone before human teams enter, but this is not always possible. Usually time is of the essence and specialized dogs can come from cities many kilometres away. The reason for prioritizing dogs in a search grid is to prevent other unnecessary scents from humans contaminating the area. The OPP will commonly deploy their own dogs in the initial search period, prior to volunteer SAR being brought in. Not only are dog teams much more successful at locating missing people and trails, they can "clear" an area much faster than a team without dogs.

Cooper and most other handlers have complete faith in their dogs, but the abilities of search canines are no good to us if they are deployed in the wrong spot or provided with incorrect data. "When a trained dog searches and finds nothing, there is information to take away." If canines cannot pick up a target odour in the search area, it means they are either not searching the correct area or that the target is no longer there.

Outside of weather and site contamination, one of the greatest obstructions for search dogs and their handlers is gaining the confidence of law enforcement. Some police agencies have yet to acknowledge the awesome power of the dog's nose. To make progress in older long-term cases, police departments need to start viewing groups like OVSARDA as an asset.

Not surprisingly, Gill agrees that the biggest challenges faced by searchers are the terrain and communication hurdles. Dense bush and rocky territory slow down search progress and interfere with signal strength. The remoteness of some locations means poor radio communications where cell phone service is non-existent. Besides the use of technological gizmos to aid searchers, the biggest change over the last 50–60 years comes down to training and awareness, both inside and outside of these organizations.

Consistent training around the province, in different environments, gives teams a leg up when they finally get the call. Teams are constantly improving their skills and acquiring more volunteers with technical and tactical backgrounds rather than just the local townsfolk. Many of the main improvements aren't coming from SAR teams at all, but instead are focused on educating the public when it comes to outdoor safety. One may be familiar with the saying, "an ounce of prevention is worth a pound of cure," and SAR agencies across the country are crossing their fingers that we have all taken steps towards that ounce. All modern prevention measures could help the rest of us from becoming needles in this provincial haystack.

Sixty years ago, people didn't wear seatbelts. Wearing a life jacket while paddling a canoe was extremely rare. Now life jacket safety is pushed at an early age, and you see them almost everywhere. Even Ontario Parks has jumped on the bandwagon with their PARKsmart initiative. This safety program is available in 67 of its parks, wherein campers can borrow a PFD free of charge. SAR teams will undoubtedly benefit from the public's increasing knowledge and safer decision-making while outdoors.

The success of many search and rescue operations depends on the knowledge and preparedness of the public. Something as simple as packing extra clothing and food on a day hike can mean the difference between life and death. These days, First Aid and Wilderness Survival Schools are increasingly accessible in your neighbourhood, which gives everyone an advantage if something goes wrong. The Search and Rescue Volunteer Association of Canada has taken initiative by creating the AdventureSmart program. This national prevention initiative focuses on reducing the number and severity of Search and Rescue incidents. The program, also in application form, is used for trip planning and to educate children and adults on what to do if they should get lost.

The target of a search operation will determine the next course of action by team members, who have laid out protocols in advance. *Lost Person Behaviour* has become the official handbook for most search and rescue teams in North America. This book outlines statistical information on where a lost person will likely be found, depending on varying factors, including the age of the person, experience and state of overall health. The book breaks down search procedures for children, adults, those who want to disappear, those with disabilities, dementia and even people afraid of dogs, to eliminate the use of K-9 units. Each grouping of individuals has a profile associated with them that indicates areas that should be prioritized in the search and the probability of detection.

For example, a missing child aged 1–3 would likely have no concept of being lost and may wander aimlessly and ignore or run from the call or whistle of a would-be rescuer. They are more likely to wander until they become too tired to continue. Children also tend to find natural or makeshift shelters in the woods that a full-grown adult would have trouble accessing, such as caves, old vehicles, and dumped appliances. Children are notorious for huddling up in small areas that adults cannot get to, or sometimes even see from a higher vantage point. A child will rarely respond to a searcher's calls because they may fall asleep easier or be afraid that they are in trouble. This age group is statistically located in a building or shelter 25% of the time, and so these places are often sought out and searched by volunteers. The information provided in this book can save precious time and prepare volunteers for what they are walking into.

Not surprisingly, children are the toughest to search for. You'd think a young child wouldn't be able to get very far on little legs, but there have been instances where a child has been found to have traveled considerable distances in the wilderness, in some cases 8 miles or more. How these children can get so far without much in the way of scrapes or bruises has been the subject of many heated debates, but the theories range anywhere from having been carried off by a cougar to abducted by a flying saucer. The amount of distance they can travel varies, especially if something of interest catches their attention, such as an animal.

We adults have just as much trouble staying put as our little ones. The only difference is the way that adults move once they become lost. Commonly, they will look for familiar landmarks or roads. This is where pride becomes a factor and poor decision making can lead to problems. Changing your position to self-rescue can have a negative effect on one's chances of being found; one can literally walk themselves out of the search area. On the other hand, many people walk themselves out of the bush every year. For those who cannot and do not walk out, the story has a very different ending. The arrival of a hunting season or a revealing spring thaw is the typical way for bodies or skeletons to be found.

Time is the friend of decay, and an enemy of investigators and coroners. They are constantly challenged when it comes to human decomposition or the lack of a body all together. Decomposition is an issue that most investigators must deal with. Time is of the essence to recover a full body of the missing before the environment can completely absorb a person into the landscape, where clues can fade, and evidence can be lost. A body will undergo distinct stages of decomposition, ranging from Fresh, Bloat, Decay, Post-Decay and Skeletal, and a variety of factors play into each one. The rate of decay is always varied due to the health of the deceased, clothing worn, environment and exposure to natural or unnatural elements.

Forest soils can be overly acidic and is one of the factors contributing to decomposition. Left on the forest floor, a body can be exposed to weather, scavengers and insects, all of which would accelerate the rate of decay. It would require an entire textbook to go into the scientific process of human decay in the wilderness. There are too many variables to consider in order to provide an accurate timeline. For example, snow covering a body would act as an insulator and could protect it, but at the same time, the thawing and freezing of remains would have a negative effect. Studies have shown that clothing also slows the rate of decay, but parallel studies contradict this, observing that clothing could accelerate decay due to the shelter it provides for maggots and beetles. Dogs and coyotes are the most common scavengers when it comes to human remains. They can alter the death scene, affect identification and even transport the body out of the search area. Distances that bones can be transported vary greatly, but coyotes have been known to carry bones up to 3.2 kilometres away in a forested environment.[9] Carnivores are not the only animals that chew on bones either, cattle and deer have left behind their distinguishable tooth marks as well.

Even in the world of the coroner or forensic anthropologist, accuracy does not mean precision. It's all based on factors related to the individual and conditions — things like gut bacteria, bone composition and scavengers in the area.

Scavenging can be delayed when a body is sheltered in heavy clothing, a sleeping bag, partially buried or submerged.

Bodies in water tend to last longer, decomposing at roughly half the rate, due to the temperature, especially if these bodies are submerged. If the aquatic environment has less available oxygen or is an extremely low temperature, the decay process could take longer and may allow time for fossilization or preservation. They would have to be deep enough in an anaerobic environment, such as a bog or muskeg, where they would be protected from insects and other natural elements. Submersion does not happen often, unless the body has "help."

Most clothing decays faster than bone, but fabrics are not without their variables either. Organic materials, such as leather, wool or cotton, may last longer in waterlogged conditions. If clothing, such as boots, have plastic components, then this of course will affect the degradation of the material.

In cases classified as long-term, if skeletal remains are not found and stored in a temperature-controlled room, they are left to the elements and eventually will turn to dust. If a living person or body is not recovered within a short time window, that person may never be located. These kinds of physical ground searches have an expiry date. Arriving decades late to some of these scenes leaves us disadvantaged. Coroners have determined manner of death of some older human remains, but many skeletons offer little clues as to their identity and what may have happened to them.

After the first 10 days or so, physical search and rescue teams are called off. There is simply not enough perpetual manpower or resources to search until a lost person is found. Helicopters and boats are expensive, and sometimes special dog handlers are flown in for a short window of time. Police may be called away to other urgent or present matters that can be resolved by their immediate action. Volunteer search and rescue teams are exactly that — volunteers — and those men and women may have to return to their regular day jobs or other responsibilities. A search effort is its strongest in the first 48 hours. After resources are drained and the police call off the search, it is an unfortunate reality that the missing person's name will slip from the headlines and quickly be forgotten.

A boots-on-the-ground approach to these cases from 50–70 years ago may result in nothing but bites and blisters. A trudge through the forest would be pointless, especially if details of the person's last known location are hazy. But that doesn't mean the pursuit ends. There are ways to approach this problem years after the person has been reported missing. On my part, many countless hours have been spent seeking out information on these individuals and tracking down family members. Digging through historical records and endless cold calls can get exhausting, but options are slim when dealing with cases decades old. Anything left to be found is hidden in filing cabinets and on poorly ink-bled computer scans. All relics from the last 48 hours of that person's life as we know it are found here, in cold case file folders.

The image of a tireless hound dog detective is usually what we think of when the idea of a cold case comes up. A thinning trench coat hangs off a tortured, intense persona. We conjure up scenes of a stakeout; they're casing the neighbourhood, going door-to-door. In reality, the day of a long-term missing persons investigator looks less like a film noir and more like a telemarketer. Cold cases are mostly desk work. There are no late-night stakeouts, no strong coffee or stale donuts. Answering the phone, if it just so happens to ring, and following up on tips that fall from the sky are pretty much all that can be done when cases go cold. It's about following leads and getting case exposure.

Each case is approached differently, depending on the leads and the status of the investigation. In an interview with the OPP, they informed me of a checklist they use to guide these older investigations. Of course they would not say what this list consisted of, but we can imagine it contains basic instructions on follow-ups and review. Since each case is unique, several investigative efforts can be used, depending on the circumstances.

> If the missing person is presumed drowned, then the investigator may ensure DNA and dental records are obtained for comparison to unidentified remains and the missing persons on Canadian Police Information Centre (CPIC) and possibly published.[10]

Investigators will also use the *Missing Persons Act* to demand access to all records on that person, something covered in a later chapter.

I expressed my doubts about any progress being made on missing persons cases 50 years old or older where no foul play is suspected. Officers admitted to me that these are the most challenging because it's not like they could utilize tips or obtain confessions. Any people with a connection to these missing individuals are no longer around. With so much time having passed, they can only check out file folders from the evidence locker and review whatever data was recorded at that time. Most of this data is incomplete, inaccurate or too little to make any progress, no matter how often it is reviewed. Police will sometimes seek out information from other jurisdictions to determine whether any details are relevant for their unsolved investigations. If all the data is available on websites like CPIC, then they can skip this step.

Police have no shortage of resources at their disposal to help clear their mounting case load. The Missing Persons Unidentified Bodies Unit (MPUB) of the OPP is dedicated to assisting frontline police officers with missing persons and human remains investigations. The National Centre for Missing Persons and Unidentified Remains (NCMPUR) is a government initiative that was spearheaded by the RCMP. Their purpose is to provide support to law enforcement agencies, medical examiners and coroners in missing persons and unidentified remains investigations. The project was put in place to address the disturbing number of unsolved cases of murdered and missing people in Canada, specifically Aboriginal women. The NCMPUR runs the website *Canada's Missing*, where case data can be shared nationally, albeit highly vague and restricted.

The NCMPUR has created and distributed a document known as *Best Practices*, compiled by experts across Canada as a guide for police officers who are confronted with a missing persons case. It's intended for agencies to use as a handbook as they revise their own policies and procedures. However, since it is not a policy document, there is no legal obligation to follow the recommendations put forward by these experts, even though it is available to all police agencies across the country.

Best Practices is an impressive, thorough and thoughtful tool, and is a terrific example of the steps that police forces should be taking. According to the executive summary of NCMPUR, it is the role of the primary investigator of a cold case to upload data and vet information for publication. The policy is a good habit for the investigator to treat all ongoing cases as need-to-know, and I believe this is the reason why all online blurbs of unresolved cases are nearly identical. When all else fails, police rely heavily on social media for public assistance.

As we flip the calendar each year, cases are only getting colder. The police remain hopeful that new technologies or techniques will give them different opportunities to re-examine their older cases:

> If there is still a chance, we would collect familial DNA to compare to our unidentified remains. Other methods include using a police sketch artist to determine what the missing person looked like, if the case involved unidentified remains; using social media or media conferences to ask the public for information; and re-interviewing remaining witnesses.[11]

Not to sound too pessimistic, but I believe the "chance" the police are speaking of is of the slim variety.

It's sad to see what even the police are limited to, especially when the disappearance is non-criminal. With each minute that ticks by, these cases get further from being resolved. The OPP and RCMP put a lot of stock in receiving tips from the public where there may just be that tiny shred of information needed to solve a case. When every remaining link of a missing person has gone, I have no idea what that coveted piece of information could possibly be.

As a member of the public, I cannot determine which pieces would be helpful to an investigator if I am not able to access details of the cases. Now, researchers, private investigators and other police agencies face new problems when accessing information about these cases. The reason for needed pressure is for the purpose of obtaining a more detailed profile, increasing exposure and focussing more eyes on the case. More eyes mean more tips from the public. But even this system isn't completely functional. In 2021, I attempted to submit an anonymous tip that could have identified human remains, however the online portal on the police website did not work and the tip could not be submitted electronically. As a back-up, the investigator listed their email on the website, but the email address was defunct so the tip bounced back.

Bureaucracy is not unlike an overgrown, unfamiliar forest. Instead of getting stuck in the sucking mud of a swamp as we search for long-term missing people, we find ourselves bogged down with sticking guidelines and swatting at pestering protocols. We must duck under the low-hanging red tape and avoid unseen pitfalls of power. All this is done with the intent to create a more detailed information profile on those that are lost for an extended period.

Although I may seem critical, I am not anti-establishment or anti-law enforcement. The findings presented here are based solely on experiences and facts presented by police organizations. The statistics and literature speak for themselves, and right now they are crying for help.

Although the public, search teams and investigative agencies involved may not get along at times, they are all working towards the same goal. When the family is involved, emotions can make the situation even more volatile. Heads will butt and procedures will always conflict with policies, but I'm sure we agree on one thing: the hardest search is the one that is called off without finding the subject.

There is one problem, though. Before these cases went cold, they were attention-grabbing stories that were a priority for police agencies and the surrounding community. Searchers would descend on the bush with high hopes, always expecting that they'd recover the missing person a little worse for wear, but alive. No investigating party or family member expects their loved one's case to remain unsolved for decades to come. OSARVA's motto is, "*So others may live.*" They donate their time and risk their safety so that strangers may be rescued and live on. But for those we cannot physically find, we still search, so that the missing may live on in one form or another, even if it is just in our memories.

3

The Freedom of Information Fabrication

"The truth never dies, but it lives a wretched life."
— Jewish Proverb

We've heard it dozens of times before. Something in your city goes wrong — a burglary, a child goes missing — and what happens? Police release the same tired statement to the media that is then broadcast into your living room. This rehearsed plea is usually along the lines of: "We are seeking the public's help in solving the case. If you saw something or were in such and such area between this time and that time, please contact your local detachment." Or, what's worse, they ask the public to solve a 35-year-old cold case, hoping that somehow, with very minimal information, decades of dust will clear and the public will present a resolution as we sit, half listening, with snacks in hand. We'll be right back after this word about a superior brand of toilet paper.

Viewers expect a speedy resolution by police within the next news cycle. After all, we don't consider ourselves to be freelance sleuths or gumshoes. It's not often that we find ourselves in the right place at the right time to provide such crucial clues to solve a case. In the collective mind of the public, it is up to the police to follow leads, uncover clues and to solve these cases in a timely manner, but that assumption is just plain wrong. Many police agencies have admitted that they rely on the public to provide new information regarding unsolved cases, but just how much they rely on us was not clear until recently.

If the police are pleading for public assistance, then it only seems fair that the public become privy to what they need assistance with. There is no way of knowing which details are lacking from these cases if the public is not privy to them. Why are we not given the more pertinent information that would not harm an investigation? It's unclear how the public is expected to know key details or fork over potential evidence in a case if we are only made aware of the seemingly insignificant fragments, at best. Despite this, I decided to take them up on their offer.

Like a pro bono private investigator, I began to source any material I could on roughly half a dozen missing person cases, ones that were so cold they were damn near freezing. I dug into everything I could for the individuals listed in the later chapters. The newspaper articles were either buried, lost, or misspelled. Sometimes they were only obtainable in person, which proved to be a challenge, as some of the libraries in question are thousands of kilometres away (some even out of province), and there was no guarantee that these articles would hold anything of value. Still, I gathered as much as I could to see if there were any links to their names. A voter list, wedding announcement or an unrelated article printed years before their disappearance would help to confirm the facts. From there, I could confirm locations, relatives and significant dates, all tiny puzzle pieces that I could stick together. I spent years at a desk sending emails, making phone calls and filling out submissions to various government bodies.

The release of records from government entities came about in 1983 with the *Access to Information Act*. Once I became familiar with the ins and outs of each file and felt confident that the case fit into the missing person criteria I cited earlier, I submitted a *Freedom of Information Act* (FOIA) request to see if I could get specific documents from the police agencies involved. That is when I hit a wall.

Police agencies are responsible for the retention and distribution of their case load. At their discretion, they can either allow or deny the public's access to records, no matter how old or relevant. Requests are formally handled by the Ministry of the Solicitor General. All denied requests have an opportunity to be appealed through the Information and Privacy Commissioner of Ontario (IPC). This is the body behind all appeals for *Freedom of Information and Protection of Privacy Act* (FIPPA) and *Municipal Freedom of Information and Protection of Privacy Act* (MFIPPA) requests.

These record-keepers know more about the individual and the details surrounding their disappearance than anyone, including the family members. This is even more true if relatives and next-of-kin of the missing person have passed on. In most instances, that is exactly the case; either that, or they moved out of province or did not immigrate to Canada with their loved one. The record-keepers will be the reason why these people are either found or forgotten.

The first time I submitted a FOIA request I got completely and utterly burned. I thought there would be no issue in getting the files, but I soon learned how naïve I was. Request after request was denied and at first, I thought I was just unlucky, but eventually I noticed a pattern. FOIA representatives would frequently drag out the process and appeared cagey or confused about my requests. They would then site codes and numbers from the *Act* that would make a layman cross-eyed. Difficulties forced me to abandon many of my attempts, but in hindsight, I should have kept pushing. I was not anticipating resistance, but every single submission was met with a surprising excuse. Something about this system was faulty, and it led me to believe that the road to free information was not as nicely paved as it appeared to be.

Every year, I would submit a dozen or so requests, anxiously waiting for that thick envelope that held a portion of Ontario's secrets, but the envelope never came. I started to feel like the whole *Act* was a scam and it was just a nice, comforting idea for the public. After all, any agency had the right to refuse a release of records due to privacy concerns and other reasons, so why release any at all? I spent a considerable amount of time on these requests, researching them, writing them and speaking on the phone with different departments about why I was denied. The admin fees and postage were beginning to add up, so if it was all just a fabrication, I needed to know.

One thing to note is that since the cases in question were related to people, I would not be able to access information because Canadians are protected under privacy laws, and I would therefore need a signed letter from the individual to access information about them. In preparation for this book, I asked one of the FOIA agents from the Ministry of the Solicitor General (who oversees the OPP) if a missing person's case file would be released if it were requested by next of kin. The answer came back as: No. Apparently, even next-of-kin cannot request records for a lost relative unless they have Power of Attorney over them. The only other way the files are released is if the missing person requests it themselves. Imagine the rage you would feel if a loved one went missing and you were completely cut out of the investigation. Normally, people don't assign Power of Attorney as a precaution if they might one day go missing. It just doesn't happen. This technicality is one towering blockade when it comes to public involvement.

I am a supporter of personal privacy for those living and dead, for a finite period of time. After all, who would want some stranger nosing into their personal record? But there are exceptions to my support of this rule, one important exception being the passage of time. Privacy laws protect a person for 30 years after death. This means that unless the missing person is declared dead, you will not be able to access their information until after this time period.

Another hurdle worth attention is with respect to "Open" or "Active" cases. During a dispute I had with the record-keepers in 2017 over the disappearance of a little girl in 1953 (a story we will cover later), I learned that they would never, ever release information related to an "Open" case. This is a crucial tidbit that we will encounter again and again. Some of their reasons behind this make perfect sense, while others I don't particularly agree with.

The most common excuse for a lack of disclosure was that the request could not be granted, as the information did not exist: "Experienced staff familiar with the record holdings of the Ministry conducted a records search. No responsive records were located." The second common cause for refusal was Section 14(1)(b), which states that disclosure of information could interfere with an investigation, and so on and so forth.[12] The third reason was Section 14(1)(f), which states that disclosure of information would deprive a person of the right to a fair trial.

I understand these concerns if the investigation were "Active," but just because a case is considered an "Open" investigation, does not mean it is "Active." There is a monumental difference. In my experience, an "Open" case may go decades without an investigator even touching the file folder. To police, this is still considered "Open" but "Inactive," and an investigator may not even be assigned. To me, however, Section 14(1)(b) cannot be a valid reason for refusal of information when there is no investigation to interfere with. Privacy is paramount if the information is required for court proceedings, criminal indictments or other sensitive matters, but I have a problem if this argument is made without proof that the case is being investigated. Based on the reasons for denial, it would seem they are assuming that all disappearances are due to homicides, but this is far from the truth. Nevertheless, their stubbornness persists, leaving me pulling my hair out in frustration, and a lot of families left without resolutions.

Here is a quick breakdown of the purpose of the *Act*:

(a) to provide a right of access to information under the control of institutions in accordance with the principles that,
    (i) information should be available to the public,
    (ii) necessary exemptions from the right of access should be limited and specific, and
    (iii) decisions on the disclosure of government information should be reviewed independently of government.[13]

On paper it sounds like a win for transparency between government bodies and the public. The only benefit to government institutions that I can see are the administration and recovery fees they impose. To researchers, historians and genealogists, this *Act* could be a potential jackpot of hidden histories. However, early on I had my suspicions that this arrangement was too good to be true.

To entertain my suspicions, I decided I had to test the *Act*. This time I submitted a request for a solved case, well over 30 years old, to avoid the normal excuses of it being under investigation and the privacy law red tape. The file in question was regarding two convicted serial killers around London, Ontario during the late 1960s and early 1970s. I figured this would be kept for quite a while for investigative, research and court purposes, and being such a large case, it was less likely to be misplaced. My submission started off well but prompted a dozen calls from the agent at the London Police Department asking for clarification each time, inquiring as to why I was interested in such things. The process was delayed from the get-go. Eventually, they asked for a 60-day extension before responding. The weeks dragged on and a copious amount of hoop-jumping was required on my part to proceed. My suspicions that police agencies actively try to dissuade requesters were beginning to look correct. Maybe the expensive retrieval fees and overall inconvenience would be enough to turn people off from asking for records.

On May 15, 2019, I received a letter from Police Chief John Pare's office granting only partial access to the records. Two full pages of reasons were given for why I would not receive full access, some as extreme as to "endanger the life or physical safety of a law enforcement officer or any other person." The last page of the letter was an estimated fee statement that would be charged to gain access to these records. The breakdown included document reproduction, search time, preparation time, offsite storage fees and mailing costs, for a total of $392.93. I have been quoted fees of up to and beyond $1,000 for cases. I refused to pay the full amount for a simple test, not knowing if the information I'd be getting would be of any use, but I couldn't help but wonder if the fees were just a roadblock thrown in the path of oncoming researchers.

After a few weeks of back and forth, I was able to lower the fee by narrowing down my request to one specific murder that this killer had been convicted of. When I asked them for clarification on the entire file, the London Police told me that the cost they mentioned was only for one individual and that other victims were out of their jurisdiction, so they did not have the records. I was dumbfounded. Keep in mind that we had been going back and forth for months, so you can imagine my frustration when I was just hearing this for the first time. Even more frustrating was that they eliminated several other victims from the requested file early in the process that were out of their jurisdiction, but for some reason this was not communicated. Was this another deterrent?

I'm sure those in the information department don't expect many requesters to drag the process out for years and be stubbornly persistent. After the first denial, they likely hope that most of us will give up. After all, the processing fees just increase from there, and in the early days of my research they certainly deterred me from continuing on a number of submissions. But, if it is a scam, it must be exposed, and the money put forth by requesters should be refunded. Of course, there is no real way to prove this claim because the excuses given are based on the judgements of the institutions, and as much as the decisions can be argued, they cannot be forcefully overturned. These institutions can choose any reason they want in accordance with the *Act*. I am certain there are preventative measures in place and strategies that prevent the release of specific records no matter what.

Before you think I've gone "conspiracy theorist" on you, other institutions have admitted to such safeguards against the general public. Dr. John Alexander of ATP (Advanced Theoretical Physics) admits that their organization took steps to avoid requests from the public through the *Freedom of Information Act,* in this case regarding UFOs, Defence and Security. Dr. Alexander explains:

> …we initiated the ATP project specifically to examine issues regarding UFOs, and what role the Department of Defense (DoD) might be playing. Like most of the general public, we assumed somebody in DoD had responsibility for studying UFOs. This was a small internal group drawn from the government and aerospace industry, all of whom were interested in the topic.[14]

Dr. Alexander's policy among his peers was to never write anything down and avoid having any kind of paper trail. If they had filing cabinets, they were empty. This was a measure taken to prevent FOIA requests, which had just come into being. They also chose a name like Advanced Theoretical Physics because it gave no clues, hints or relation to the topics that might be searched. This is just one example, but it shows you the power and aggressive preventions that we may be up against. Who knows what other barricades stand in the public's way of information?

But is it a conspiracy against the people or simply bureaucratic incompetence?

Many of my other requests were dragged out by officials for a year or more. In some cases, I was asked to pay outrageous amounts of fees; in other cases, the records were just gone, and police claimed to have no knowledge of them, even though a considerable amount of money and police resources were used during the initial search stage. You would be surprised how often my submissions for records were declined because they could not be found in the system. For "Open" or "Active" cases, those of historical significance or cases that involved a lot of manpower, one would think records would be kept on hand or digitized and stored for study, training or for future generations. After all, the various archives, collections and police museums in the country are all in place for such material. But this assumption is wrong again. It sounded like records weren't being kept at all.

My emails and phone calls would go unanswered for months, leading me to think that I was purposely being dodged. Even in the later stages of the research for this book, FOIA agents and police continue to delay my requests after numerous extensions.

From my years of experience of trying to break down these communication barriers, I learned that there was more than just a problem with the actual *Act*. There seemed to be glaring insufficiencies with the system itself. This included the way records were kept, maintained and communicated between the institutions involved. As it turns out, the police face the same problems as we do, just on a different level. They can only act on information they receive, and if it is not shared with them by the public, coroner's office or other police agencies, then they too are left in the dark like the rest of us.

One phone call was a real eye-opener that caused a fair amount of aggravation. In a conversation with an agent from the London Police Department, I was told that they did not have case files for two or more of the victims because the individuals both had out-of-town addresses. This meant that they were out of their jurisdiction, and therefore the cases were handled by other municipal departments. I inquired that surely they must have a copy of the files. Given the same man was convicted of both slayings, the files would have been useful in the court proceedings. The agent said they never had copies and hadn't even seen them before. What this shocking revelation means is that neighbouring police departments aren't communicating with each other to the degree that we all expect them to.

I think we all picture police working together to bring down the guilty parties and locate our lost citizens, whether they wandered over the county line or not, but the reality is starkly different. During investigations, many police departments do not share files, tips, interviews, leads, witnesses or even communicate regarding possible links, no matter how related they are. This is known as Linkage Blindness and is a term that isn't talked about nearly enough. Linkage Blindness is when police forces are unable to link crimes or missing persons cases to the same offender or other jurisdictions. It can occur when police administrators and investigators will not admit or do not know that a resolution is beyond their immediate jurisdiction. It's attributed to lack of cooperation and is often cited as a reason for criminals to continue operating for long periods of time — or, in this case, for missing people to remain missing for decades.

No wonder there are so many unsolved missing persons cases. No wonder there are so many unidentified remains waiting to be named. The police don't even talk to the police.

This is a serious problem that is known by police and officials, but persists nonetheless. The misconception that police forces are working towards the same goal is false and should be acknowledged. Police have made steps towards increasing communication and accessing information within law enforcement agencies with the Canadian Police Information Centre (CPIC). This site, which is only accessible by police and partners, is a repository of data on wanted individuals, missing persons, stolen property and other crime-related data from across the country. Here, the public can submit tips, but it does not allow them to view any of its unsolved cases. On this database, more than 7,800 people are listed as missing in Canada and approximately 1,657 people are listed as missing across the province of Ontario. South of the border, the United States has the National Crime Information Center (NCIC), which provides the same flow of information. Even with these databases in place, we still have people falling through the cracks.

Studies have shown that existing databases like CPIC have several drawbacks. The information can be out of date, neither clear or consistent and can be reported differently from one jurisdiction to another.[15]

On websites where the public does have access to cases, like *Canada's Missing*, the missing person's profile will have very basic information, and some of it is not helpful in leading to a resolution. Usually, it describes a very general area of where the person was last seen and a few articles of clothing that they may have been wearing. Sometimes there is no information at all, save for a name, and in some cases these names are spelled incorrectly.

It is the NCMPUR's opinion that information on missing people or found remains should be publicized if it will not jeopardize the investigation, with which I wholeheartedly agree. That said, there is information that is still being withheld that could be released to the public:

> Providing it will not jeopardize the investigation, the coroner/missing person investigating agency should request publication to the national missing person and unidentified remains website for any unidentified remains where there is information suitable for publication and reason to expect the public may have information that could help identify the individual, as soon as practical at the investigator's discretion.

Section 4.8.9 of *Best Practices* goes on to say the purpose is to illicit the public's help in solving the case.

Another outrageous discovery I made in my examination was that the record retention period for most of these institutions is much shorter than the privacy period for FIPPA. For example, the retention period for the RCMP is only two years. If the public can only request records that are 30 years old or older, one would expect the retention period to extend beyond the privacy period. This makes absolutely no sense. It is disheartening to know that this was probably not a coincidence. We cannot give these organizations the benefit of the doubt, as there is evidence to show that they are aware of such harmful discrepancies. In section 4.7.9 of the RCMP-managed NCMPUR document, all team members are made aware of the importance of the *Privacy Act* and retention periods, and yet we still run into this problem:

All records may be subject to federal and/or provincial access and/or privacy legislation and should be managed accordingly. RCMP files including MC/PUR and CPIC information are subject to the collection, usage, disclosure, retention and disposal provisions set out in the federal Privacy Act. RCMP files are also subject to the federal Access to Information Act. All provinces have similar Privacy/Access legislation and agencies should be aware of these provisions in their jurisdiction.[16]

A missing persons case will, without question, go inactive if there are no new leads over time. This is where the term "cold case" comes from, and it refers to the fact that every tip and lead has been followed up on. Therein lies another problem when dealing with family members of the missing. Relatives of the missing may not hear from their police contact for quite some time, which would signal that the investigation has stopped or stalled without notice. Therefore, some families may become more proactive and launch their own investigation, hire a private detective or launch a website or campaign. In an interview with the OPP, I asked them about a police policy that dictates when a missing person file can be declared inactive if no new information is obtained. Their response was that they will never close a homicide or a missing person investigation unless it has been resolved. All leads and tips are followed up on. They didn't address my question about inactive cases, which are cases that are not reviewed or assigned to an investigator for active follow-up. We can confirm they exist based on information published by the NCMPUR, and the fact that not all missing people are listed on the missing person list.

The information on the OPP website is not consistent with the information on *Canada's Missing*. Why is the information not shared between sites and how is the public expected to help solve cases with a limited profile online? I posed this very question to the OPP, who told me that the investigating officer publishes their missing persons cases at their discretion and initiation. The OPP works closely with the RCMP to keep the website updated with new information to ensure accuracy. But, if other investigating agencies are publishing cases at their own discretion, how can the information remain consistent across the board? If all agencies aren't following NCMPUR's *Best Practices*, then what good is it doing?

The OPP has stepped up their media presence tremendously in the last decade and works closely with the press to broadcast cases in relevant communities. Social media is relied on heavily, where a person's face can be distributed globally with one click. Especially today, we are receiving AMBER alerts via our smart phones. We can't underestimate the power of social media, but at the same time we can't be sure if it actually works in solving these cases because the data is not kept, studied or distributed.

It wasn't so long ago when police were just as hindered by privacy laws as the public today. Each province used to have a different privacy policy when it came to missing Canadians. Most provinces blocked officials from accessing medical, financial and telephone records as a way of protecting the public, but since 2019 all provinces in Canada have adopted new legislation that removes information roadblocks for police, allowing them to create a full victim profile that can lead to clues on the person's whereabouts. This includes information on everything from school records to Internet searches, and even the last time the missing person received medical services or filled a prescription.

As of 2013, Nova Scotia had one of the more relaxed privacy exemptions for police, but now Alberta,[17] Saskatchewan,[18] Manitoba,[19] and British Columbia[20] have adopted similar legislation that allows police to access the following:

(a) records containing contact information;
(b) records containing identification information, including a physical description and any distinguishing marks;
(c) telephone and other electronic communication records including, without limiting the generality of the foregoing,
    (i) records related to signals from a wireless device that may indicate the location of the wireless device,
    (ii) cellular telephone records, and
    (iii) text messaging records;
(d) internet browsing history records;
(e) global positioning system tracking records;
(f) photographs;
(g) video records, including closed-circuit television footage;
(h) records from a school, university or other educational institution;
(i) records containing travel information;
(j) records containing accommodation information;
(k) records containing employment information;
(l) records containing health information;
(m) records containing financial information;
(n) any other records that the justice considers appropriate;

This list is essentially copied and pasted in each province's *Missing Persons Act*. Finally, on July 1 of 2019, Ontario jumped on board with the legislation and has mirrored the same policies.[21] The road to the legislation in Ontario is one I know well. It all snowballed from a recent tragedy that was relatable to me. It started when 28-year-old Daniel Trask went on a solo adventure in the Temagami area of

Ontario in 2011 and did not return. Daniel seemed very much an outdoorsman and a lover of the wilderness, like myself, so the story hit home with me and hundreds of others who enjoy Ontario's beautiful forests every year.

He was reported missing by family and the OPP was involved in a search. In an article from 2019, Daniel's mother, Maureen Trask, is quoted regarding the frustrating roadblocks that she and police faced while looking for Daniel. Trask first checked local hospitals to see if her son might have been injured and was checked in. She was told that since she did not have Power of Attorney for her adult son, she would not be eligible for such information. When she asked the police, they too admitted that they did not have authority to check hospital beds. This meant that hundreds of hours and resources could have been wasted in the wilderness of Temagami, only to find out that Daniel was laid up in the hospital. They were unable to check his bank accounts and credit cards to track his movements and would only be limited to eyewitnesses who last reported seeing Daniel last, "Without having that information, it's very difficult to track their movement, including things like [CCTV] video, perhaps at places where they were last known to be," Trask said.[22]

Maureen Trask battled for four years to change the way privacy of missing persons was handled. This only comes in to play for adults— of course parents of young children have authority over them. Keep in mind that this new legislation is helpful to police to gain more information without a court order, but does nothing for the general public, meaning that if your loved one goes missing, you will not be able to gain information on them. This act gives the police more power but does not help the public in assisting with long-term missing cases. In my opinion, more work needs to be done here.

Daniel's remains were found in 2015, but even then, we still didn't have all the answers.

Police Practices and Myth

Even with the advancements made by the *Missing Persons Act* and an increased amount of police presence, databases and support agencies, there are a swarm of factors that prevent case resolutions.

Across the country, belief and rumour stand in the way of recovering missing people. There is still a common assumption that a person must be missing for 24 or 48 hours before a report can be filed, however none of the police policies I reviewed across Canada subscribe to any such rule. There is no time restriction on when you can report someone missing. Previously, in Ontario, it was law that one must wait 24 hours from the time of last seen before contacting police, but since the *Missing Persons Act*, this time restraint has been revised. NCMPUR asserts this notion to law enforcement around the country.

> A police agency should not turn away a report of a missing person on the basis of time elapsed since they went missing. There is no waiting period for reporting a missing person. Under no circumstances should a reporting party be advised that they must wait a specific period of time before a report can be made. Any delay has the potential to negatively impact the investigation and the likelihood of success. To suggest a waiting period is to pre-judge the risk assessment.[23]

Sadly, we live in a world where there is a difference between written policy and police actions. For example, even in the face of a "no-waiting" policy, police could ask the person submitting the report to wait 24 hours. In a discussion report prepared by Dr. Melina Buckley, there are some situations where police might not refuse to take the report but may blatantly share their doubts in the seriousness of it and discourage people from making a formal report, which would only delay the investigation further.[24]

Regardless of the individual or time frame, the investigation begins once law enforcement is notified. It is the police agency's job to now determine if that person is missing and complete an assessment. The police agency is required to take on the investigation and forward the case or any tips to other policing forces or active and interested jurisdictions. In no way do these responsibilities fall on the public.

There is also a belief that only the family of the missing can make the initial report, but this has also turned out to be false. That is not to say that these shared misconceptions are baseless. In fact, it used to be a requirement that only family could be involved. When this law was enforced across relevant institutions, they did not factor in how this blanket protocol failed to consider variables like who last saw the missing person, estranged family members, persons traveling or persons without family.

Once again, we look to *Best Practices* for top-notch protocols that police forces would benefit from:

> A police agency should not restrict who can report a missing person. A report should be accepted from anyone who is concerned that the person is missing. In the past, some agencies would only accept a report from a family member. Yet, in some cases, the missing person is estranged from their families so the family may not even know that the person is missing. Rejection based on who is reporting the person

missing runs the risk of failing to investigate a legitimate missing person situation.[25]

The belief that only family could report the missing was not a public fabrication, after all. These were all once policy rules that stood in the way of case resolutions and we still see their lingering effects today. We have instances that show how some police forces have denied investigating missing people for this exact reason.

When Sarah de Vries went missing in Vancouver, British Columbia in April of 1998, her friend Wayne Leng approached police to report her missing. Police told him he was unable to do so because he was not a family member.[26] Even more surprising was that Leng admitted being the last person to see Sarah de Vries alive, but the police waited two weeks before calling him in for an interview.[27] One would think that Leng would be a person of interest in this case, but for whatever reason local police did not share this view. DNA was later found on serial murderer Robert Pickton's pig farm, which officials confirmed matched Sarah de Vries. We can only wonder what would have happened had police begun the investigation when it was brought to them, or if protocols were less restrictive at the time.

In her thesis work, *An Awkward Silence*, submitted in 2013 at the University of Ottawa, Maryanne Pearce offers many examples of how police error and baseless policies have only added to this country's missing person problem. Her overtly detailed and thorough work has been regarded as a massive leap towards justice for missing and murdered Indigenous women in Canada. Through impeccable research, Pearce presented jaw dropping facts on the subject that gained national attention.

Pearce cites a second case where 17-year-old Amanda Bartlett had gone missing from a group home in Winnipeg in 1996. The group home did not report her missing, perhaps since she was known to leave unannounced. Bartlett's mother contacted the police to report her missing numerous times that same year but was turned away. In one instance, an officer told her sister, "We don't do family reunions,"[28] and refused to initiate a search or even add her name to the list. It wasn't until 2008 that Winnipeg Police Service had finally classified Bartlett as a missing person. It took 12 years and the help of Amnesty International. As of April 2022, Amanda Sophia Bartlett has never been found.

It is the responsibility of police to never turn away a missing person report. In hindsight, despite the price tag, on a human level it is better to front-load an investigation at the risk of being wrong rather than take the report seriously weeks, months or even years later when the chances of a positive resolution have diminished.

As each minute passes, the chances of finding a missing person alive fade. It is the general opinion of police that the first 24 hours after a person goes missing are the most crucial in the investigation. This is even more so for children, where the first 20 minutes are critical. In Canada and the United States, the majority of kidnapped children are killed within 3 hours.[29]

There is ample data to back this opinion, and yet we still have upsetting stories like Bartlett's and dozens of others. These stories are important to retell here because they offer a perspective not often seen by both the public and the victims. People generally operate under the belief that if they were to disappear, the authorities would stop at nothing to bring them home. In reality, this is not the case. Imagine if people like Sarah de Vries and Amanda Bartlett knew of these stories and saw how their cases were handled.

There is substantial police literature that ensures that the public will not face difficulties when reporting a crime or missing person.

> A police agency should not turn away a person wishing to provide information on a case on the basis of jurisdiction. Complainants should contact the law enforcement agency having jurisdiction for the case, but they should be able to provide the information to ANY police agency. The information should be taken in wherever it comes in and by whatever means, and must be passed on to the agency of jurisdiction. It is not the responsibility of the public to determine jurisdiction or understand whose case it is, nor are they always capable of doing so. We must not make it difficult for people to provide helpful information.[30]

Police agencies agree that there should be no obstructions to the flow of information, and yet it is still happening. With NCMPUR already doing most of the heavy lifting and laying the groundwork, it only takes the individual officer to follow the steps provided. I cannot fathom why these *Best Practices* are not mandatory procedures.

We have made great strides of improvement with countrywide Missing Persons legislation, but still readers may be able to detect my frustration. This stems from the significant fact that not only are the public relied upon to solve cases, but they are responsible for the majority of cases that are solved — not detectives.

Suddenly, the plea from detectives on the evening news is starting to make sense.

This truth is not realized by the public at large, but in an objective, independent research study done by the Rand Corporation, researchers Peter Greenwood and

Joan Petersilia exposed the surprising data that, "most cases are solved by means of information spontaneously provided by a source other than those developed by the investigator." While police are no doubt involved, it is up to the public to solve the case: "...the three most common groups that assist in solving crimes are the public, patrol officers, and detectives, in this order."[31]

In a follow-up report, the same authors concluded that, "Nearly half of investigators' case-related activities are devoted to post-arrest processing." Greenwood and Petersilia also reveal that,

> ...it is not appropriate to view the role of investigators as that of solving crimes. They do not spend much time on activities that lead to (case) clearances, and much of their work in this connection could be performed by clerical personnel ...our review of individual case folders persuaded us that actions by members of the public can strongly influence the outcome of cases... Sometimes they recognized the suspect or stolen property at a later time and called the investigator. In other cases, the victim or his relatives conducted a full-scale investigation on their own and eventually presented the investigator with a solution. Collectively, these types of citizen involvement constitute a sizeable fraction of cleared cases. Possibly many more cases could be solved if the public were made aware that they cannot depend on the police to solve cases magically but rather must provide the police with as much information as possible.[32]

There is no question that the police are better equipped, highly trained and more resourceful than members of the public are, and yet here we are with a huge undertaking put on us, many of us not even aware that we have.

The Rand study found that the public's perception of police investigators has proven to be a problem. Thanks largely to an abundance of police television series and movies, the public sees the investigator as a tortured, gung-ho, "boots on the ground" Sherlock, when in reality their role is far from this image. The study found that investigators' time was occupied mostly by paperwork, filing reports and other administrative duties, rather than chasing down leads and running around town with a magnifying glass. Their role only intensified during the prosecution phase of the investigation if a crime was resolved or was before the courts. In reality, investigators sit and wait for someone to call them with a tip.

By painting a realistic picture of how crimes are solved and understanding the true role of investigators versus the popular portrayal of them, we can dispel stereotypes and reengage the public's interest in cooperating with police and being helpful members of their community.

This cooperation is the most crucial at the time of reporting the incident, when the responding patrol officer records the first details from the public. The more details conveyed at the beginning of an investigation, the better chance of solving the case.

Although this research done by Rand was conducted decades ago, the findings still hold true today. We still hear stories every week on how instrumental the public is in solving a cold case. In an article from the *Toronto Star,* Detective Sergeant Steve Ryan admitted that a simple phone call from a member of the public was the key that unlocked a murder mystery going back almost two decades. The charred remains of a teenage girl were found in a suitcase in Vaughan, Ontario on September 1, 1994. A forensic anthropologist noted she had sustained severe injuries and fractures prior to her death and was likely tortured, however they could not obtain fingerprints or identify her by other means. An anonymous phone call helped police identify the 17-year-old girl and have the guilty parties arrested. The article quotes Detective Sergeant Ryan praising the power of public influence on these cases, "It goes to show the power of a phone call. It's a difficult case."[33] Ryan believes that this case should provide hope for others connected to unsolved cases.

Crime Stoppers is a civilian, nonprofit organization run by a volunteer board of directors. They are an intermediary between the public and police that offers an accessible avenue for tips to be submitted anonymously, and until recently, they paid reward money for any tips that led to a case being solved. There was now an incentive for the public to come forward with information. For those that are not comfortable working with police (and there are many) this provides a great alternative.

As of February 2021, Crime Stoppers' statistics showed that 273,981 cases were cleared because of public tips. I reached out to them multiple times for a comment and statistics involving missing people, but they remained evasive and dismissive and were surprisingly unhelpful. For an organization that works with police departments across the country, it seems that some of the law enforcement behaviours have rubbed off on them. If we compare Canadian websites to websites like the National Missing and Unidentified Persons System (NamUS) in the United States, there is a glaring difference. The success of NamUS is published and made crystal clear on the front page of the website. That does not happen in Ontario. NamUS also publishes the exact number of missing and unidentified bodies reported every year; these are statistics that Canadian police can't accurately state.

Crime Stoppers is a great improvement, but I would like to see more transparency to the public with their data. After all, if it weren't for the public, they would have no data.

We can't know how often tips from the public are responsible for solving missing persons or unidentified human remains cases in Ontario, because the OPP and agencies like Crime Stoppers do not have or track this statistic. There is no provincial direction that requires them to do so. Understandably, when it comes to closing a case, this information is less of a priority, but I for one would like to know. Without an exact number, we can be sure that the public has a huge involvement. Websites like *Crime Stoppers, OPP,* and *Canada's Missing* are a valuable way for the public to be in the loop, but only if the information is presented accurately and efficiently. States the NCMPUR:

> The purpose of the web site is to solicit tips from the public, which is of great benefit to the investigation. The longer the delay in publishing, the greater the chance that valuable information will be lost.[34]

I was able to speak to the OPP about why they thought the accessible information being posted for missing persons was so scarce. They claimed, again, that whatever is available is made public at the discretion of the investigating agency. They can only provide as much information on the missing person as they are provided. It could be speculated that initial interviews with witnesses and relatives are less thorough in some cases and result in this lack of information. Perhaps this is because police and family members are pressured and eager to get out searching while the trail is still hot. It would seem that it is not the fault of individual police officers, but more of a problem with the system and antiquated practices.

The proof that sharing information can lead to case advancement and resolution, is, as they say, in the pudding — or, in the instance of human remains cases, in the bones. When the public are finally able to access, review, share and actually see the information with their own eyes, only then will we start to bring these lost souls home or give a name to unclaimed remains.

Historically, presently and based on my own personal encounters with accessing data, it seems we are in the middle of an *Info War*. Knowledge is both the key and weapon when it comes to public assistance, and I for one will not give up, after all, a man who has tasted knowledge can never be full. After laying out the difficulties involving privacy, transparency and the costs associated with them, it seems that information is not free at all. As these unfortunate crimes and disappearances happen, we learn that information is a valuable commodity that is very hard to come by.

4

Vital Vachon

"Lost in that camp, and wasted all its fire, and he who wrought that spell!
Ah, towering pine and stately Kentish spire,
Ye have one tale to tell!"
—Bret Harte

As migrant workers populated the north country in search of precious timber and ore, bush camps began to pop up sparsely throughout the lumberwoods. The guttural sound of chainsaws and the chopping cough of the axe was all one would hear from daybreak to nightfall. If not for the plunder of raw timber, then they came for the tantalizing gossip of gold in the ground. Serious prospecting began in 1906 after traces of gold were unearthed near South Porcupine, one of five wards that make up the town of Timmins. The discovery sparked a mining industry and brought in droves of immigrant workers. These labourers came over with the dream of carving out a life, and in most cases left their families behind. The timber industry had a similar effect on the region. Only the strongest could handle the demands and hardships of the bush. The town required its people to be as tough and spiny as the name suggests. The labour was lonely and intensive, and after a day's work, men would often return to the solitude of their bachelor camps… and in one of these unmapped lumber camps was the last place Vital Vachon was seen alive.

Vital Vachon was of French descent and had been living and working in the area for years. On paper, his occupation was known only as a "bush worker" — sadly we don't know much more than that.

On May 1, 1973, Vital Vachon left his bush camp somewhere in Lucas Township and traveled into Timmins to purchase a new chainsaw and a few bottles of liquor. A witness reported that around 6:30 p.m. he left town and returned to his bush camp by way of Vet's Taxi of Timmins. Vachon dropped the chainsaw off at the main bush camp and made his way, by taxi, to a trailer occupied by another someone whose name was not released. According to reports, the pair socialized and drank an unknown amount of liquor. Vachon left alone around 8:15 p.m. and proceeded to his bachelor camp, which was another mile and a quarter further into the bush. He was observed by fellow workers to be heading in the correct direction, without any cause for worry. They did not report him drunk or stumbling.

On May 7, the foreman ventured into the bush towards Vachon's private camp and couldn't find a trace of the man anywhere. He returned and informed workers that Vachon was not there. The foreman inquired about Vachon to another employee who had his camp right next to him. The worker stated that Vachon had not been at his camp all week. This was reported to the property owner who then reported it to police.

In order to find out who Vachon really was, I contacted police for the case file back in 2017, but I was denied it based on nine different sections within the *Information Act*. Most of the exemptions had to do with interfering with an active law enforcement investigation, highly sensitive information and multiple claims to the invasion of privacy. I don't know how they can argue the latter, given that the event took place in 1973; I am unsure of whose privacy they are protecting. They seem adamant on protecting all names even though the reports were filed over 30 years ago. Despite the secrecy, police claimed to interview several workers in the area, but it is impossible to tell who police spoke with and what these people said. As I was unable to get the report, I was forced to push the investigation to the back burner and continue on with other research.

On a hunch, I decided to resubmit for this case in 2019. I had some serious doubts that this was an active investigation as the police had claimed. I wanted to learn how active it really was. How often were police reviewing the Vachon file? In April 2019, I received a response letter from the OPP, who had now granted me partial access to the records. Now I was really confused… I could not understand why they would release case files to me now and not in 2017 when I initially requested them. Clearly their reasoning for the first denial still stood and would apply two years later, so I was curious to know what had changed.

Upon my review of the file, there were at least four fully redacted pages of information, as well as other redacted statements, names, locations, descriptions and other snippets within the text. Nevertheless, I was able to confirm just how active this case was and how much of a priority Vital Vachon had become. According to scribblings on the file, the case appeared to be last reviewed on October 27, 1998.

The first police report I accessed was from May 10, 1973. The report filed by Constable William (Bill) Alexander Archibald #2434 included the statement from the foreman. Archibald conducted the initial search as best he could. In early May, there can be a fair amount of snow still left in Ontario's bushland. Heavy tree cover and lower temperatures prolong winter conditions making spring arrive a few weeks later than locations further south. It may have slowed search efforts and made it difficult to track on the forest floor. Archibald went on to say, "As thorough a search as possible due to the bush conditions at this time has been conducted without success. A search helicopter [middle of sentence redacted] has also proved fruitless." The investigation included interviews with co-workers and witnesses, and foul play was not suspected. All names of interviewees were redacted from the police report, including the initial witness and the foreman.

Constable Archibald went on to say that "the search will be continued when weather and land conditions improve." There was no indication of weather events at the time, but he could have been referring to snow melt.

However, not a single report indicates that a search and rescue ground team was deployed to beat through the bush after the missing man. SAR teams are capable and trained to operate rain or shine and in all seasons. If they can search for missing people in the dead of winter, why not in early May?

Constable Archibald had an interesting theory as to what happened to Vachon, "I strongly suspect that Vachon became lost in the bush and may have fallen into one of the nearby creeks or into the muskeg and is dead."

After more than a week later, police officers still could not locate next-of-kin: "To this date I have been unable to locate any next-of-kin and although VACHON has lived and worked in the area for the past few years, there appears to be no one who new [sic] him well."

Vachon was a single man and, as far as I could gather, had no children. Could it also be that he had no other family in the country? In a follow up report, the police became so desperate to find relatives that they placed an ad in the *Timmins Daily Press* looking for information on Vital Vachon and for next-of-kin to come forward and identify themselves.

In my years of researching these subjects, I have never heard of police taking this approach. In the past, it was common for the coroner to hold an inquest and display clothing or other identifiers to see if locals knew the man, but in a case where there is no body, I guess running an ad in the newspaper is the next best option.

If next-of-kin were eventually located they were not included in this, or any of the follow up reports. All reports ended with a signature from "Sgt. Robert (Bob) Stanley Rose #1425."

> **HELP WANTED**
> Ontario Provincial Police of the South Porcupine detachment are asking the help of the public in securing information about bushworker Vital Vachon, who has been missing for more than two weeks in the Lucas Township area. Police are seeking personal facts about the man, family, rela t i ve s, where he came from. Anyone with information, is asked to contact the detachment at 235-3345.

* May 17, 1973, Timmins Daily Press.

Police continued their search of the bushland where Vachon was last reported to be seen on May 23. There was no indication of an organized search party being formed. Police stated that nothing was found and they would return to the area once it, "dries up."

The police had two conflicting locations that were mentioned in their search, one of them being Buskegau Creek. When I asked a local resident about Buskegau Creek, they had never heard of it, nor could they locate it on the map, and try as I might, I couldn't find it either. There is a Buskegau Road, which intersects the Buskegau railway point but it's not near South Porcupine. There is a Buskegau River but it does not go through Lucas. It's possible that the creek in question is a seasonal waterway, only filling in the spring and draining in the summer heat. Regardless, not a shred of evidence was found that he was in either area.

I called the town of Timmins, Black River-Matheson, Iroquois Falls and Cochrane and none of them had heard of Lucas Township. It took a few years of digging, but eventually I was able to get my hands on an old map. South of Cochrane and East of Highway 655 was a blurry, black and white rectangle marked "Lucas." It was 53 kilometres north of South Porcupine. The map shows two main rivers in the area and a wetland to the southeast. I had tried to gain access to the property, but during my search I learned from the Ministry of Natural Resources and Forestry, that the area is privately owned. This makes any follow up searches to the location exceedingly difficult. Officers returned to the property again on July 9 and July 13, hoping that drier conditions may reveal some sign of Vachon, but they did not.

On August 22, both Sergeant Rose and Constable Archibald returned to the area where Vachon disappeared. They retraced previously searched locations, specifically the path between the trailer and the bush camp and asked other men who were still working in the area if they had recovered anything. Unfortunately, no new information was gained, and the officers concluded that Vachon must have wandered far from the area he was expected to be in and was now deceased. I would think that all workers would be requested to be removed from the area and work to be shut down until Vachon was found, but for some bizarre reason this was not the case. How were they expected to track a missing man when others were working in the area, making trails, cutting trees and walking over clues?

Not only did work continue in the area since May, but it was frequently visited by locals and hunters, who reported no evidence of a body or of Vachon's belongings. It's not clear to me why police would have put so much trust in the remaining bush workers and hunters that entered the area to turn over evidence or approach police with information. How could they notify every visitor to the area that they had a missing man in the bush and to keep a look-out? With this in mind, Archibald concluded his fourth report stating that, "It can only be assumed at this time that VACHON wandered a considerable distance from the area, and can now be presumed deceased." With no evidence that he had walked anywhere in the area, I don't see how this could be assumed. Police were unable to find a single footprint or article of clothing so there is no indication if he was far or near. He could have left in a taxi, or he could have walked in a different direction. Again, from what I could gather, no formal search was carried out and no search dogs were deployed to the area.

Pages 14, 15, 16, 18 and 20 were excluded from the police report for various reasons.

Sergeant R.S. Rose did two further write-ups on the matter, the first one dated November 8, 1973, in which he stated, "it is unlikely that his remains will ever be located." The letter was signed off by inspector A.B. Forster.

Whether he was basing this on a hunch or a tip, this is a pessimistic and gloomy outlook by the investigating officer. It sounds like Rose did not believe it was worth a continued search effort and wanted the matter finished or moved to someone else. Dead bodies don't move on their own, so if Vachon is dead in the bush it is only a matter of time until his remains are found — not the other way around. Same goes for the theory of him falling into the river — unless he was trapped beneath a log, his body would have surfaced. Sergeant Rose then went on to confirm that no relatives of the man were living in Ontario. This resulted in a sad end for Vachon. Perhaps his remaining family was still overseas and had not even heard that he was missing. The absence of family means an absence of pressure on the police department to do more.

Based on this point of view, Sergeant R.S. Rose recommended that the office of the Public Trustee take the case over. To my knowledge, the office of the Public Trustee would oversee finances of those who could not act for themselves or had no known relatives; they would step in as an executor. I have no way of knowing if it is common for police to make such recommendations, but I felt it a bit tacky that Rose was already thinking of the man's estate as if he were certain he was dead. Keep in mind that not a single clue was found to indicate that Vachon was deceased. It's important to mention here that in all of the missing persons cases I have researched in the province of Ontario, I cannot think of one where the police gave up so quickly (only six months) and presumed with confidence that the missing person was dead based on absolutely no evidence. Out of all the Open cases I have seen, no matter how old, it never, not once, states that the person is presumed deceased. Police will usually treat the investigation as if they are looking for a living person. I can't say what it was about Vachon's case that was so unique. However, even with Archibald's belief that Vachon was dead and the recommendation by Sergeant Rose, the police file was still left open and treated as a missing person. Either a superior officer kiboshed the idea or no one took action on the recommendation. This is one of the weirdest cases I've come across.

Sergeant Rose concluded his report on December 17, 1973, confidently stating that, "VACHON became lost in the bush while intoxicated and is dead." Clearly, the sergeant is stating his own beliefs here and they are not based on found evidence. As I stated before, it was not mentioned in the police report that Vachon was drunk. Without a toxicology report they could not determine if he was intoxicated. This is also an assumption by police that Vachon vanished that first evening on the way back to his camp. The reality is that Vachon could have vanished on the third day, fourth day or any other day up until he was reported missing on day seven. This is why the theory of Vachon being intoxicated does not hold up. I also find it odd that no one reported Vachon missing for seven days. Did the foreman or fellow workers not notice that he did not show up for work for an entire week?

The last few pages of the police report were nothing but revised templates with the same basic information on Vachon entered into the boxes. No new information was added over the next few decades. One thing that bothered me was that there were a number of blank pages included in this report for no reason I could imagine. I'm not talking redacted pages; I'm talking about literally blank pieces of paper, some of them with pen scribbles at the corners. How are these relevant and why are these in Vachon's file? There is also a contradiction with Vachon's age in the report. First, he is being reported as 59, then 69, then 55 and finally 70 years old, but if his birthdate is accurate, he was clearly 56 at the time of his disappearance.

When compiling an information profile on a missing person, there are critical identification factors investigators must hit. A physical description is a must in case the missing person is still alive and has left the area and could have been seen by others. At least one recent photograph should be on file and distributed to media and the public. These are simple practices that are recommended to police agencies. It is not a requirement of the investigator to follow them, but it damn well should be, as stated once again by the NCMPUR:

> The investigator should ensure at least one recent photograph of the Missing Person is on file as soon as possible. More than one photo is desirable. Photos are used in all publications and alerts. Photos are an excellent way to recognize someone. Studies show that on a missing person website, cases without photos are rarely visited.[35]

If investigators know that cases without photos are rarely visited by the public and out of jurisdiction investigators, why then is this not being made a priority? Why do we not have a photo of Vital Vachon or others who have been missing long-term? Vachon surely would have had a passport photo at the very least, but nothing was on file. If Vachon was known to take taxis in and out of town for supplies, then distributing his photograph to local drivers would be a great place to start.

Vital Vachon is described as 5-feet 7-inches tall, weighing 160 pounds, Caucasian with brown hair, brown eyes and wearing a beard and sideburns. He wore both upper and lower dentures and was of a slender build. He spoke with a French accent and was said to be "loud" and "vulgar." He wore rough clothing, likely due to his profession. The police report stated multiple times that he may have had a silver plate in his skull. Other than the plate, Vachon had no known physical or mental dependencies.

Police officers returned to the area multiple times, leading us to believe they combed the bushland thoroughly, however, they do not state if they dragged the local rivers. Vachon was reported to have a metal plate in his skull and if Vachon was in the area, then the metal plate would still be there. I wonder if police ever used a metal detector in their search. It would be amazing to me if this detail was overlooked because the metal plate was mentioned in the police report at least three or four times.

I could confirm all these details when they released a partial police report to me, but they still refused to release any search and rescue reports, interviews, statements or anything else that may give me a better understanding of this man's life. I was able to get my hands-on Archibald's day journals for the months he was involved, but there was not a single mention of Vachon or the investigation. I figured there had to be more information out there so I filed an appeal only a days after to try and get the non-redacted report.

I went through the appeal process and one day was called by the mediator between me and the OPP regarding the case. They stated that there may have been new information found that was just redacted. She admitted that police were eventually able to find next-of-kin, but that's all they would say. It's probable that they were living in another province or country, which is why it took months to locate them. I was never able to locate these family members to confirm if they existed or were even alive. Some of the redacted information were statements from family members, co-workers and those involved, and are still subject to privacy laws. Details involved what to do with and where to send property owned by Vachon. These are details that I am not interested in, but I would like to know the ins and outs of the search and what his fellow employees saw, especially the one he supposedly drank with and the individual that camped beside him. I put more pressure on the mediator to reveal the statements without the names of the witnesses or relatives, but she stood firm that in the case of Vital Vachon I would not gain further access.

The two exemptions that were given to me by police were as follows: 14.1(l): Police processes. This means they are unwilling to share the steps that police took and would likely include SAR tactics and resources. Perhaps they want to avoid criticism in their efforts. Secondly, was section 15 (a, b, c): Information related to other governments. I'm wondering if that is a European government who cooperated to confirm Vachon's immigrant status and locate next-of-kin. I am still of the opinion that more would have been done if Vachon had family living close by. The files are now locked away and will only be seen by members of the police, should they choose to look at it one day.

Unless I'm reading this wrong, the police documents indicate that Vachon's file was revisited on October 27, 1998. It is recommended that police list and document regular checks on the file. This includes maintaining the listing on various websites like CPIC and renewing contact with the family every 12 months in long-term cases and then every 24 months. Also, at the annual anniversary of the disappearance and significant dates like birthdays, NCMPUR advises that police get in touch with the family. Moreover, in the past, police have created short videos or media releases in an effort at renewing public interest. The goal is to create more awareness of the case and have a file that can be shared and discussed amongst the public. It's clear that many detachments aren't taking NCMPUR's recommendations seriously.

Recently, a video campaign like this was done for a woman who went missing in London, Ontario, and I remember they had even put up billboards. But why hasn't this been done for people like Vachon or others mentioned here? Other than what was previously stated, not much is known about this man. I was able to discover that Vachon once lived at 173 Algonquin Blvd East in a rooming house. His fellow tenants were cut from the same cloth and consisted of other bush-workers and two cooks that were likely part of the same outfit. I would love to know if any of these people were interviewed, including the rooming house owner. This building is now a thing of the past; a parking lot stands in its place. Outside of the classified ad posted in the *Timmins Daily Press*, there isn't much left that connects Vital Vachon to this world.

Unless family members come forward and reach out to me, we will never learn more about this man. He is one of the many migrant labourers that have been swallowed up by the bush and forgotten to time. Because of the lack of willingness to share information with the public or other departments, it won't be long before the name Vital Vachon will fade into history and be completely forgotten. We can only hope that the police do not give up, although it looks like they may have already.

Sergeant Rose sent a report to his detachment commander in Rainy River, Ontario in December 1973 with a copy to the superintendent. The report was a brief rundown of the incident, with the lower paragraph removed for a collection of reasons, those being: The disclosure of the record could facilitate the commission of an unlawful act or hamper the control of crime, the personal information being highly sensitive, and was compiled and is identifiable as part of an investigation into a possible violation of law, except to the extent that disclosure is necessary to prosecute the violation or to continue the investigation. However, below the redacted section, Rose punched out a single revealing sentence from his typewriter at the very bottom of the page: "We know very little about Vital Vachon."

I couldn't agree more; and sadly it looks like things are going to stay that way.

5

Sander Lingman

"Claim posts fallen, with tags askew, Blazes gone, except for a few. The sides of the pits have all caved in — The traveller wonders what lies within."
—Frank Holley

The bizarre disappearance of Sander Lingman is one that will haunt the forests of northern Ontario indefinitely. It's a perfect example of the mystifying vanishings that have captivated me for decades.

The Lingman family came over from Bollnäs, Sweden, and after living in various Ontario towns, finally settled in Nakina. Nakina was officially formed in 1923 as a station yard on the National Transcontinental Railway. It is a place of adventure and discovery, known for abundant mineral mining and home to world class lakes teeming with fish. Today, the population sits at a quiet 500 or so residents. It's the kind of place where most had wished they'd grown up, but at the same time are relieved they didn't. You will only hear good things about Nakina.

Sander Lingman was born to Karl and Anna Lingman and was one of five siblings, Albert, Wendell, Charles and a sister, Ruth, who sadly suffered from leukaemia and did not live to her third birthday. Sander was born on September 1, 1925 in Nakina and lived there for the remainder of his life. The Lingman's were hard workers and known throughout the northern tip of the province for their hunting, trapping and mining achievements. They also guided others through the wilderness that was now becoming as familiar as their backyard. From all accounts, they were the embodiment of outdoorsmen.

If you look on a map just north of Opasquia Provincial Park, you will find a lake named after prospector Johan (John) Lingman. The lake was discovered by Lingman prior to 1930 and was officially mapped in 1936 by O.A. Seeber and G.M. Robson, assistants to J. Satterly.[36] It was officially named Lingman Lake in December of that year.

Since its discovery, Lingman Lake has been the battleground for mining companies, and remains a high-grade gold deposit to this day. The lake is as remote as you can get, with no roads or railways nearby. The arduous trips into the interior are a testament to the Lingman character. Another relative, named John Lingman was one of the first to reach Laird Lake when there was news of a gold strike in 1937. The family wasted no time in making quite an impact in the region soon after they landed in Ontario in the early 1900s. Like his descendants, Sander Lingman had an explorer's spirit and was quite a young businessman. These tales of adventure and pioneering only deepen the mystery of his disappearance.

Lingman didn't have what some may call a formal education, but he along with his brothers were competent and hardworking bushpeople. Not only was he reported to be a wilderness guide, he was also a trapper, and had a shop that sold snowshoes and other equipment that one would require when venturing into the outdoors. He was a bachelor, somewhat reserved, I'm told, and had recently been hired to work for a mining company called KRNO Mines Limited, based out of Toronto.

He was on contract with the company for an undisclosed period of time. It is not uncommon for mining companies to hire locals due to the benefits they come with — the obvious being that there would be no need to provide long distance transportation for workers, and they would possess an intimate knowledge of the area. KRNO was created by Vincent Feeley and Joseph McDermott, who came to the north and sought out Lingman directly to help stake claims for them. It is unclear why they specifically went after Lingman, but it was likely based on a recommendation from Tom Church, a reputable prospector in the north.

Prospector W.N. Baker discovered new copper deposits south of Gripp Lake, 43 miles northwest of Nakina in the fall of 1954. This sparked a staking rush from locals and competing companies. A total of 8,390 feet of drilling was completed in at least 20 drill holes by 1955. Further deposits of zinc were discovered. Word quickly traveled to the south of the province and KRNO became incorporated on September 10, 1959 to get in on the action. KRNO was hastily put together, and as we'll find out later, wouldn't be around for long.

On Sunday, October 30, 1960, Lingman was hired by Tom Church to retag mining claims for KRNO Mines around Gripp Lake. The job was to take three to four days and was to be done quickly before the lakes froze over. This expedition was different because the men were supposedly flown into the area by helicopter. Typically, staking work that was in hard-to-reach places was accessed by float plane, canoe or foot. The use of a helicopter for prospecting would have been unheard of in those days.

Staking claims is literally what it sounds like — marking the area of interest with wooden stakes. It was a way of claiming a plot of crown land to explore mining opportunities. It was usually done with wooden posts or stakes, but could be done with natural fixtures in the environment, such as the side of a boulder or stump.

To complete the staking, one would put up the corners as a property boundary, marking each with an identification tag (preferably metal) that would withstand the elements. Tags were key to making and maintaining the claim. Each of these tags would indicate the direction of the claim, the time created and completed, the date, post number, name of the prospector, and so forth. Tags must be re-staked every year or the area would be forfeit and up for grabs from other prospectors, in what was an extremely competitive profession. The re-staking by Lingman in 1960 should have been routine, but something went terribly wrong and instead Sander Lingman would vanish off the face of the earth.

The area of his disappearance is remote. It's an overgrown wilderness, full of ankle busters, and countless lakes brimming with walleye. As November approached, the grassy edges of the Gripp would have begun to bow and wilt from the cold. The men had already been camped in the area for two days. The group consisted of his brother Wendell Lingman and two unnamed persons, likely a mechanic and a cook, who were all employed by the same company, but probably not locals. Tom Church may have been one of these individuals. There is reason to suggest that one of the company owners, Vincent Feeley, was on site as well, along with someone named, Ed Vannchette, whose name was barely legible in the officer's field notes. Try as I might, I could not find any information on this man to corroborate his involvement.

On Tuesday November 1, Sander and Wendell Lingman left the KRNO bush camp around 11:15 a.m. to retag the claims roughly 2.5 miles away. Both being familiar with the area, the brothers decided to split up around 11:45 a.m. and agreed to rendezvous back at the camp at 5:00 p.m. Rain fell all afternoon, turning to blowing snow in the evening.

After a day's work, the men returned to camp, but Sander Lingman failed to show up. Knowing Lingman was bush savvy, the men decided to wait awhile longer before sounding the alarm, but as the minute hand ticked beyond 5:00 p.m., his companions became anxious. The men kept their eyes on the tree line but there was no sign of the prospector, and now dark was slinking in fast. Having enough, Wendell Lingman grabbed a gas lamp and marched into the woods after his brother. He thought maybe Sander had broken his leg or had taken a fall and needed help getting out. Knowing his route for retagging, Wendell went to each staking location and discovered that all of Sander's tagging had been completed, yet there was no sign of his brother.

Leaving all his overnight gear at the camp, Wendell knew his brother was not prepared for a night out in the woods. At this point, he knew that something serious must have happened for Sander to become a no-show. The sky darkened overhead, and a veil of snow transformed the surrounding forest. The flame from

Wendell's lamp was a frantic flicker that struggled against the twilight and the November chill. He walked a nearby tote road that twisted through the staking site, but found no sign of his brother and was eventually driven back to camp by wet, blowing snow. Wendell returned from the forest and informed the others. Their calls for the missing prospector bounced off the opposing shoreline and were overcome by the gloomy darkness that closed in. They started up the helicopter every two hours to give Lingman some bearings in the event he got turned around in the weather.

The newspapers reported that Sander was last seen at about 3:00 p.m. that day, but no further information was given beyond this. It's believed that Wendell saw Sander carrying out his work from a distance, but police did not confirm this.

At daybreak, Lingman was still nowhere to be found. Feeley took to the skies in the helicopter to look for any indication of the man. Finding nothing, he flew to Auden, 27 kilometres away, where he telephoned the Ontario Provincial Police.

Constable William Jack Hayes (#2051) learned of the incident at 1:30 a.m. on November 3, after returning from court proceedings in Port Arthur. Hayes was a 37-year-old veteran of World War II, who came from the Rainy River District of Ontario. While serving overseas, Hayes was wounded in action in Normandy. His family confirmed that he suffered a shrapnel injury to his back and leg, but this didn't seem to slow him down by any means.

By 1960, Hayes had been on the police force for 10 years but was brand spanking new to Nakina. In fact, this was his first day on the job in Nakina, and he would be the only officer stationed there for quite some time. In a letter from District Inspector Martin William Ericksen of Port Arthur, Hayes had been transferred from the Terrace Bay detachment to the Nakina detachment, effective November 1, 1960 — the day that Sander Lingman vanished.

Hayes was going to be living at the detachment and be responsible for the upkeep, operations and any prisoners confined there, but before he could even unpack, the call for assistance had come in. Gripp Lake is roughly 96 kilometres from the Nakina police detachment, as the crow flies. There were no roads in to Gripp Lake and it could only be accessed by air.

Not being a licensed pilot, at 8:30 a.m. on November 3, Hayes drove to the Austin Airways base where he would grab a seat on one of two aircraft that had been arranged to fly in that morning. Fourteen men, including five from the Department of Lands and Forests, had accompanied him.

Before leaving, W.J. Hayes got in touch with Staff Sergeant L.E. Lellave of Port Arthur, who advised for Hayes to proceed to the area, obtain all information and return before nightfall.

Despite it being his first day in Nakina, Hayes would have been a great asset to the search. He had a lifetime of experience as an outdoorsman. His father was an Indian Agent and he grew up with Indigenous youth, giving him a leg-up when it came to navigating and tracking in the bush compared to the average policeman in those days.

Hayes reviews a photograph.
* Courtesy of the Hayes family.

The Austin Airways Norseman cut across the surface of the isolated lake leaving a spraying gash in its wake. The aircraft engine sputtered as it ferried towards the shore, where it coughed and died. Hayes caught his first sight of Vincent Feeley as he waited at the edge of the bush. Hayes climbed out of the float plane and was briefed on the situation, scribbling down the details in his notepad.

The hastily assembled party of 19 volunteers raced into action. Constable Hayes wrote that the helicopter ran its engine as often as it could to give some sort of bearing for Lingman to follow back. But if Lingman was in the area, he did not or could not follow the noise out. As the first official day of searching came to a close, Hayes made a few passes overhead before leaving the area, without results.

Among the group of searchers were a number of Lingman's relatives and friends. In addition to his brothers Wendell and Charlie, his uncle Axel, and cousins David and Wilfred had joined the search and rescue operation. Family friends Donald Downey and Ivor Lassie joined to help as well, lamps in hand. To make matters worse, the snow kept coming as searchers set out. Their lanterns splashed a timid glow through the Canadian woods, intermittently giving away the ominous pines and the rocky shore of Gripp Lake.

Snow mixed with rain continued almost unabated for seven days. Volunteers returned to camp soaked to the skin, shivering from the onset of hypothermia. Constable Hayes was unable to get a flight into the area on November 4, leaving the family members and bush-workers to themselves. The Department of Lands and Forests advised that their Beaver aircraft was standing by, but could only be put to use if officially requisitioned by the OPP.

When the snowfall lightened up, search aircraft returned to the sky, but their visibility was now obstructed by the boughs blanketed in thick pillowy snow. Elmer Ruddick ran the Austin Airways base and was likely responsible for flying the searchers in and out of the area.

Hayes got a ride on the next Austin Airways flight on November 5, that was scheduled to bring supplies in for the searchers that were left behind. Hayes was given a progress report by Axel Lingman, who had taken over as the leader of the search: still not a single trace had been found. Axel stated it would require more men to cover the ground properly and that time was running out. Hayes conducted an aerial search for two and a half hours with hopes of spotting smoke from a fire or any indication of Lingman. As the light faded, Hayes returned to Nakina along with four other searchers who were flown out due to exhaustion.

Searchers believed that Lingman was not lost but had fallen and was hurt. Everyone involved praised him as an excellent bushman. His partners stated that he left camp with a sack of food that he could have rationed if he ran into trouble. He also had a compass and matches in his possession. His wilderness experience helped to maintain high hopes of his survival and yet, after days of searching, there was no sign of Lingman.

Based on my interviews, Feeley wanted to leave the area and return to the city, but Hayes prevented him from doing this. Since Lingman could have had a broken leg, a heart attack, or other life-threatening injuries, they were counting on the helicopter to be able to fly him out.

At dawn, the familiar distant drone of the Norseman's engine broke through the cloud cover. Hayes squinted out the window into the abounding wilderness below. This time he was accompanied by six Indigenous woodsmen to assist the search effort, with another load of fresh volunteers waiting back in Nakina to be airlifted in.

With the overnight temperatures dropping sharply, many of the lakes were beginning to freeze over, making landing difficult. The lake ice had to be broken in order to reach the camp. This seeded a feeling of dread among searchers, who knew that time was against them. Once the lakes froze, it would make access by boat and float plane impossible, leaving only searchers with snowshoes to traipse through the dense, hazardous forest that was now layered in two feet of snow.

Searchers thoroughly scoured the area 16 miles north of Auden with support from the air, when possible. Newspapers printed that an Austin Airways helicopter was used, as well as the helicopter employed by KRNO and conventional aircraft. Constable Hayes recorded in his notes that Feeley flew the company helicopter for a total of 8 hours and 40 minutes on searches from November 1 up to November 6.

Feeley informed Hayes that the KRNO chopper was overdue for its 100-hour flight check and would need to be flown to Port Arthur in accordance with flight regulations. This inspection was said to take between two and seven days to complete. Searchers worried that with the loss of the helicopter and the worsening weather, no further volunteers should be flown in. Most of the men at camp were so exhausted that they would not have the energy to walk out on their own if the helicopter could not return to pick them up. Four more men were removed from the camp due to exhaustion.

On November 7, Constable Hayes received a telephone call from Tom Church in Auden. He stated that the search party found what appeared to be blood roughly a quarter mile from the mining camp. He had the sample of alleged blood with him in a bottle. Constable Dorigo from the Beardmore OPP detachment drove to meet with Church and collect the sample.

All scheduled flights were grounded on the morning of November 8, due to heavy snowfall. As the skies cleared around the noon hour, an Austin Airways Beaver aircraft was able to safely land on Gripp Lake in order to deliver a radio to stay in contact with the search party. Five more men were pulled out from the cruel, merciless bush.

The suspected sample of blood was sent to Fort William where it was tested by District Pathologist Dr. Albert E. Allin. The laboratory sent a letter of results on November 9, where Dr. Allin stated:

> We examined this fluid which was very dark brown in colour. It failed to show the presence of blood even in the most minute amounts. It was therefore useless to examine it further as to its possible origin as there is no suggestion that this was blood or other fluid related to the

human body. We are unable to determine what its origin may have been.[37]

There was still no sign of Sander Lingman after eight days of searching. Austin Airways flew over the camp on November 9, but was unable to establish radio contact with the ground team. Another fly over was scheduled on November 10, but ice conditions prevented planes from takeoff at the base. All aircraft were removed from the water and equipped with skis and would have to wait for the ice to thicken before resuming patrols to the area.

By November 10, Constable W.J. Hayes addressed the media with, "Nothing new to report." As he was quoted in the *Daily Times Journal*, "…so far as I know they are still looking for him." This implies that Hayes had taken a step back from the search at this point. It's unclear how involved he really was after the initial period, but it's very possible he got called back to Nakina for other matters. One would guess his war injury might have prevented him from carrying out arduous schleps through the bush, but this was not the case. Constable Hayes was the only lawman in that jurisdiction at the time. He was one man, with one cruiser and one gun, patrolling hundreds of kilometres. The borders he patrolled were far and wide, wooded and challenging and it would be impossible for him to remain on the scene for any long periods of time. His jurisdiction included First Nations reserves, which could sometimes become volatile when locals and non-locals would have disputes. And in those days, calling for backup was never an option.

In addition, Hayes was required to return to his post at the detachment for daily duties. There were four jail cells at Nakina, which usually held prisoners overnight or even for several days, both of which needed supervision. Mrs. Hayes would often cook food for the prisoners to lighten the load of her husband. His family was a witness to his full days, as he patrolled his territory and returned for office work. Years later, when he made corporal, Hayes would request an additional two officers to help patrol the vast region.

The searchers that remained at Gripp Lake, returned to camp soaked to the skin, unable to uncover a single trace of Sander Lingman, as if he wasn't in the area at all. Sadly, on November 11, Axel Lingman, Sander's uncle, walked out of the bush and announced that the search would be officially called off until further notice. Axel broke the news to Constable Hayes over the telephone from Nakina around 7:30 p.m. The plan was to return with ski equipped aircraft once winter had fully taken hold in the north.

As the year came to a close, Constable Hayes expressed his opinion on the early days of the search effort with his superiors.

There is very little if any hope that Sander Lingman will be found alive. On the possibility that he did hurt himself and unable to reach camp, if more men could have been airlifted to the scene at the start before the weather prevented same, there is a good possibility he would've been found in time. If a flight is made in the spring just after the snow melts, his body may be found by watching for a concentration of ravens.[38]

Family and volunteers went back in the spring to resume the search after the snow had melted off. Except by this point they were looking for a body.

In May of 1961, bush pilots flew overhead looking for a black cyclone of buzzards that might hint at the site of some remains. On May 17, a search party of 10 men, led by Axel Lingman, returned to Gripp Lake. The searchers stayed in the area until May 23 and did a thorough sweep of the staking route as well as the shoreline, but nothing of interest was found. A second visit to Gripp Lake took place on June 16 with four men searching the land for a day and a half. The next day, search crews focused on the waterways, using canoes. They scanned the shore, the trails that led down to the lake and even dragged the waters with irons where Lingman was last seen. They returned with nothing to show for their efforts. A man, reported to be living on nearby Marshall Lake, conducted small searches periodically as he made trips into town, however he never found anything to indicate Lingman was in the area.

The local airlines were asked to watch daily as they passed through on their route, but no signs of scavengers were ever found. This gave searchers and family the impression that Lingman was not in this area. Hayes reported that relatives were at a loss to explain Sander's disappearance. He ended his report stating that, "Axel Lingman is of the opinion that any further searching would be futile."

Here was a man fully equipped to be in the outdoors with a lifetime of experience and yet he completely vanished without any clue. Not only was this incident mysterious, it was literally unbelievable. No trace of Sander Lingman, alive or dead, has ever been found. No footprints, no clothing, no equipment, no backpack and no bones. Some may argue that the search wasn't as organized as it could have been, which resulted in a lack of results. However, all members were knowledgeable and retraced the man's route; the reality is that there were not many places he could have gone.

To further shed light on this perspective, another search operation was underway during this time that resulted in a successful rescue. In the same week, three hunters were reported missing in the Finmark area, slightly north of Thunder Bay. With similar efforts deployed to find the lost men, it took just a few days to locate them alive. A search plane spotted their trail and directed ground crews to the area. Given the location and it being the same time of year, this should have been a resolution shared with Lingman, but for reasons unknown this did not happen. To this day, he is still categorized as a missing person and the case remains unsolved.

The Gripp Lake area is still an active site for prospectors. While it hasn't changed much since the 60s, there is now an uptick in human activity. Hundreds of mining employees, canoeists, fisherman, hunters, locals, and forestry workers have visited the area since 1960, and not a single fibre of Lingman's existence has been recovered. How is that possible?

As mentioned in an earlier chapter, it is up to the responding officer to create a detailed profile on the missing individual, but for whatever reason this was not done. Not only did Lingman's age fluctuate on the police report from 30, to 32, to 34 to 35, to 59 there was no information collected regarding his height, weight, hair colour, eye colour, medical information, personal items he may have had with him, clothing of any kind or any notable identifiers, all of which would have been valuable for searchers then and now. If anyone found an article of clothing in the area, we would never know if it was tied to Lingman or not. It would have been easy for police to obtain a physical description of the man, given the fact that most of his family members were involved in the search since day one. Perhaps since time was of the essence, Hayes initiated the search right away without conducting the proper interviews. But after the first shift of bushwhacking, why wasn't a detailed profile created? Why did police never obtain a photograph of Lingman? Try as I might, I could not track down a photograph of him from relatives or any of the archives, now more than 60 years after his disappearance.

In defence of Hayes, the police practices we have now were not as rigorous as they were in 1960, and if they were, they were not applied as vehemently as they are today. That being said, it is fundamental to create a detailed victim profile as early as possible, based on interviews with every individual at that camp. Whether due to Hayes being spread too thin in such a huge area or the optimism that Lingman would be found promptly, this profile was not done. We can only wonder if Lingman would have been located had there been more police officers available to help. At least one could have stayed behind to lead an organized search and complete interviews.

When an expert bushman goes missing in his own backyard, my mind races to all the possible theories of what could have happened. Is it possible that Lingman had fallen in an unmarked drill hole? While no exact number could be found, the 8,390 feet that were drilled in the 1950s likely doubled by that point, given the buzz of activity. Obviously, an excavation site is a hazard to walk through, but there is no indication that Lingman was in the area of the drilling. Also, he had been in the area before and knew his route, so the likelihood of that happening is slim. Same goes for drowning. He would have been aware of the hazards in the area and drowning victims always surface after a few days or would be found during the spring thaw.

Knowing where the claim lines were, searchers retraced the route Lingman had taken. They discovered that he (or someone) had completed the retagging, meaning that whatever happened had occurred on his way back out. In less than five hours — a reasonable timeframe to cover the last time Lingman was seen to the time he was missed — something extraordinary happened to this man.

A potential injury is a sure way to slow down an experienced bush-worker, causing him to miss his rendezvous time, but this theory is just as weak as the others. He would have been within the search grid and could have called out for help or built a fire. It was as if he was walking along and just dissolved out of existence.

I got to work right away and contacted the Ontario Provincial Police about the case, but my request for records was denied. In their eyes, the case was still open, and they could not cooperate on it. They listed several excuses for the rejection, such as it may deprive the person of the right to a fair trial, it could interfere with a law enforcement matter, it could commission an unlawful act or hamper the control of a crime, or infringe on three counts of an unjustified invasion of personal privacy and other such nonsense. Without the police report, I was unable to confirm how thorough the investigation was.

Given that the case is from 1960, I argued that everyone involved is now dead. All witnesses and searchers are now deceased and there is no primary source of information. If there were deathbed confessionals to be jotted down, they would have happened years ago. Just because the case is marked "Open" doesn't mean that anyone is looking. You'll notice this ongoing theme with all older missing person incidents, such as Vital Vachon. After my initial denial, I felt discouraged. I had received the same response so many times and I knew this was a hurdle I could not pass.

In March of 2019, I tried to access his records through other means as a backdoor way of gaining information. Knowing he was employed by the mining company, I thought perhaps there were still employment records lying around. I tried the Canada Revenue Agency, the Ministry of Labour, Employee Services, and the Central Production and Verification Service Branch. Unfortunately, their records are only kept for seven years. That meant I couldn't track employment records, incident reports, property or staking maps.

What about KRNO Mines Limited? They were involved in the search and dollars were clearly spent, and when dollars are spent, typically there is a paper trail. There should have been flight hours logged for the helicopter that was flown and sat idle, waiting for Lingman to be pulled from the bush. Or perhaps, they even donated money to the search effort or compensated the family in some way? The more I dug into this mining company, the more I saw that these ideas were unlikely.

In one way, KRNO mines was a dead end. They were only active for a short time and were cancelled by the Ontario companies branch, but I couldn't find out why. The company seemed to be erased, just as Lingman had. There was no living paper trail or former employees that I could track down for interview. Through some persistence, I was able to locate the incorporation ID number, which was proof that they existed at one time and exactly what I needed to trace them through Government Services.

In the winter of 2019, I made the walk in the cold and took the escalator up to a Service Ontario location for corporations located in downtown Toronto. This is where businesses are incorporated and assigned ID numbers. I waited in line with optimism, on the green, salt-stained carpet. I imagined a wealth of information on this company that was being guarded by the clerk behind the desk. When it was my turn, the clerk's face scrunched up. He searched the incorporation number I provided, and I waited anxiously, watching his continual head shake. There was no wealth of information that waited for me. Other than a single page of dates, the company seemed especially hollow. This was going to be harder than I thought.

I did leave the service desk with one piece of information though: The reason KRNO went defunct was noted as, "Involuntarily dissolved by non-compliance." As small as that tidbit of information was, it did tell me something. A declaration of non-compliance meant they broke government regulations, either willingly or by neglect. Is it possible they just abandoned the company? KRNO had officially piqued my interest and the next step was to reach out to the mining community to see what they knew.

The entity turned out to be a ghost. I contacted every mining association I could track down to pick through their records or institutional memory banks. Starting with Mining Associates, I worked my way through the Ontario Mining Association, Prospectors and Developers Association of Canada (PDAC), The Ministry of Energy, Northern Development and Mines, and even a senior geologist still working in the area north of Nakina. None of these companies had any mining records or recollection of Lingman or KRNO. They weren't able to help, but that single clue of "non-compliance" was enough to keep the trail hot. Later, through my own means of research, I was able to uncover much more.

KRNO became incorporated on September 10, 1959, by Vincent Feeley and Joseph McDermott, who apparently held extensive mining claims in the Thunder Bay district. They appointed David Humphrey as president, Charles Philips as accountant and John P. McNamera as officer, according to an official report from the Legislative Assembly of Ontario. Even though Feeley and McDermott started the company, they listed themselves as 'Vendors,' which is not typical and a bit eyebrow-raising, and soon I found out why.

It turned out that both Feeley and McDermott were self-confessed professional gamblers and dangerous players in organized crime. While this is likely not related to Lingman's disappearance, it's clear that, unbeknownst to him, Lingman had entered into a shady agreement with some colourful characters. Feeley and McDermott were members of an illegal gambling ring and were known to police. This would explain why they both wished to remain under the radar, not wanting to be president and vice president of the company. Feeley and McDermott also had their hands in other mining claims in Big Duck Lake, about 170 kilometres northeast of Thunder Bay. Reports supplied by KRNO indicated that they had bought up several mining claims and bored extensively. There is even evidence to suggest that they sat on claims that were not bored.

Was it possible that Lingman got in the way of a criminal plan or perhaps angered the wrong people? According to a *MacLean's* article from September 1963, Joseph McDermott had a violent streak about him. Feeley and McDermott ran an illegal casino in Cooksville, had ties to the Mafia and were cutting Detroit members in on the action. Keep in mind that all forms of gambling weren't made legal or regulated until 1992 with the *Gaming Control Act*. That didn't stop Feeley and McDermott, however, who ran other secret clubs in Toronto, Windsor and Fort Erie, decades before.

Southwestern Ontario was a hotbed for organized crime in conjunction with surrounding major cities like Detroit, Hamilton, Guelph, Montreal and Niagara Falls. McDermott was an intellectual and a crafty one by all accounts. He was well-read and studied the law, which made him fully equipped and prepared to run profitable gambling houses. According to the article, when McDermott was charged with breaking and entering in 1940, he officially joined the army so he could appear before a judge in uniform to manipulate the decision. The pair also had a history of bribing dirty cops, known as "an edge," to receive tips in advance of OPP gambling raids. It turns out the pair had caused quite a racket in the south as gangsters and professional gamblers. But they weren't exactly city slickers either. The pair had their hand in another illegal gambling house in Timmins and would travel throughout the province in a private aircraft. On September 30, 1958, they, along with six other known mobsters from Michigan, went to Moosonee on a "moose hunting trip." They stayed at the James Bay Goose Club until October 4.

I'd be naive to believe that their intentions were to hunt moose, hence my quotation marks.

In Stephen Schneider's book *ICED*, Feeley was reported to be just as crafty. It was said that he forged his discharge papers so he wouldn't be drafted into World War II. He confessed to renting safety deposit boxes under fake names so he could conduct business in private bank cubicles. Their illegal gambling ring prospered with the help of tip-offs from paid OPP constables, and they were able to gain power and a pretty penny.

Feeley and McDermott were both licensed pilots and had a private airplane for getting around to each of their enterprises. This makes their exploits in the north a little more believable. In 1959, they purchased Airgo Limited, which gave them additional aircraft at their disposal,[39] one of which was a float-equipped Cessna, which would have given them unlimited lake access. Feeley and McDermott were careful not to identify themselves early in the deal to purchase; instead, they sent their lawyers, David G. Humphrey and Hugh Locke, who paid for the company in a large sum of cash. The sale was not disclosed to the Air Transport Board or the federal Department of Transport, which directly conflicted with federal regulations.

Oddly enough, they kept the Airgo company for only a year and sold it in November 1960, the same month of Lingman's disappearance. Apparently, McDermott purchased a helicopter for $44,000 in cash, which he brought in a suitcase in hundred-dollar bills.[40] On their way to make the purchase, they swapped the $44,000 for a money draft to avoid suspicion. In order for the chopper not to be traced back to them, they purchased it in their lawyer's name. On paper it would look clean. The helicopter was no doubt the same one used by the men to look for Sander Lingman.

In a final head-scratcher of suspicious aircraft activity, McDermott and Feeley actually gave away an aircraft to their lawyer and solicitor, Mr. David Humphrey. He stated that he never wanted the thing, but that they both insisted he take it, and they registered it in his name.

There is more evidence to suggest that the pair knew the Nakina area better than one would expect as gamblers and used their resources to explore heavily wooded sections of the region. In the minutes collected from a debate in the Legislative Assembly of Ontario, a geologist was contracted by KRNO Mines Limited to make a survey in the summer of 1960, just months before Lingman's disappearance.

> During the course of the field work valuable assistance in the provision of camp facilities and transportation by helicopter was rendered by J.

P. McDermott and V. T. Feeley of KRNO Mines Limited. On several occasions the use of the helicopter facilitated the examination of the mineral deposits in the area and the traversing of sections where access was difficult.[41]

When I first uncovered this information, I wasn't sure if I was dealing with a stunning coincidence or an unsolved homicide. McDermott's record of a convicted gambler, conspirator and liar doesn't necessarily make him a murderer, but it is interesting that Lingman was working with criminals who walk that shadowy line when he vanished. The OPP has never disclosed if Feeley or McDermott were suspects in the disappearance, or if they were even questioned. We know that Feeley wanted to cut and run back to the city once they called police, but Hayes wouldn't let him go. We also know that at least Feeley was there for the search effort — exactly how involved he was is anyone's guess.

We will never know the nature of the contract between Lingman and the gangsters of KRNO. We don't know how legitimate the work in the area was or if they were involved in his disappearance at all. There just isn't any hard evidence. If Feeley and McDermott were involved, what reason would they have to eliminate one of their employees? Did Lingman know more than he should have? Did he find out the criminal nature of his employers and feel the urge to expose them? And did it have something to do with the mining claim that he was working on? There was evidence to suggest that the mining enterprise was just a ruse to defraud the public out of money.

As written in the Official Report of Debates in the Ontario Legislature, longtime politician Donald Cameron MacDonald revealed an intriguing possibility of further criminal intent by Feeley and McDermott. MacDonald stated that after the departmental geologist visited one of their mining claims, their findings were published in a report. Printed on the bottom of the front cover was an underlined note that stated, "This report has not been edited in order to allow immediate publication." Knowing that this was not a common practice for a geologist to rush out a professional report, MacDonald suspected that the geologist knew something was wrong with the mining claims and was trying to protect himself from some type of blowback. I was able to get my hands on both the edited and original version of this report but failed to find any major inconsistencies that would suggest illegal activity. But then again, I'm no mining expert. Just what that inconsistency was we can only guess, but MacDonald had convinced himself of one theory. One week after the rushed publication of the survey was released, McDermott and Feeley applied to the Ontario Securities Commission for permission to release the vendors' shares of KRNO for public sale. From the write-up, it looked as if the two men were trying to create the illusion of rich gold prospects in the Thunder Bay district.

Unbeknownst to the public, the area had been prospected over and over, and industry veterans believed that there was no more gold to be found. It seems as if they were trying to start another gold rush, and by doing so, would collect on the money for the vendor shares, which as we know, both men controlled. In June of 1962, both men would be charged with this exact crime when they defrauded Keevil Mining Group into buying up a $25,000 option in KRNO claims. The judge later dismissed the charge on grounds of reasonable doubt. Refuting testimony from Tom Church and Minister of Mines, James Maloney, likely swayed the decision.

I uncovered a number of mining records that show Feeley and McDermott had returned to Gripp Lake in the years that followed Lingman's disappearance. A survey was done at the north end of the lake on claims KK24195 and KK24194, where a total of six holes were drilled in 1962. In fact, Feeley was active in the area into 1965 and owed 3 kilometres of land north of Deeds' Island on Marshall Lake. Seven more drill holes were made on the property. According to the geological survey, McDermott also got his hands dirty based on a labour report he filed for rock pit mining in the Gripp Lake area in the 1970s.[42] During these two decades, their work amounted to 1000s of feet of drilling. We can speculate as to their reasons for returning, but we will never really know.

After 1963, Feeley's criminal record included everything from forgery to breach of war industries control board regulations. McDermott's rap sheet would include everything from breaking and entering, theft, possession of an unregistered firearm and conspiracy. But to my knowledge, neither one was ever convicted of a murder. Last I heard, Feeley and McDermott were locked up in 1964 for their 'edge' with police officers. After 1970, both characters disappeared from the headlines and out of the public (and police) eye. McDermott eventually got jail time, but I couldn't uncover any kind of paper trail for the time afterwards. Eventually, I traced Vincent Feeley to Mount Hope Cemetery. His stone said he died on August 1, 2007, at his home, at the age of 84. I found a number of stones for McDermott, but since his story seems to have ended publicly in the 60s, I was unable to confirm 100% if any of these markers belong to the man in question.

There is no doubt that the delinquent duo raised a few eyebrows in the mining world. The thing that stuck out to me the most was the enormous amount of Big Duck Lake and Little Duck Lake deposits that had been bought up by Feeley and McDermott that had little-to-no mineral value. The duo had attached themselves to dozens of veins in the North that had very low (or in some cases zero) gold content. Furthermore, in several acquisitions, KRNO had acquired veins but had not bothered to sample or drill them at all. This all would have been obscured knowledge to the general public, who would have had to take the mining company's word for it. But Sander Lingman was no average Joe.

Is it possible that Lingman found out about this mining scheme? He certainly must have sensed red flags, seeing that he was a local with prospecting experience in that district. Those in the mining community would have had a heads-up on the contents of these veins because of a geology report that was first conducted in 1914 and 1915 by Percy E. Hopkins. Hopkins stated on multiple veins that were then in the possession of Feeley and McDermott that, "...the gold content is low."[43]

The newspaper coverage on Lingman's disappearance soon dried up. A year after he vanished, the Lingman name popped up again on the front page of the *Daily Times Journal*. There was an article from the April 24, 1961 issue that stated an employee of the Department of Highways had made a gruesome discovery. The body of Sander's brother Wendell was found pinned under his Dodge station wagon 38 miles northwest of Nakina. The report stated that there was some malfunction with the steering on his car and he failed to navigate a sharp turn. Constable W.J. Hayes arrived at the scene on the Anaconda Iron Mine Road at 12:30 p.m. with a doctor. They discovered Wendell deceased, laying on his back off of the east shoulder. He was wet and covered with a blanket and coat. An investigation revealed that, Wendell had been employed by the Department of Highways on a "slashing project". While heading south, Wendell lost control on the west soft shoulder. His vehicle travelled 300 feet, crossed to the east shoulder and then careened over a five-foot drop, rolling 75 feet over boulders. The station wagon came to a rest on its roof in a pool of water. Fellow workers discovered the crash at 11:00 a.m. on their way to the work site and pried up the car to free him, dragging him to the spot where he was found. Wendell had survived the rollover but died minutes before the doctor could arrive.

I was taken aback at the news and how devastating this would have been for the family at a time when the anniversary of Sander's disappearance was looming on the horizon. This family was no stranger to tragedy. I asked myself if there could be some kind of Lingman curse. I was reaching for something that could explain all of this. How else could a family have such bad luck?

I attempted to track down any survivors who participated in the search for Lingman, but unfortunately all the primary sources involved had passed. His siblings were all dead and so was officer Hayes.

Through some random luck, I was able to locate a cousin named, Millie Bourdignon. As next of kin, Mrs. Bourdignon would be the first to be notified should the police make a breakthrough on the case. Bourdignon operates a successful air service in Nakina and is an accomplished bush pilot. When I first found out about her, I was pleasantly surprised that she was eager to talk.

For being around 10 years old at the time, Bourdignon knew quite a bit about Sander's story. She wishes she was a bit older to fully understand the flurry of action that was going on outside Nakina at that time, but what she does remember and was told is still very valuable. Her father, Axel, was an integral part of the search party, as we've learned.

Like me, she was perplexed by the disappearance of her cousin. She confirmed that "Sander was excellent in the bush," as well as many of the other details in the story.

It appeared that the family was suspicious from the onset of the investigation. From multiple conversations with Bourdignon, she shared a story with me that her father told her. When Axel was coming into the camp after a search, Feeley was waiting there. He approached Axel and asked him what he thought happened to Lingman. Axel replied, "I have my suspicions, but I can't say." It was unclear if the Lingman family knew of KRNO's gangster connections at the time, but it's clear that Axel felt Feeley was involved. The belief hasn't changed over time either. Bourdignon and her family have always thought Sander was murdered, even though a body was never recovered: "We do think that they killed him somehow." Bourdignon told me, "I think maybe he found something out when they were in the camp."

Feeley and McDermott had a longer reach into the north than one would initially think, so is it possible that Lingman was removed from the Gripp Lake area that day? Could this explain why searchers came up empty? We have on record that the helicopter owned by Feeley and McDermott was used to explore difficult sections for geological surveys, and they had extensive claims that surrounded the search area. If their other claim areas had been included in the search radius, I wonder what searchers would have found. Perhaps police were looking in the wrong spot. Bourdignon believes that they could have picked him up in the chopper and pushed him out the door somewhere. Given the timeline and the remote location, it would not be impossible. There is endless wilderness and many lakes in the region that Feeley would have flown over a dozen times before.

This theory is particularly frightening to envision: Feeley asks the young man to climb aboard, and they fly a few kilometres north above an uncharted middle-of-nowhere. The door is slid open; they're hit by a blast of November wind. Feeley draws a gun, forcing Lingman out of the helicopter 100 or more feet above the ground. There is just one problem with this theory — wouldn't Wendell have heard the chopper take off? Depending on the topography, sound doesn't travel well in the bush, but you'd think if he heard a helicopter's engine, Wendell would have reported it.

Apparently, there was more odd behaviour from his shady employers. Axel revealed that there was a dispute afterwards between himself and Feeley and McDermott. He said that the men did not want to leave Lingman's wages with his family before they took off back to Toronto. Axel argued that they still had people out in the bush searching for Lingman so what would happen if he showed up or was found? Why would Feeley refuse to leave his wages? Surely, he must have thought this would have looked suspicious. Did Feeley somehow know that Lingman would never be found? It's not clear how the family got KRNO to cough up the money, but they eventually did.

While investigating the disappearance, I came upon a rumour of a court case regarding unsolved murders and missing people in which Feeley and McDermott were involved. It was scheduled for the spring of 1961 in Toronto. Interestingly, Wendell had made plans to go to it and speak about his brother and how he felt that these gangsters were responsible. In a bizarre turn of events, Wendell was killed in the vehicle incident mentioned earlier before he could take the stand. I could never confirm the rumours of this court case involving murders and missing people, and Constable Hayes gave no indication that Wendell's death was anything but an accident. Like his brother, Wendell was a young man and not married, so there is not much family left connected to this tragedy that I could follow up with.

There is no evidence that Vincent Feeley or Joseph McDermott were ever responsible for the disappearance, it is only discussed at length here because it is an interesting connection. If we are left to believe that they were involved, it doesn't take much of an imagination to consider that they could have influenced the situation in their favour. After all, they were reported to have connections with James Maloney (Minister of Mines), multi-millionaire E.P. Taylor and CNR president Donald Gordon. They seemed to have a long reach throughout the province and could have bribed whomever they deemed necessary to get that "edge." Why not? They'd done it before.

As we have learned in previous chapters, police are encouraged to be in contact with next of kin at least once a year or on the anniversary date, as stated in the guidelines created by the NCMPUR:

> At the annual anniversary of the disappearance, the investigating agency should consider renewing contact with the family. The agency should touch base especially on anniversary dates and significant dates such as a birthday. Anniversaries of the disappearance are difficult for the families of missing persons and so the contact is good management of the relationship with the investigation.[44]

According to next of kin, police have not been in touch since 2006.
Some years after the disappearance of Sander Lingman, police did approach Bourdignon for her opinion on a discovery they had happened upon. While working in an area southwest of Gripp Lake, a tractor train rode up from Auden

along the railroad tracks with the intention of staking claims. The tractor was going through the bush and as it turned up the soil, an old hat popped out of the ground. Police shared the find with Bourdignon only to have her confirm that it was not Lingman's hat. The hat found was a dressier one with a buckle, not something that would typically be worn in the bush. When Lingman wore a hat, it would have been a baseball cap. It's possible that the hat is not related at all, but I mention it here because it is a piece of the story. Perhaps it blew off a rail passenger's head or perhaps it flew off of Feeley or McDermott as they soared through the November sky that evening, we will never know.

Sander Lingman left not a single trace behind. The way I see it, two things need to happen if we are to put an end to this mystery. First, we need to find bones. Second, those bones need to be identified. That is a job for a forensic anthropologist. But without a DNA sample, how would it even be possible to confirm who they belong to? In my discussions with the family, no DNA was collected from any of the Lingman relatives. I would like to know how police expect to identify the remains of Sander Lingman if they are ever found. There are multiple mentions of the importance of this in the police guidelines, which again illustrates how worthwhile these practices could be if they were mandatory.

> If there are suspicious circumstances or if the person is presumed dead, the investigator should immediately collect samples that could credibly provide DNA of the missing person. The investigator should collect and protect personal effects as soon as possible, and/or DNA from relatives of the missing person as soon as there are reasonable grounds to suspect that the person may be deceased, as established by substantive investigation or witness, or when other means to locate the person have failed to do so. The collection of DNA should be a matter of course as investigations reach this point. In some cases, the correct timing will require judgement taking into consideration the attitude of the family, circumstances of the disappearance, and the availability of other means. In general, it is recommended to collect DNA samples as soon as possible. Personal effects that might contain DNA are much more difficult to collect intact and uncontaminated as time goes by. Relatives' DNA is also more difficult to track down as time passes (people move, pass away). DNA can be used to confirm identities which may not be possible if DNA can no longer be collected.[45]

The importance of this clause cannot be underestimated. Even the literature conveys a tone of urgency, so it's astonishing that police have not tried to collect samples.

The battle for information on this case is still ongoing. After having my FOI request denied in 2017, I resubmitted in 2020, a process that was painfully delayed for six months.

A 60-day extension was required and granted on November 16, 2020. I still did not receive a response after January 15, 2021 and continued to follow up for weeks. My calls and emails were not returned. Finally, I connected with the senior program analyst, and I agreed to give an additional two more weeks before I followed up with them, even though no official notification of extension was offered to me. I acted out of good faith, as the *Act* clearly states they have 30 days to produce the records or a letter of extension. This two-week grace period passed and another full month (all of February and into March), and I still heard nothing.

Weeks later, I received their response, which nearly caused me to hit the floor. I was denied the Lingman file yet again, but not because the case was still "Open." I was denied because, "the OPP have confirmed that no records exist." There are a few things wrong with this statement, the most glaring being that I was denied in 2017 based on the grounds that records did in fact exist. This either means they lost them since 2017, or someone wasn't being truthful. They cannot legally destroy an open case file or close it without a resolution. This statement also confirms that police are not looking into the case any longer, but for reasons unknown, are giving the illusion that they are by leaving it up on the website and denying FOIA requests.

Are police giving the public the illusion that these long-term cases are being investigated, but in reality, are not? If police have given up on the Lingman investigation then next of kin must be notified, because as of 2021, the family and the general public are under the impression that the police are actively working towards resolving the case. With the obvious problems brought about by this decision letter, I had no choice but to make an appeal through the Privacy Commissioner. I drafted a concise and thorough appeal letter that highlighted the glaring issues of the matter and did not hear back for another three months or so. The OPP again confirmed that there are no records in existence regarding the Lingman case. They further went on to reiterate that they do not purge information. This is a direct contradiction, because I have already proven that a file did exist at one time and more than one investigator was assigned to the case, so if it wasn't purged or lost then were did it go?

In 2006, the OPP sent a letter to Mrs. Bourdignon saying they would highlight the Lingman case on their website. It indicated that they not only had records, but that a new investigator was assigned who was mentioned at the bottom — Provincial Constable R. Taylor. Secondly, a case file must exist somewhere because Constable Hayes was assigned to the case and took detailed notes, which then would have been transcribed to a police report (I have the notebook). Thirdly, an online profile of Lingman would mean that they are getting their notes from that police report.

To be completely thorough, I attempted to reach the detective at the Greenstone OPP detachment. I was able to connect with Detective Sergeant Gaston St. Onge, the officer who now handled the Lingman case. Sergeant St. Onge assured me that Lingman's file did exist and could not understand how the OPP, through FOI, could tell me that it did not exist. Sergeant St. Onge could not comment on the case but did review the file prior to our call. He said that the case is ongoing and would be checked against any human remains found in the province that may match Lingman's profile.

At the time of this writing, I have escalated the appealed discussion to an adjudicator, who I hope will appreciate these facts. I am still waiting for the final word on the matter, as the review could take months or years. The process has revealed shocking new information and those interested in learning more on the Lingman file can see Appendix A.

When details of an individual are scarce, it puts them at a greater risk of being forgotten. I hope I have done the man proud and given him enough here to be remembered by.

There was, however, one shred that Lingman left behind for us as a link to his existence. It's not a dramatic revelation, like a secret child or a lost diary. Thankfully, this piece was preserved within the Archives of Ontario. I thought it funny that the staff do not know that they hold the final piece of Sander Lingman's life within a mountain of withering banker boxes.

I took a trip to the archives on February 8, 2020 to see it with my own eyes. There was a single file folder that was hidden among a few dozen others in a box of bygone mining records. They were coloured from age and softly ripped at the edges. The taped-over labels were tarred brown and weathered by time. The tears were soft and dry, and I wondered when the last time was that someone had set eyes on these files. The folder was labeled: *Sander Lingman v. J. & H. Koski, Appeal from Decision of Mining Recorder, K.K.*" What waited inside was a time capsule from 1955. It was a dispute of a mining claim between Lingman and another prospector. This was his appeal to the Ontario Mining court. The typed ink was smudged in some areas, but otherwise perfectly legible. The folder included formal judgements, letters and a number of telegrams to the applicant and respondents.

The material stated that Lingman appealed to the Mining Court that J. Koski and H. Koski re-staked six mining claims that belonged to him in March of 1954, when the claims in question were not open for staking until May 1, 1954. Lingman stated that the Koskis, "disregarded posts and claim lines which were well defined at the time."[46] He had reached out to the Mining Court in the fall of 1954 but did not hear back on a decision until September 1955.

I couldn't believe my luck at finding a paper trail that Lingman had left. I was pleased that I was able to pin something to this mysterious man. It was written on letterhead that locals believed belonged to Ken Wai, a local repairman who would fix electronic appliances. I had wondered if Lingman once worked alongside Wai in his business or if he was just a friend.

Although it barely improved my understanding of this person, it was a tangible thing that tied him to the history of mining in this province. I admit, you cannot tell much from a letter, but there are subtle hints that give me a tiny insight into his personality. The most important part for me was a small gift that Sander Lingman left behind for us all. There, at the bottom of his politely typed note was a handwritten signature, which I feel is all too fitting to end his story with.

*Courtesy of the Archives of Ontario

6

Geraldine Huggan

"It's just the waiting — and the nights — and knowing that she's out there in the rain and darkness."
—Ann Huggan

The odyssey of Geraldine Huggan is one of the most heartbreaking, blundered and brutal stories of epic search and rescue that you've probably never heard about.

I first came across the story while doing research in Northern Ontario, long before the idea of this book. I have always felt unsettled about this forgotten story because of its gut-wrenching details and unsatisfactory ending. This was a tragic black spot in Ontario's history that has been swept under the rug. It seemed that no one was talking about Geraldine any longer, even in the North. But after hearing of the struggles of searchers, the anguish of family and the untold story of what the youngster endured, it is my goal to make sure she will never be forgotten.

The story begins in July of 1953, when Mr. Jared Huggan drove from downtown Winnipeg with his wife Ann and four little girls to spend a few weeks at the family cottage. The couple was married years earlier, on October 26, 1940, and Geraldine was born on November 24, 1947.

The cottage was nestled in Wade, Ontario. Wade is neither a town nor village, it is simply described as a place or railway point in the Kenora district. It lies just south of the Canadian National Railway line (CNR) and is heavily forested and remote. It is tucked in the bushland of the north and could easily go undetected by non-locals. The cabin itself was behind a large rock face and belonged to Jared's father, Robert Huggan, a retired railway worker. The cabins in the area are without telephone lines and power, with the exception of a generator for some.

Five-year-old Geraldine, or "Gerry" as she was known, was the second youngest child in the family. She made the trip each summer with 11 year-old Judy, 8-year-old Linda and 3-year-old Sandra. Reports stated that all the girls were accustomed to the outdoors; having grown up there, they knew the property well enough. The cottage was 6 miles west of Minaki and 110 miles from Winnipeg (the family's home). The family arrived on Saturday afternoon around 4:30 p.m. and looked forward to summer vacation, a familiar feeling for many of us. The Grays, relatives to the Huggan's, were staying at the neighbouring cottage. The first week of July is important to most Canadians as they celebrate Canada Day and take extended vacation. The promise of beer, barbecues, fireworks and family gatherings are looked forward to by many.

On Sunday, July 5, Huggan, along with her sisters, left her grandparent's brown painted cabin and walked to their neighbours', the Grays, which was the third cottage in the row. The paper at the time reported it was about 75 yards from the Huggan property. The children were playing in the yard. Her mother recalled that Huggan was seen chasing some feral cats. Her father was busy working on the outboard motor for the boat trip they planned to take on Fox Lake, about 2 miles north of the cottage, which crossed the railway tracks. On this fateful day, Huggan was described as wearing a plaid shirt, running shoes and blue jeans. Her aunt painted a loveable image of her, telling the papers she was, "very chubby and healthy," with brown eyes.

For an unknown reason, it was believed that Huggan returned home by way of a forested path between the cottages. To this day, the family is not sure why she set off walking towards the cabin, Geraldine could have been playing, wanted to go home or had become impatient and set off to Fox Lake by herself. Regardless of the reason, it is a short path between the two cottages, a path she had walked countless times and would not have gotten lost on.

All the sisters knew very well that they were never to venture over the railroad tracks alone. At 10:30 a.m. that morning, the parents called to round up the children, but Geraldine had vanished. We cannot be certain how long Huggan had been unaccounted for. One newspaper claimed it was only 10 minutes until the family realized that Gerry was no longer in the yard with the other children. Her parents called out to her, but after minutes of unanswered shouting they quickly realized something was wrong. Neighbours and campers joined in, checking under cottages, outbuildings, down wells, under cars and in sheds. Any place that a little girl could possibly hide.

It must have been a horrifying search initially as the dangers were aplenty. The high-speed trains could whiz by at any minute and the forest is thick, swampy, and home to dangerous wildlife and natural hazards. Nothing in the immediate area was found, which forced the family to spring into a wider, and more official search operation. Reports indicated that a forestry lookout tower was first notified of the missing girl, who then radioed the Ontario Provincial Police. At 6:00 p.m., police arrived from Minaki to organize a search, which would be helmed by Constable Ken Wilson. Both vacationers and workers were recruited to search that afternoon. Rain fell. When the posse called it quits at dark, her father Jared kept searching through the night, lantern in hand. At around 11:00 p.m., he returned; in what would signal the end of the first day of the official search.

To give a little more perspective, a 2006 report by the U.S. Department of Justice found that the first three hours are the most critical to locate a missing child. After that, the likelihood of finding them alive decreases significantly.

The Huggan parents anxiously waited for the sun to rise, and when it finally did, the searchers were refreshed and ready. Jared Huggan was out searching by 6:00 a.m., along with seven others. Soon, a line of 70 volunteers marched out on Monday morning in the first full day of an organized search. There were 50 more men by the time the afternoon sun hit its peak, including three on horseback who trotted the logging roads. Corporal E.B. "Red" Bailey of the RCMP arrived by freight train with a tracking dog named "Buddy" who was eagerly pulling at his arm.

Even with additional manpower, unfortunately nothing was recovered on the second day of the search. By nightfall, rain had swept in again and the temperatures had dropped to a chilly 7 degrees Celsius / 45 degrees Fahrenheit. A dangerous situation for anyone without proper clothing or shelter.

Constable Ken Wilson with RCMP dog.
* Winnipeg Tribune, July 8, 1953

By the morning of day three, the searchers had covered more than 4 square miles, but Geraldine was still somewhere out there. Pounding rain hampered the efforts overnight and searchers were forced to sit and wait. Tracks and traces were smudged out, washed away in seasonal weather. The group of volunteers expanded to include 12 forest rangers, local bushmen, Indigenous guides, nearby campers, a handful of RCMP officers, and neighbours.

Searchers Return From Futile Hunt

All day Tuesday these searchers hunted in vain for 5-year-old Geraldine Huggan, of Winnipeg, missing from the family summer home at Wade, Ontario.

Dense, Wet Bushland Refuses To Yield Up Missing City Child

*Image published in the Winnipeg Free Press, July 8, 1953

There were reported to be about a dozen camps at the railroad settlement, as well as two lumber camps in the area, which all pitched in, totalling about 100 searchers. Neighbour Marcelle Warren was quoted in *The Winnipeg Tribune* saying, "I can't stop. I know what it's like. I have children of my own. It's like Geraldine were my own child."

Her fear, like many others, was due to the weather and nighttime temperatures. While the average overnight temperatures for the month hovered about 10 degrees Celsius, this can be down-right teeth chattering if you aren't wearing the right clothing or are soaked to the skin. Media correspondents from around the country gnawed at their pencils and waited at the edges of the tree line for a searcher to emerge with the girl in their arms, but by the end of Tuesday, "No dice," was the only update police had brought out with them.

By the fourth day, the search became desperate and intensified. Two additional OPP officers were put on the case to aid Constable Wilson. One of them, Constable Llewelyn Burritt of the Hudson detachment, was not as optimistic: "I give her one more day, then we'll have to assume the worst."[47] But not all involved were as pessimistic. Murray Campbell, a doctor from Winnipeg, believed that the child could have survived the initial freezing nights and even a few more days of discomfort.

One might be surprised to know that this was not the only mysterious disappearance in the area. In fact, there were multiple. During the hunt for Huggan, Jake Macdonald, a medicine man who lived on the reserve, was confident that she was still alive. He believed this based on another child that was lost in the bush years earlier. In 1951, a seven-year-old Indigenous boy was lost for 40 days in the bush south of Kenora. He had wandered away from the school yard at Cecelia Jeffrey on Airport Rd. The boy later described going ten days without food until he found a remote cabin and broke in. He ended up losing a foot to frostbite.[48] But he lived.

The search ballooned to a monster level. The *Brandon Daily Sun* printed that an army unit from Fort Osborne in Winnipeg was dispatched, along with extended family from the South and nearby campers. Every able-bodied man and woman was enlisted in the search. The Department of Lands and Forests had volunteered two seasoned game wardens, four timber cruisers, four more forest rangers and local bush pilots. Two forestry planes flew low over the swamps and muskeg hoping to catch a glimpse of some clue, some trail, followed by a third plane from Parsons Airways. Fifteen local rail employees dropped their hardhats and hammers and joined the search along with eight other men from Transcona, Winnipeg. It's important to note the Indigenous guides mentioned in the newspapers referred specifically to Joe Cameron and Cornelius McDonald of White Dog Reserve (otherwise known as Wabaseemoong), an Ojibway First Nation band located about 51 kilometres northwest of Minaki. Both Cameron and McDonald were accomplished bushmen and had lived and breathed the woods around them their entire lives. They had tracked and trapped all around Minaki and would continue to do so in their older years. McDonald was crucial to the effort because he was an expert tracker and could distinguish animal and human footprints, as well as physical disturbances in the environment. McDonald and Cameron would also have critical knowledge and skill to navigate the wilderness. I was fortunate enough to connect with the daughter of Cornelius McDonald, who was able to share the perspective of her father during and after the search. Once McDonald and Cameron arrived, there was already a small posse deliberating how the search would be conducted in such a tough area. McDonald recalled that they were instructed to walk side by side at arm's length, like soldiers, so nothing would be overlooked.

Cory Kilvert, a reporter for the *Winnipeg Free Press* and member of the search party, captured the moments in time as Constable Wilson and Corporal Bailey addressed the dozens of volunteers: "Lets get together today fellows." "No further than arm's length apart and watch the man on your right. Take it slow. Look under every bush. Don't pass up any place a small child could be hidden."

A somber and eager silence gathered among the searchers as they heeded their instructions. Then a booming shout from Constable Wilson was heard down the line: "Okay, hit it!"[49]

The line of men and women swept south of the train tracks, towards the cottage, slowly and thoroughly. They kept the line as straight as they could, navigating the tangles of brush and briar. The line of searchers would bend and break through the thick patches, as the search leaders did everything they could to control it. "Hold on the right!" they'd be heard shouting. They would constantly pause to fill any gaps between them that the harsh landscape had pried open. The wilderness was their enemy and threw no shortage of obstacles in their path — giant deadfalls of spruce and birch, tripping undergrowth, jagged rock and hidden holes of water shielded by ferns and moss. Granite ridges, knee high swamps, chest high brush, skin shredding thorns, underbrush so thick you'd lose sight of your feet as you walked. How could a child possibly make it through?

Corporal "Red" Bailey was in the lead, while Constable Wilson followed from behind, scanning the line for any signs of breaks. To the far left was Constable Burritt, to the far right was bush-savvy CNR man, Johnny Rheault.

The pleading calls of searchers echoed through the backwoods labyrinth of cottage country, replacing what would normally be the sound of summer birds. They stabbed the soft forest floor with sticks, lifted limbs and poked rock crevices and waterfalls, all while they were continually smacked in the face with brush. Their hands were constantly bit by branch and bugs and their feet gave way under camouflaged trapped doors of misleading footing. Searchers battled through an onslaught of blackflies and mosquitos.

Alice Morrison, the girl's aunt, was quoted saying, "The little girl is used to the outdoors. The family spends every summer there, and the children know the settlement well, but have never wandered beyond it before."[50]

Then a tiny clue emerged from the jungle-like bush and word made its way back to civilization. Small, child-like footprints were found on a mossy high ridge on the shore of Fox Lake. Searchers spent an hour scouring every inch of the rock. When they followed the tracks, they petered out in the direction of a swamp.

On the fifth day, the newspapers of the time reported that an Inspector Corsie of the OPP made an official plea for the army at MD 10 in Winnipeg to send units to assist in the rescue. We are unaware if they received an official response. Word spread like wildfire and soon strangers from near and far were flocking into Wade to offer any type of help. Another large posse of men were flown in from Kenora, as well as Murray Campbell, the doctor from Winnipeg. Members of the Winnipeg Fort Rouge Legion arrived on July 8 and took to the bush immediately. In the height of summer, this place would have been packed with vacationers, so it would be very possible to gather hundreds of people because they were all within reach. All available police, including the RCMP, were called in for assistance. In short, the search for Geraldine Huggan was massive. Four more tracker dogs were brought in from Kenora and Minaki and yet even trained dogs could find nothing…

On day six, 65 soldiers descended upon the bush with walkie-talkies and heavy gear, a scene you'd expect to see in a Hollywood movie. They all volunteered from the Royal Canadian Horse Artillery in Winnipeg. But yet again, the wilderness surrendered no clues.

By the seventh day, temperatures soared, making the intense search even more nightmarish. Royal Canadian Air Force (RCAF) helicopters roared overhead, giving the whole area the energy of a full-scale military operation. The searchers coordinated with two-way radios, from the sky to the ground, from basecamp to the Huggan's cottage and to those that stayed behind to feed the droves of volunteers. The hope of finding Huggan alive was beginning to evaporate in the stifling July heat and authorities guessed she could only live without shelter for another few days. Ontario Fish and Wildlife employee and bush-worker Ray Simcoe admitted it was the toughest search he had ever experienced, as stated in the *Kenora-Keewatin Daily Miner and News*. He had also brought a dog with him to aid the search. The search re-combed previous ground and then widened to include Myrtle Lake (approximate 4 kilometres southeast) and Catastrophe Lake (nearly 3 kilometres to the south).

Troops Join Hunt For Missing Girl

* Image published in the Winnipeg Free Press, Friday July 10, 1953

Interest in the area grew when a piece of red lint was discovered snagged on a fallen tree that led to Catastrophe Lake. Huggan's parents examined the fibre but could not determine the source. By July 11, the Huggan story began to slip from the front pages as a lack of leads thwarted the searchers. When searchers halted due to darkness, the Huggan family would sit around in the evenings and speculate on the mysterious disappearance of Geraldine. Her aunt thought she could have been lured off to pick wildflowers, perhaps planning to make a bouquet for her mother, something she was known to enjoy.

Late on Sunday July 12, Joe Cameron and Cornelius McDonald returned from a new search area from the south. They were worn down and hungry from an entire day of bushwhacking. As both Ojibway elders from White Dog had rejoined the others at Wade, they brought back uplifting news. They had found a child's tracks 2.5 miles southeast of the search area. The helicopter was encouraged to keep flying overhead and the dogs were called back. Soldiers from the 2nd Regiment Royal Canadian Horse Artillery went back into the bush, just as they were about to return to Winnipeg.

The tracks were followed for 50 yards, lost on hard ground, and then picked up again and were estimated to be made on Friday or Saturday, making them about a day or two old. Cameron measured the print with a stick and believed they were about the same size.

The thought that Huggan could still be alive gave the search party a breath of fresh air. Their confidence was restored, but the tracks were an unusual find. They were far outside the search area, depressed in white moss and appeared to stagger, leading southeast to Myrtle Lake. Yet again, the dogs failed to get a scent. The search intensified and the army moved into the dense bush around Myrtle Lake, but the positivity was short-lived.

These prints were met with contention. Were they actually that of the child's? Later reports stated that it could have been a false lead that wasted precious time. Experienced officers from the RCMP believed that the footprints were not those of a child, but perhaps an animal or even an adult human that had shrunken or weathered in the elements. In a search and rescue operation, I would think it'd be safe to trust the expertise of the Indigenous trackers, specifically McDonald, who had been tracking animals for years.

He lived till he was 97 and still enjoyed venturing out to track in his old age, until his family members voiced their concerns about his solo adventures. By all accounts, you'd think he would be able to determine a child's footprint from an animal's.

From the beginning, McDonald and Cameron were not pleased with the way things were handled. They felt it too restricted — walking dead ahead with no trail to follow.

* Cornelius McDonald, circa 1980

They figured if a five-year-old girl was going to walk, she'd likely walk where there was no rough terrain, where the woods weren't so thick. McDonald's daughter, still a resident of White Dog, said: "My father and Joe Cameron were bothered by the way the search was conducted, arm length to arm length late into the night, that's when both decided to do it in their own way and the only way that they have done when tracking..." Perhaps they felt the effort was too clumsy and the long line of searchers were destroying possible tracks.

I also found it odd that the expert trackers weren't given more control over the logistics. Why recruit an expert tracker and not let him advise the teams on how the search should be conducted?

The Brandon Daily Sun reported on the story with captivating headlines such as, "Fruitless search for missing girl in stifling swamp land." They stated that so much traffic had entered the forest that local guides, familiar with the area, found it unrecognizable and impossible to follow a trail. Rumours stated that they needed to use red paint on trees and rocks to mark off areas that had been searched.[51]

Despite this, the group slogged through the choked wilderness. Jared Huggan was in the literal thick of things. He never gave up on the search or sat on the sidelines, sometimes searching 18 hours a day. He scaled over rocks with the rest of the searchers. He waded through swamp land and endured the hordes of biting insects until dark. The terrain is so difficult here, that the average rate of the search was a quarter mile per hour (roughly 400 feet). Searchers admitted that they would sometimes lose sight of the man beside them when they'd be just over an arm's length away.

By Tuesday the fourteenth, the men were prepared to give up the search. The RCAF helicopter would do one final sweep of the countryside and if nothing was found then all resources would retreat back to Winnipeg.

PLAN SEARCH: Leaders of the search for five-year-old Geraldine Huggan, Capt. R. N. McKay, in charge of army search troops, and Const. Ken Wilson, of Ontario provincial police, look over a map to plan the day's search around Wade, Ont. for the missing girl.

*Image published in the Winnipeg Free Press, July 14, 1953

It is at this point that the newspapers really make a mess of things. The story differs not only between news sources, but also between locals, family members and search volunteers. There is a jumble of dates that make it impossible to accurately state which event took place first. Newspapers credit a man named Harry Hawes with making a discovery, however they do not accurately describe how. Instead, they tell how Indigenous trackers were responsible for picking up the trail of the little girl. It is not uncommon for newspapers to mix up details when they're up against deadlines and both versions are compelling. Somewhere within all these stories is the truth and because of this, and for the sake of history, I will present all of the alternate endings that I was able to uncover.

First, let's tell the story that the newspapers told. The *Winnipeg Free Press* paralleled the coverage along with the *Kenora-Keewatin Daily Miner and News*, *The Winnipeg Tribune* and *Brandon Daily Sun*. Upsetting rumours that a body was found began to circle on July 15. Several papers stated that the girl's body was found, yet the next issue on Thursday July 16 says that no body was recovered, "The body of the child, who wandered away from her grandparent's cottage a week ago Sunday, was not recovered."[52] *Kenora-Keewatin Daily Miner and News* admitted that the previous reports, "were sketchy."

In their haste, I believe the papers were a bit overzealous in printing updates that had residents of both Manitoba and Ontario on the edge of their seats. What they were describing on the fifteenth was a scene in which evidence of the girl was found that might have indicated that she had perished, but no actual remains were found.

Fifty-one-year-old searcher and prospector Harry Hawes, along with friend Joe Bynski, raised money from Kenora locals to hire a bush plane that would take him into Long Lake. The newspapers reported that Joe Bynski accompanied Hawes into the bush, but through further research by both myself and the Hawes family, I was able to confirm that Hawes went in alone. No further information on Joe Bynski was found, and I could not determine if he has any living family to interview. Hawes's family are adamant that Bynski was not with him when he searched for the lost girl. It seemed the newspapers got that wrong too.

Bynski, a local plumber, just seemed to be involved in the fundraising. Hawes was acting on a "hunch" that if the child was anywhere, she would likely be found in the vicinity of Long Lake and Catastrophe Lake. Hawes was adamant about Long Lake but would never tell others why. Hawes would only refer to his intuition as a "hunch," maybe because he was protecting himself. In an area with dozens of lakes, what drew him specifically to Long Lake?

Hawes arrived in Wade on Monday and flew into Long Lake on Tuesday morning via arranged float plane. Here he would spend two nights camping and looking for clues. It wasn't long until the hunch paid off. Hawes reported to find footprints and the imprint of a small face in mud that ran along the edges of Long Lake. The evidence suggested that the girl had stumbled. He was confident the print was made by running shoes worn by Huggan when she disappeared. It's assumed that these prints were only a day or two old. Behind the footprints were red, blue and grey lint fibres, believed to be from the clothing Huggan was wearing. They were caught up in the branches of a deadfall spruce. When comparing them to an identical plaid shirt her sister was wearing, police determined it was a direct match. The trail was hot again, but time was running out.

A short distance up ahead, another footprint was found and again it appeared to match the tread of the young girl's shoe, but this time with a split down the rubber sole. The bushland had scraped and clawed at her at every step, tearing her clothes and shoes so badly that her tiny toes now poked through the top. The area in which they were found had been previously searched, so it appeared that they were following Huggan in a circle. Constable Wilson stated the significance of the find: "It indicates Geraldine might have walked south on the logging road to Long Lake, then turned along the shore."[53] Oddly enough, with search crews in the area, she never responded to their cries.

The search and rescue teams had convened on a point 1.25 miles west and 1.5 miles south of Wade. OPP Sergeant Martin Erickson flew out to the location along with Coroner Dr. D.J. Mason. This would mark day 10 of the search.

Now concentrating their efforts further west, south of the CNR tracks, the searchers followed the mud until darkness fell and then resumed the search at dawn. Another batch of 24 volunteers flew in from Kenora. More than 75 others drove in. Fifty more searchers came from Redditt, Ontario.

Shortly before noon, the child's clothing was found. Deep in the middle of the forest in a swampy area, Indigenous trackers located her blue jeans and plaid shirt, along with tufts of hair. A body had not yet been recovered. The discovery was half a mile east of where Hawes's hunch had materialized, but oddly enough they reported finding more footprints later, on the northeast side of Long Lake.

Trampled down spots gave way to speculation that perhaps the girl had slept in a hollow overnight, but there was no way to prove it. Perhaps more upsetting than the discovery of the clothes, were the marks made on the ground. Following the marks led to more clothing, including the blue jeans with one leg pulled inside out and torn pieces of underwear. The signs pointed to the girl dying of exposure, possibly while she bedded under the alders and then being discovered by the wolves after death. Indigenous trackers guessed that the wolves then dragged her through the mud and out of her clothes and devoured her body. They pieced the tragic tale together with scraps of clothing, strands of the girl's hair and wolf fur from the area. The Ojibway tracker's story was accepted by all, including the coroner, as the men gathered at the site near the edge of a swamp. According to Dr. Mason, "There was not enough left for either a proper burial or an inquest."[54] Interestingly though, the investigators reported that there was no blood on the clothes or in the area. The coroner concluded that she had likely been devoured 48 hours earlier.

Three-gun shots echoed in the summer air, spooking a pack of buzzards skyward. The operation came to a screeching halt. More than 200 men walked out of the bushland with their heads low and their eyes red. An aircraft cruiser flew overhead broadcasting on a loudspeaker that the search was over. The railway workers returned to their tracks, the forestry workers retreated to their offices and Wade would never be the same again. Constable Ken Wilson breathed his thoughts to the press as he pulled himself from the northern woods, "I guess this is the end — and what an ending."

Despite the temperatures being close to freezing on the first two nights, officials believed the girl survived on her own for eight days and lived off water and perhaps berries. Frustratingly, the area had been thoroughly searched in the early stages of the hunt and the location of her clothing was only about 2 miles from the family cabin by map.

Constable Ken Wilson was not satisfied, however. Even after the search had ended and the family had all returned home, he could not get the case out of his head. The discovery of clothing and drag marks was not enough to put the matter to rest. Reports printed on July 20 stated that four days after they declared Geraldine Huggan dead, he recruited four men to head back into the treacherous swamps to find some proof of the girl's demise. They needed remains for complete closure.

When they returned to the area, they were able to locate the den of a she-wolf. Around the den were the scurrying paw prints of wolf pups, but no evidence of Geraldine or other human remains. The five-man team scoured the vicinity, ducking under tree limbs and swatting at insects.

A gruesome discovery was made only 100 yards south of where the clothing was found. There, in a lonesome heap, was whatever was left of young Geraldine Huggan. It was not specified what body part was recovered, but it was only a single piece that was then shipped to Coroner Mason in Kenora. The newspapers of the time used words like 'mauled' or 'mangled', but unfortunately this colourful language never depicted the truth. Her father returned to Minaki the next day to identify the remains and take them home to Winnipeg.

CORNELIUS MCDONALD

Now that I have shared the story told by the newspapers, there are other versions that require our attention. In an interview with the daughter of Cornelius McDonald, he explained how he made the discovery of the body, which conflicts with the story told by *The Winnipeg Tribune* reporter Bob Metcalfe and others who were writing daily updates, as well as prospector Harry Hawes.

McDonald explained to his daughter that as frustration was mounting in the north woods, he and Joe Cameron got permission from the search supervisor (likely Ken Wilson) to set out on their own to take a stealthier, less destructive approach to the search. The next morning, they set out and by early afternoon they found the first major clue. They came across a broken pink barrette and immediately went into "high alert mode." This find was never mentioned in the papers because trackers kept the find to themselves for fear of a giant wave of searchers erasing a possible trail made by the girl. Without telling anyone of the find, they scrutinized their surroundings for a couple hours until coming upon another barrette and a piece of white cloth. This discovery could have been made before or after Harry Hawes got involved, but because it was never recorded to the papers, we can't accurately place it in the timeline.

Although clothing was recovered, no mention of the child's shoes appeared in the reports. Both McDonald and Cameron stated that any rumour of kidnapping or abuse was not substantiated by the scene or the remains of her body. Oddly enough, during the recovery of the clothing and her remains, McDonald and Cameron were repeatedly told to stay back from the area as to not disturb any of the "evidence." Witnesses claimed that superior officers came, took photographs and then left. Evidence is often not a priority when a child is lost without indication of foul play. If these claims are true, I thought this observation to be both interesting and contradictory.

Perhaps it was this version of the story that had locals whispering about foul play. Well over 60 years later, there is still rumour about the cause of her death, many still believing the girl was kidnapped and murdered. This gnawing feeling in the minds of locals was not touched on in any of the newspapers. The way the clothing was recovered only added to the speculation. Newspapers claimed that they found her blue jeans with one leg pulled inside out. Animals would not cause this because they do not remove clothing before devouring people. They would either tear through them, swallow them, or both, and in this case, there was torn underwear nearby. Even if the body was dragged by a wolf, it would not explain the one pulled-out pant leg. If dragging was the explanation, then both legs should have been pulled out for the pants to be removed. McDonald, Dr. Mason, nor any of the searchers comment on this, so they must not have seen it as suspicious.

After discovering the scene, McDonald and a small group of searchers returned to the Huggan cabin. He remembered the sad moments that Ann Huggan shared with them about the last time she saw her little girl.

> The baby's mother stood at the kitchen table when the news was delivered/brought to her, she was overcome with emotion, she said 'last time I seen my baby I was standing at the kitchen sink doing dishes, I smiled as I watched her chasing a bird who was hopping around. The bird, it seemed like was playing with her, everywhere the bird hopped my daughter was right there. Then the train sounded its whistle and I remembered to go get my baby.'

Funny thing about that bird — after hearing that story, both McDonald and Cameron said something to the Huggans that I found to be quite eerie: "It's the bird that took the baby girl away."

THE HARRY HAWES LETTER

What are we to make of the hunch pursued by Harry Hawes that led to the discovery? Somehow, he knew exactly where to look and yet this detail was shrugged off. To fully explore this hunch, I made an effort to learn as much as I could about Hawes.

It's interesting to note that Hawes was also successful in finding two other missing children in 1947 after a search of 200 men failed to bring them home. He picked up the trail of a boy and girl in muskeg and was able to locate them alive. Research indicates that these were the children of Henry Stone, but I could not confirm much more than that. I spent considerable time trying to learn more about Hawes to present an accurate profile of him. I wanted to find out more about this mystery man who had not been given any recognition for his northern escapades.

It's odd that a man responsible for recovering three missing children, when so many others had failed, was not revered or publicized as a local hero. After all, the "hunch" was a big piece of the puzzle, and only Harry Hawes had that piece. I couldn't find a lick of information other than his brief mention in this newspaper. It looks like nobody gave him a second glance. Through some persistent digging, I was able to track down his daughter and granddaughter in 2020, who were still residing in Ontario.

Harry Hawes was a remarkable character with a colourful past. His daughter and granddaughter shared some interesting facts about the man. In 1945, Hawes ran for the leadership of the then Labor Progressive Party. He prospected all over the northwest, gaining him excellent skills as a woodsman. He found gold in 1949 in the Lake of the Woods area, and even did extensive prospecting around Wade. He was a "rags to riches to rags to riches" kind of guy, often coming into money by staking a mining claim and spending it on his next adventure. His family described him as being generous to a fault.

He was the original inventor of the snowmobile, and claimed that Bombardier stole his patent, a fascinating fact that I badly wanted to believe but naturally had no way to confirm. His granddaughter, Deb Cantrell was kind and generous with her time. After speaking with her for awhile, I began to feel like I had known her grandfather. From what I had gathered so far, I knew that Hawes was an above average man, so I thought there could have been a slight chance that he had kept a journal, memoir or had at one point written down something about the legendary search effort for Huggan. It would be a piece of the puzzle that had been missing from this story for over 50 years. You could imagine my elation when Cantrell told me that such a document did exist. It turned out that Hawes had written up a report of the events years later, in 1960, for a woman who was doing a story about it. His write-up was later passed on to OPP Constable Bouché (spelling not confirmed) who had reached out to the Hawes family for advice on how to search and locate another missing child. That in itself is remarkable. With permission from the family, I include Harry Hawes's story here, unedited in its entirety. You'll have to look past the typos as Hawes recorded this on his typewriter. Some details are graphic and upsetting, and for this reason I had reservations about including it, but for the sake of history and for the sake of finality of this story, I felt compelled that this is something I must do. The story Hawes leaves us is very raw and real, and I believe it to be accurate.

You'll notice right away a discrepancy in some of the details. For example, the age of the girl and the dates and time she went missing. When I questioned the family about said discrepancies, they confirmed that Hawes only printed what he had heard from nightly radio broadcasts at the time and so not all the information was correct. Hawes was listening to the radio — not reading the papers. At the time of his intrepid decision to search, he was 50 years old and laid up in bed on doctor's orders. He had been immobilized by blood clots, or as he describes in the letter, "thrombosis." As I stated earlier, the media, while sometimes excellent at reporting the facts, is not always correct. This will be the first time Hawes's version of the story has ever been told, and like me, I think readers will find his trip into the woods simply astounding:

I received your letter on the 19th inquiring into the story of the Wade episode when the little girl went missing and one of the greatest searches for lost people in this part of the country ever took place. It was July 5th, 1953 when hundreds of men and women took part in this which I think was one of the biggest manhunts or I should say little Girlhunts ever organized in this part of the country. The search party consisted of 500 civilians at first, under police supervision and experienced woodsman directing the search for five days and nights. As many became exhausted tramping the rugged terrain, and the line started to weaken, the army was then called out to take over.

For another five days, over 1000 men combed the bush country in the vicinity of the lost girl covering roughly 20 square miles of rugged rocky, swampy bush lands, with no success. At this point the authorities decided to give up the search and close the books with an unsolved mystery. Where did the little girl, 8 years old, from Wade, on her summer holidays dissapear [sic] to, between the hour of 6 and 7 p.m., the night of July 5th, 1953. "Lost", came the flashes over the radio, "an 8-year-old girl at Wade, Ontario." The search began immediately by the entire neighborhood. Indians and whites in the area join forces and started the gruesome hunt, all night searching brought no clue as to what could have happened to the girl. Was she drowned, was she lost in the bush, or had a wild animal devoured her? Perhaps she was kidnapped, or had got into a sinkhole of quicksand and disappeared? All or any of these things could have been responsible for her disappearance. On July 6th the call came for every able-bodied men to volunteer to join the search. The response was to the tune of at least 500 able bodies men and women, organized by the authorities and professional bushmen. Directed by these men they searched for five days without any success, or any clue to the mystery of the lost girl.

The Army was then called to take over and continue the search. Every effort had been made and every detail was disclosed to the army commanders and officers. They organized and started to continue the search for five more days without success. At this point the army and authorities decided to give up the search and close the books once again on a unsolved mystery in northern Ontario.

Unfortunately, at the time of the search, I had been confined to my bed at home under doctor's orders as I had suffered three thrombosis from 1947 to 1953, but I kept a record of the search and mapped every detail as it was broadcast every night. I was quite familiar with the country in general as I had prospected at one time or another mostly all of north-western Ontario in the past 25 years, and had been on other searches in the past and was very successful, it just seemed as though I had an affinity for finding lost people.

Now that the big search was over with no success, I went against all doctor's orders and shouldered my pack and borrowed enough money from friends to charter an aeroplane and fly me to a lake near the scene of the Big Search and I pinpointed the spot where I wanted to land. I arrived at my destination at 9:15 a.m. July 17th, 1953 with grub for three days. The plane was not out of sight yet when I had picked up the first sign of the little girl's route of travel. I found her track on a game trail along the lakeshore in the swampy low ground somewhat obliterated, but still obviously her track to me anyway. Next I came to a windfall where she had crawled over and fell in the mud on the other side, her hand and foot prints were evident. With great care I then was convinced I was on the right track. I started to observe everything very closely, missing no bets, I examined the windfall she crawled over and found hanging on a knot, a few threads of cloth. They were so fine I had to use my magnifying glass to identify the colour of the threads which proved three different colours, comparing to the cloth in the little sweater she was wearing at the time of her disappearance. I carefully put the threads in my glass case and then made notes of everything in detail. Suddenly I thought I had better go back to the first sign on the track I had found and cover it with birch bark so it would not become obliterated in case I would have to prove my facts. I did this and did likewise to all my discoveries along the way. I found many of her tracks along the game trail in muddy places, but all were many days old which was the most disappointing thing after almost a mile of signs along this game trail. Here adverse conditions confronted me, a large floating bog with a creek flowing from the north with muddy banks and low ground draining from a big swamp, long wild grass and tag elders, a jungle you might say, where tracks were hard to pick up. I started to tire a little so I made a fire and boiled the can and had something to eat. While I was eating my lunch I noticed there were a number of buzzards and owls further on in the centre of the swamp making a lot of noise. This drew my attention. I had to decide my own course of action, and I had to plan very carefully so as not to loose [sic] any ground that I had already explored with much success. Up to now only a portion of the creek banks had been explored, so I decided I would finish the creek and then if no other clues were found I would pursue the possible clue of the owls and bussards [sic], they were not hanging around for nothing in one spot like that. I carried out my plans up and down the creek banks, both sides, with no encouragement, no more clues. I went back to the last track I found on the game trail. I scratched my head for something more possitive [sic] in the way of clues as to where she could have gone from this floating bog. Did she try to go through it and mire? No, I finally made up my mind she did not attempt to go into the bog. Then on second thought, maybe it was dark when she was here and did get into it and became hysterical and waded in and got in to a hole and drowned. So I tried to make sure and went into it up to my waist and searched every possible clue I could think of with no encouragement. I gave it up and considered my previous clue, the buzzards and owls. I stripped and wrung out my clothes and boiled the can and had some tea. I was reviewing my notes when suddenly I came across an empty cigarette package and a chocolate bar wrapper some 30 feet north of the game trail and a blaze on a small tree as if done with a hunting knife. I thought for a minute and decided that it was a mark made by the searchers for sure. But how is it I never saw any adult footprints on the game trail. Well I put it down to this, possible inexperience was my answer. The game trail meant nothing to them. But I was not satisfied with this explanation. I am going back to that point and check further away. I backtracked once again and I came to this blaze off the game trail 30 feet, checked everything closely, came up with the same answer the searchers had. Now I am still not at lands end. The buzzards and owls in the big swamp. I sat down for a minute, went back to my childhood days (psychologically). What would a child do when they would be confronted with fear, exhaustion? No doubt if it was daylight when she came to the bog, no more trail, lake on one side and bog in front of her, would she go back or would she cry herself to sleep right here, wake up and start to wander perhaps in the dark. I started a very close examination of everything. A sloping hill to the north, a not too rocky southern slope, the sun would be shining nice and warm during the day, the lake in front, blueberries growing on the side hill although still green, will be refuge temporarily until the pain of hunger and solitary confinement together with the human instinct and memories of home would build new temporary vitality to go and find home. Stopped by the bog, decided to go around or over the hill the least line of resistance would be her path. All this came into my mind while I rested at the blazed tree.

I decided on the latter, the least line of resistance would be her path. I started off again looking for any and every possible clue. At last I found the clincher. Some quarter of a mile around the nose of the hill I found where she had relieved herself. Upon thorough investigation I noticed she had been eating green blueberries and leaves and grass. Seemed to be at least a week old. I blazed the spot and covered with birch bark and went on around the hill. To my own surprise when I came around the hill I was again in sounding distance of the buzzards and owls. With no more clues I decided to investigate the merrymakers and see what they were preying on. The swamp was very wet but the hill or ridge surrounded the swamp so I kept to the hillside as I came closer the buzzards panic was evident. They flew up in numbers and the owls quieted down. I stopped suddenly as I got a wiff of a very distasteful odour. I was about half way up the hill and there was slight breeze from the direction of the buzzards. As I approached the swamp the odour got stronger and the buzzards got noisier. There was long grass and a more open spot. I could see the swamp was not so wet in this spot so I proceeded towards this open little hay meadow which was the size of a city lot. I would say as I came closer I noticed the alders were sparsely scattered among the tall wild hay and were broke off about two feet up and suddenly I noticed some black hair wound round the broken stubs. I immediately examined the hair and was convinced it was human hair. At a second glance, behold here was a very conclusive clue as to what happened to the little girl. A pair of little bue [sic] jeans turned inside out. I examined my find confident I had solved the mystery. Then I started to look some more and found a little pullover that compared in every way to that of the little girl's. The odour was strong over a little further and the long grass was tramped as flat as a floor. I proceeded to this spot where at last the mystery was solved. Here was the partial remains of the little girl, dismembered as it were, the main trunk and skull were intact although badly devoured beyond recognition. Moving with magots! [sic] Then came the moment of decision for me. I looked at my watch, four o'clock, the afternoon of July 17th 1953. Three miles from Wade Ontario were the parents of this little girl who had come to enjoy the summer vacation with their children, one of whom no one knew the whereabouts but me.

I started to ponder at this stage of my exploration trip and to look for a sympathetic and understanding way which to approach the broken hearted parents of the little girl. Conscious of the fact that I had three miles to walk through the rugged bush with positive evidence in my pack sack as to the fate of the little girl, I was the only living person that could solve the terrible tragedy and mystery that had shrouded the northwestern part of Ontario in the past two weeks.

I drew my conclusions together quickly with a terrible restraint of resentment on my own part for being obedient to my doctor's orders and staying home at the beginning of the search. Why hadn't I gone and saved the little girl's life? It was a weakening moment. I turned and took another look at the weird setting and suddenly discovered it was not complete. I had to cover what I had found to keep the savage buzzards and canibals [sic] from any further destruction. This I did, fully aware that a lot more had to be found yet to complete the picture. The legs and arms were not around although I had searched considerably without success. The time was getting on and I had three miles to get out of the bush. I realized a search party that could be mustered up in the small village would be the best thing to try to find the rest of the remains, and this could not be done until the next day in any case, so with this decision, I started with my full bag for the day. As I trecked [sic] on through the bush, up and down over the rocky ridges and through swamps, I was not thinking of the three miles at all. The first thing I knew I was at the railway track just a quarter of a mile from Wade. The time went fast as my mind was occupied every minute and every step of the way. I came around the bend and I could see Wade Station. What am I going to tell the people? How am I going to tell them? Tired and very nervous, knowing my own condition, could I stand the ultimate impact that was to come?

Suddenly I saw a handcar coming towards me. Knowing it would be section men working on the track I was getting close to the station and I thought this would be a good shock absorber if I could only stop that handcar and make known to these men my mission, and let them relay to the parents the grisly news. This I accomplished very well. I stopped them and told them about my mission to Wade. One man spoke up in broken English "Where you find out about this, lots of people been look for this little girl?" They advised me to tell the police at the station. He said "You find her out where she is?" Yes, I found her, what was left of her. He accompanied me to the station, it was only a short distance to go. The section man was very talkative. I asked him his name and he said "Nick". "Where you come from" he asked me and I told him "Kenora". He said "Ha, lots of people was here from Kenora. Lots of soldiers been here just go away yesterday" We had come to the station by now and I told Nick to go in and ask the police to come out, that I would like to talk to him. He was anxious to help and I stayed outside awaiting the police. Nick of course had to break the news as I had hoped he would. The police officer came out and I introduced myself and told him my mission. As the Police had no residence in Wade he was waiting for the night train to go to Minaki where he was stationed. He thanked Nick and asked me to come into the station where he could interview me. Thanks to Nick and the police, I had two shock absorbers. I presented the clothes and the hair and told my story to the police constable. Well, well, he mumbled, its too late to go out there now. Yes, I replied. I have had a very strenuous day and I would like to retire. Well I'm sure, he replied, but I would like to have these clothes identified by the parents and I would like to have you with me if you wouldn't mind. I explained my condition to him and told him I didn't think I could stand the shock, and felt the parents might go frantic when they saw the hair and the clothes and heard the story. He agreed, and said he would get the agent to go with him as he must have a witness. As the agent had heard the whole story, he quickly agreed to go. He asked me to stay at the station until he returned which I agreed to do. It wasn't long until I had lots of company. The moccasin telegraph had gone into action when Nick got the handcar going. The neighbors soon gathered around and went to console the parents and get all the news they could gather. Naturally they were around my [sic] like flies.

However, the police officer returned to the Station, and called me to the side. We went into the station office and he asked me to help arrange organization of a small search party for the next day to try to locate the rest of the body. In the meantime, news was cabled to the police headquarters at Kenora and arrangements were made for the coroner to be at the lake by plane the next day at 10:30 a.m. I would be there to direct them to the scene and also get a small search party going within the surrounding area. This I helped to carry out and get under way before the Coroner arrived. Fourteen men took part, mostly Indians. Before the coroner arrived, all members had been found. The Indians found them scattered within a short distance of the original discovery. The coroner arrived shortly before 11 a.m. and I was at the shore when the plane landed and came in with the coroner, the late Dr. Mason, and Sergeant Erickson who promptly congratulated me for my magnificent work. I thanked him, but told him of my regrets at not going out at first, but the sergeant was fully aware of my condition and sympathized with me and said you have done well, you have opened a closed book and enabled us to close it again with a sad mystery solved. Only for the parents good it is comforting and to the many people who sympathize with them, so I say again — Harry you have done a good job for the whole community, Congratulations." He then asked me where do we go from here. Just follow the blazed trail and I will lead you. I have a trail cut and blazed out for you. I was thinking of Dr. Mason when I made this trail. "Very thoughtful" spoke up Dr. Mason, who had one stiff knee which made it difficult for him to travel in rough terrain. We hadn't far to go, about a quarter of a mile. Everything went well and we got there quickly. The sergeant

made his notes, and we picked up the remains and placed them in a plastic bag and returned to the plane and took off for Kenora. I flew back with them. When we landed I had a lot of friends there to congratulate me and of course newsmen. My story was brief as the cameras flashed from all angles, I kept moving towards home. At last I got home where everyone was waiting anxiously to hear the news first hand. They got it and I quickly decided to have a good hot bath and roll into bed. I was tired and nervous but happy. But I had one more little job to do before everything was finished. It wasn't a nice job. I was requested to go to the Undertakers and identify the remains as a matter of form. This I did and my job was completed and another chapter written off in my life, but stamped in my belfry forever.
—HARRY HAWES

Line by line, I was amazed by Hawes's recollections. The details tell of someone who was there and greatly affected by the entire situation. His family can vouch for his credibility, saying that he was always very honest and not known to embellish. Thinking about it, why would he? Harry lived an adventurous life and had no need to make up tall tales. Any fabrications would have never measured up to his true experiences as an adventurer. If any inaccuracies surface in this letter it is likely that it is due to the passage of time and recollection of the facts.

Some readers, like me, will still be stumbling over a confusion of dates. As Hawes mentions, twice, he launched his solo search days after the newspapers said he did. If we assume that Hawes simply got the date wrong, then the other stories seem to fall into place. The extraction group of 14 men that met up with Dr. Mason on the lake likely included Cornelius McDonald and Joe Cameron and, as Hawes states were responsible for finding the other remains, "Before the Coroner arrived, all members had been found. The Indians found them scattered within a short distance of the original discovery."

As Hawes mentioned in his letter, it was likely that the local newspapers were printing stories before the full matter had unfolded. Sometimes there were multiple issues per day. This could be why many of the later articles contradict the previous ones. It is possible that Harry Hawes, Sergeant Erickson and Dr. Mason returned to the area on Wednesday the fifteenth, which would make sense given the story of the Indigenous men who discovered the site. If Hawes arrived in Wade on Monday, joined the search party Tuesday, and found signs of where the girl was headed, it would make sense for him to fly into Long Lake on the Wednesday. It seemed the papers weren't getting the full story. Out of those 14 trackers that accompanied Hawes back to the site on Long Lake, four of them were said to break off from the main line and make further discovery of the remains and partial clothing. They were credited with finding the blue jeans, but clearly it was Hawes that found those a day earlier. Newspapers also mentioned that Hawes spent the night in the woods, but I found no evidence of this in his letter.

The four men credited were named in the July 16 issue of the *Winnipeg Free Press* and *The Winnipeg Tribune* as, Charlie Fisher, 28, a guide at Minaki Lodge; Albert Kelly, 44, also a Minaki guide; John Thomas Henry, a 51-year-old counsellor from White Dog; and Pat Lecoy, 58, of Great Falls, Manitoba, a veteran of World War I.[55]

Left to right: Charlie Fisher, Albert Kelly, John Henry and Pat Lecoy,
* Winnipeg Tribune, July 16, 1953

They supposedly swept east from Long Lake inland to find drag marks and torn underwear of the child. Why McDonald and Cameron are not mentioned here is not known, perhaps there comes a point when the *who* and the *what* no longer matter.

One aspect Hawes never explains in his letter is his so-called hunch that brought him to Long Lake in the first place. Whatever it was, it was strong enough to motivate him beyond his injuries and doctor's orders. The nagging question is, was this a premonition? Did it come in the form of a dream? I often wondered how early he got this "hunch." In the letter, he states his regrets for not acting earlier, as if he knew the spot where Huggan was wandering, and could have made it there in time before her little life was taken away. It makes me wonder if Huggan was "supposed" to be found alive.

I had to question his family about this so called "hunch," because as of now we had no way of telling if Hawes was spiritual in this sense of the word. To my surprise, Cantrell, after discussing it with her mother, told me that, Harry was known for his premonitions:

> Mom couldn't remember anything specifically, but she said he was always predicting things that eventually came to be. Mom laughed when I asked her about this because she said, 'your father was always saying, "one day the world would be hit by a catastrophic pandemic."'

Let me state here that I interviewed the Hawes family in the summer of 2020, when the world was hit by the Covid-19 pandemic. Even after decades gone-by, Harry Hawes proves to be a fascinating man.

If we are led to believe that Hawes had a premonition or a dream, it would not be completely out of the realm of possibility. There are other cases to suggest this could have been the reason, and it could explain why he was so hesitant to disclose his sources. Oddly enough, all of these other cases I am referring to involved citizens of Manitoba. What is so special about residents from Manitoba and why are they "taken" from us, later to have their location mysteriously revealed to random citizens? These stories are so remarkable and cannot be ignored. They must be somehow related to Huggan's case. For more on this, see Appendix B.

A few final notes on Harry Hawes before we close this chapter. His full name was Harry Horatio Nelson Hawes. He had a heart condition and died of heart disease on November 20, 1960, at the age of 58. When his daughter was asked about the theory that Huggan was abducted, she said, "Harry never said a word to suggest that this was anything other than a child that wandered off, got lost, and was eaten by wolves."[56] Having said that, Cantrell, had the impression that Hawes believed there was something more nefarious to the story. Just what that was will remain a mystery.

Harry Hawes, 1960.
* Courtesy of the Hawes family

LOCAL PERSPECTIVE

I came upon a considerable amount of rumour while investigating this historical episode. Since the police records have all been destroyed, I have no way of confirming the testimony I received from local residents or family members.

Many things strike me as being very odd about this case. When the footprints and clothing were found, they were in an area previously searched. That in itself is odd. It seemed that Huggan was circling civilization a day or two ahead of her parents and would-be rescuers. The location was not far from the cabin or railway tracks where most of the searchers were camped. Some train cars were used to house an army unit for a number of days. The clues were within hearing distance of the searcher's calls, not to mention the planes and the recognizable voice of her father. On the other hand, her father, Jared, admitted that Huggan was afraid of the dark and would likely stay put after dusk and might not respond to rescue calls. This is a perfect, real-world situation that is echoed in the data of *Lost Person Behaviour* that we touched on in earlier chapters. We can't tell why she wouldn't respond, but it's a note worth mentioning, since her father would know her best.

Since the area was already searched, is it possible that clues were plopped down in such a way that they would be found? It's an idea that was entertained by some. I had heard stories that there was a man's bootprint in the mud close to where her remains were found. If a bootprint was discovered, in my mind, there would be enough reason for the police to dismiss it as belonging to one of the searchers. However, Harry Hawes never mentioned any other footprints or tracks in his letter as he crawled along the shores of Long Lake. However, he did mention the cigarette packaging and the chocolate bar wrapper, which he believed to be left by inexperienced searchers. Odd that footprints did not accompany those items, but perhaps the wind blew them there. I feel he would have mentioned footprints if he saw any.

When speaking with one local, he remembered a peculiar man who had a cabin at Wade. He was a fire ranger known to locals. As a tight community, the adults used to get together quite often to play cards in the evenings. When the ranger would come around, he made the others uncomfortable, staring at the children a little longer than what was considered polite. It wouldn't be impossible for a man to snatch up a little girl as she walked alone down a wooded path.

The searchers walked 4 square miles in the first four days of the search, and nothing was found. It's as if she didn't wander away but was scooped up and dropped outside of the search zone. How?

The last fact of this case is that young Huggan knew the area and had been there many times before. Her family vacations were six-week stints, which was ample time to become acquainted with the surroundings. When and if she came to the railway tracks, you'd think she would have stopped. If she ventured past the tracks, she would have known that turning around and retracing her steps would lead to her family's cottage.

What about the fact that more footprints were found further north after the discovery of the clothes? On July 16, The *Winnipeg Free Press* is quoted saying, "Other footprints were found farther north-east along the Long Lake shoreline. These prints were well north of the first." The whole story was strange. Did something sinister happen to Geraldine Huggan? Was she taken by something or someone? It's interesting to note that no distinct adult human tracks were in the area. What made her wander away without the company of her siblings in the first place? Unfortunately, we will never conclusively know.

Jared and Ann Huggan continued to stay together after the incident and went on to have more children. I thought it was very possible that some of their children were still alive and willing to speak to me about this.

Huggan's siblings were all sisters, so it made tracking them down all that more difficult. Moving away from Winnipeg was likely, and I had no way to know if they were alive or dead. I would also be dealing with the very real possibility that most of them would have changed their last names if they were married. Now, with whispers of murder and sloppy police work, I was desperate to know what the family thought about this. It took me more than a year, but one day my efforts paid off.

To my surprise, the Huggan property is still being well taken care of by Debbie Huggan, Geraldine's first cousin. Debbie was born after the disappearance, but her thoughts were integral to the story and helped to gain a more accurate understanding of who Geraldine really was. Her father, Walter, was involved in the search back in 1953.

Debbie Huggan was able to confirm many of the details already discussed when I spoke with her in October of 2019.[57] As Debbie's version of the incident goes, Geraldine's parents told her not to take the path between the cabins on the way back because it passed through the neighbour's property — this was the path mentioned in the paper.

Debbie believes that instead of taking that path, she walked behind the cabins to avoid getting in trouble. To avoid walking on the neighbour's property, she overcompensated and walked too far, passing all of the cabins in that row. This would mean that instead of the children walking in a line of three, as some retellings suggest, at one point Geraldine ventured back on her own.

The path mentioned in the newspaper is a wide-open path where houses can be seen, but the alternate path wasn't a path at all. This was the first mention of a second "path." Although I referred to it as a path, Debbie corrected me that it was only thick bush. There was no access and no trail. It would have been a bushwhack back to the Huggan cabin. I felt a new kind of heartbreak once I heard Debbie's explanation. It had a degree of innocence that had been overshadowed by the mystery of it all. Perhaps, when her mother and father called out to her, she didn't answer because she thought she was in trouble, and after that she just kept walking. Is the more tragic cause the most plausible — she simply walked too far?

Debbie didn't mention the fire ranger character, but she was aware that there were loggers or road crews in the area and could understand how someone from the crew could have grabbed her. With no evidence, it's hard to give this theory much credence.

I can't begin to imagine the heartbreak and loss this family must have felt. From all I have heard, Jared and Ann Huggan never spoke about the incident once their daughter's remains were recovered. When Debbie would visit the Huggan home, she never saw any pictures of Geraldine. In fact, the first time Debbie saw a picture of Geraldine was from the newspaper article I sent out a week before I interviewed her. No one in the family ever discussed it.

After some painful searching, I was eventually able to track down another family member.

The family member asked not to be identified, to which I will oblige. I telephoned her late one evening at our prearranged time. There was an immediate sadness in the voice on the other end that weighed heavily on me. I was hurt by it. I was trespassing through her personal heartbreak, and I felt very guilty with it. The heartbreak suddenly felt very fresh, as if we were discussing the tragedy at the funeral. I clammed up. It's hard to make someone understand that you're coming from a good place. I was already at a disadvantage, she had never met me; never read anything I had written and couldn't understand why a stranger would be interested in this story. I tried to explain how much this story had meant to me, but when the words left my mouth, they sounded so flat to my ears. Here I was, waltzing in from out of nowhere asking questions. That was a very hard conversation for me, but the whole time I kept thinking about Geraldine and why I was doing all this work. After all, I was only going at this with the best intentions, to honour her memory and to uncover the truth. Her memory must age well. It must be preserved, and if I upset people in the process, maybe it's worth it. Wasn't it better to keep her in the front of our minds instead of pretending like she never existed?

Once the conversation began to flow, I was able to get a different perspective on it, one you'd never find in the newspapers. The family member did find it odd that Geraldine's parents never liked to discuss the disappearance. She admitted to me that Gerry's mother was completely devastated by the loss, which might go to explain why photographs and mementos were removed from sight in the home. There was one piece of Geraldine that remained behind though, a little teddy bear that belonged to her and was kept on her bed. Since they didn't discuss the tragedy, the family never attempted to access records of the autopsy, or search for the police report. In their minds, they knew what happened and did not require anything further. I must confess that as time went on, I couldn't determine if the negative feeling I had initially felt in the interview was because of my prying or because this person didn't know for certain what had happened to Geraldine. Perhaps she felt cut off from the incident, excluded from the grief.

There were two versions of the story that she was told over the years. The first was that Huggan got lost in the woods and eaten by wolves. The second was that an OPP officer had kidnapped her, raped her and left her for dead. It's obvious that there was some mistrust in the area, and perhaps some of the family felt that the investigation into what happened to the little girl was not as thorough as it could be. To be clear, the papers did not report any suspicions of foul play. Dr. Mason, the coroner who did the autopsy, did not publicly state that there was evidence of an assault on her body and no inquest was held.

When I asked which theory she thought was most likely, she told me that she hoped there was no one waiting in the bush to grab her that day. Hypothermia or an animal attack would have been much less upsetting than an assault on a helpless little girl.

Eventually, Geraldine's older sister Judy heard that I was writing up the story and got in touch with me. Her memory of the incident is far from perfect, having taken place so long ago, but Judy was there when her sister disappeared, so I felt it was very important to speak with her. Judy told me that they got rid of all the data, photographs and news clippings once her father died. Like many others, she regretted it now. Being 12 at the time, the memories had been clouded over — that, compounded with the fact that most of the children were hidden safely inside the cabin and were limited to what they were told while the search was underway. They would receive daily visitors to keep her and her family company, while they waited for police to bring their sister home. There was nothing dramatic about how the day unfolded. Judy had been on the swing in her grandfather's yard, while Linda, her younger sister, took Gerry down to play at their Aunt Lil's cottage. The path they took was down the rock at the front of the cabin, across the back of the Walker's cottage and into Aunt Lil's yard, which would be right there. The path was wide, clear and used daily. For whatever reason, her sister decided to come home. Instead of returning the way she and Linda had gone down, Geraldine took the back route behind the cabins. Judy believed that she must have taken a wrong turn and got lost: "That's exactly how it happened. She went off by herself." Why she went the back way is beyond Judy. The family could not understand it. The newspapers would print up a variety of reasons, none of which can be confirmed. One report stated she had gone to pick wildflowers for her mother, one report stated she was chasing a bird, another said that she was following a cat.

There are just as many reasons for why she wouldn't hear the desperate calls from her father and the searchers. It was reported that she was only gone for 10 minutes, but Judy believes it could have even been longer. Linda came home without her, so the family didn't know she was missing until then. Even if she was only gone 10 minutes it's likely that she still wouldn't have heard the calls. You can get pretty far in 10 minutes and sound does not travel well in the forest. In an area so thick, where there's so many rocks and trees, it's not out of the realm of possibility that the calls didn't reach her. I remember playing in the forest when I was younger, and I would only be able to hear my parents call me when I was on a hilltop. In 10 minutes, you could easily be out of earshot.

"You have to realize how thick the bush is here and how easy it is to get turned around," Judy told me. Judy remembers the day that they found her sister. She had gone up to the train station and heard it from searchers. She recalled coming home and telling friends of the family that they found her. Of course, they were relieved, but they knew that it meant she was dead. As for the rumours as to what happened, Judy stated that they never paid any attention to them. They knew what happened and the rest didn't matter.

Oddly enough, when I spoke to Debbie Huggan she described a situation in which she was at a function the week before I spoke to her and overheard two men speaking about the disappearance. From what she was able to catch, they both subscribed to the theory of a bear attack. Perhaps it will never be properly settled in the history of Wade either but getting people to talk about Geraldine Huggan is a sure way that she will never be forgotten. Her journey through the rugged wilderness will not be hidden from time.

AFTERMATH

To try and stamp out some of these rumours, I undertook a thorough archival search for records. It was touch and go with the director at the Office of the Medical Examiner in Winnipeg for a copy of a death certificate or autopsy report to get a final answer on the matter. I wasn't sure if they would tell me anything since I wasn't a blood relative of Huggan, but I thought maybe I'd get lucky. A few months after my initial request was made, the director told me that no records could be found.

In 2017, I submitted an extensive *Freedom of Information Act* request to the OPP and included all my findings. I was looking for any official documents, such as a police report, a search and rescue report, surviving photographs or interviews. After months of digging, I found nothing. When I opened the letter of denial, I felt quite defeated. Police failed to provide a single page of the event, citing that nothing could be found. How fitting, I thought, but also how unacceptable. This was the biggest search and rescue operation at the time and received international attention, how could not a single shred of it exist in the system? I seemed to be the only one left on the planet that was looking for poor Geraldine Huggan.

Keep in mind that this story made daily headlines across Canada and even spilled into the United States. In fact, almost every State in the continental U.S. had printed the story, and often it was on the front page. These include even the most southern states like California, Arizona, New Mexico, Texas, Louisiana, Alabama and Florida. Clearly, this story had an impact all over North America, but then it was quickly forgotten about.

I searched every archive that I could and every group that was involved. Library and Archives Canada turned up nothing. The Archives of Manitoba had zip. The Archives of Ontario provided diddly-squat.

The Minaki OPP detachment closed years earlier and sent their files to the office in Kenora, but they too did not save them. Nor did the *Canadian National Police Service*. I even sought out the family of reporter Bob Metcalfe, going so far as tracking down his children and writing a letter to his widow in British Columbia, but that trail turned up nothing.

My FOIA request to the RCMP was continuously delayed. I sent a few emails and called their office, but always got the same voicemail. They exceeded their time limit of 90 days, after which I called every day, and almost every hour for three days, until finally someone answered on May 1, 2019. Although they had reviewed my request, a response to my file was still pending. There was nothing more I could do but sit and hope. A few months later, they revealed that nothing on the matter was found. I probed them over and over and asked that they check again, to which they responded with some surprising results. The retention period for the RCMP is only two years. I couldn't believe it. I was beyond surprised, and my hopes of finding a shred of an official write-up was quickly going to pieces.

In missing persons cases, the police can play God. In a way, they can erase all memory of a person, just by throwing out their files. It's tragic to think that someone's life has a retention period. In a way, it echoes our very mortality in that, after a while, none of us really matter.

Am I wrong to put the responsibility on the police? Perhaps, but I don't expect them to shoulder my wrath alone, after all they are only doing their jobs. They are not a museum of Ontario history, but if they were, we would know a lot more about our past and province. Speaking of museums, I even checked the OPP Museum in Orillia, but they had no helpful records. I went as far as submitting a request to the Winnipeg Police Service, who were surprisingly helpful, I should add. They gave me some promising news that they had 14 reels of microfilm from 1953. How could I not get excited? Surely a snippet of Geraldine's story was on one of these reels. I would never be able to forgive myself if I had not done a complete and thorough check of all the agencies involved. Time ticked on and I started to feel a bit confident. I had convinced myself that somewhere out there was an ending to this story, and this might be it.

But whatever confidence I had was destroyed when I received yet another skinny letter in the mail. The results of my search stared back in a dull black ink, and my heart sank:

> After consulting with our Records Compilation Unit, we have determined that the requested records could not be located. Therefore, access is refused in accordance with s. 12(1)(c)(i) of *The Freedom of Information and Protection of Privacy Act*...[58]

Every attempt felt like I was getting two steps closer to closure and two steps back. I was really scratching my head now. There were 14 microfilm reels from 1953 and not a single shred mentioned the case of Geraldine Huggan — the largest search in history. Multiple army units and police detachments were involved and yet nothing was saved. What else happened in 1953 that would be worth keeping above all the rest? This is not an issue of a short retention period because obviously they were keeping something of importance from that year, but to not include the Huggan story seems totally baffling. Would a few pages more really be too much? I felt utterly robbed of my conclusion that I was so confident was waiting for me in those reels. I was chasing a memory, something that no longer existed, like a shadow rounding corner after corner until I hit a dead end.

As much as I wanted to find something, all of my attempts to source official documents on the case have been in vain. It was becoming quite clear that there was nothing on Geraldine Huggan to be found.

For an unknown period of time, there was confusion between Ontario and Manitoba on whether this was a closed case. I was getting mixed answers from provincial police and was leaning towards it being an open case. After all, this was one reason why I was initially denied cooperation with my first FOIA attempt.

Somewhere along the line, there was clearly a breakdown in communication between officials and newspapers all over the country. When Ken Wilson went back for a final search, he clearly found human remains, because I was able to track down the final resting place of the young girl to Brookside Cemetery.

I was not able to personally make the trip out there to visit the little girl that haunted my mind and broke my heart for so long. I was saddened that I wouldn't be able to pay my respects in person. But being Canadian comes with more advantages than just clean lake water and pure maple syrup. I thought I may be able to count on a friendly and helpful Winnipegger to visit the cemetery on my behalf and take a few photographs for me. I posted an ad online and almost fell out of my chair when I saw the response. I received 84 views on one online ad and 1,116 on a second ad. There were well over 30 replies, some within hours of posting. It seemed everyone was eager to help, or at least curious about my request. A man named Darren stood out among the group, and I directed him on where to go. It was he and the beautiful people of Winnipeg who helped me find a certain kind of ending. A day or two later, when I received the photo, it was a new and strange feeling that I could not describe. Was this some type of closure? When I saw the marker with her name on it, a bittersweet wave came over me. It hurt, but it was accompanied by a strange relief, probably because I knew she was not still out there, alone in the wilderness.

When the story is all laid out, it's shocking that the searchers could not come up with more clues or a distinct trail. Highly trained professionals, army units and trackers came up with almost nothing to say the girl was even in the area. It's highly abnormal when tracking dogs are not able to find a scent. Searchers blamed the rain for washing away possible scent trails in the first crucial night. Perhaps there were too many volunteers involved in the search and they inadvertently tampered with the scent. Just imagine 1,000 people converging on a single area at one time. We will never know, and we are left with a number of oddities that will forever keep us head-scratching.

The disappearance, search and untimely death of Geraldine Huggan still painfully echoes in Ontario's history. Even with all these years past, I feel the sting of the loss of this poor Canadian child. It started off as a very ordinary situation, something we have all done in the past. Long summer days at the cottage in a familiar setting that promises memories and endless joy. I smile when I think of her excitement as she arrived at the cabin and strolled the secluded property.

I can only imagine how the search must have really felt to those who were involved and related. We must never forget their pain or suffering; most importantly we should not forget Geraldine Huggan. She should be a reminder to us all that life is so precious. Hold fast to your children, "don't let them out of your sight," Judy ended our interview with. Advice that we should all abide by.

GERALDINE HUGGAN

*Published in the Kenora Miner and News
A division of Postmedia Network Inc.

I will end Geraldine's story with a loving tribute from her parents, which was printed one year later:

HUGGAN — In loving memory of our darling little daughter, Geraldine who fell asleep July 11th, 1953. Time rolls on, and we are reminded of a day our hearts were crushed, when God took you — oh so quickly and we all in gloom were thrust. In the bud of life and death claimed you. In the prime of childhood days. But we hope someday to meet you and be with you always. — Lovingly remembered and sadly missed by mommy and daddy, and sisters Judy, Lynda and Sandra.[59]

7

Pierre Michaud

"We discovered the tomb of Hélène Michaud here in Richer, but we did not know where her husband was."
—Patricia Gendreau

While neighbours, police officers and bush-workers around Wade turned the woods upside down looking for Geraldine Huggan, some locals couldn't help but be reminded of another mysterious disappearance that took place years earlier.

On July 19, 1946, at the age of 79, Pierre Michaud vanished without a trace in the exact same spot.

Very little is known about Pierre Michaud. He was born in La Limouzinière, France and immigrated to Richer, Manitoba (formally Thibaultville) in the early 1900s. Michaud's property was close to (and bisected) the historic Dawson Road, the first all-Canadian land and water route linking eastern and western Canada. In 1903, Michaud donated 17 acres to the parish of Enfant Jesus to build a church, a convent, a parish hall, a rectory and a school in an area that would be about half the size of Richer.

Michaud always dreamed of becoming a farmer, but the rocky terrain that surrounded his home made this impossible. Instead, he decided to raise sheep. He and his wife Hélène had no children but would end up caring for his sister's children when she died during childbirth. Michaud's wife Hélène passed away on February 5, 1944, and so he decided to rent out his home in Richer and leave Manitoba to live with his niece, Marcelle Warren in Wade, Ontario.

Michaud would live with Mrs. Warren and her husband, George Warren, a section foreman for only a short time. On July 19, 1946, at the age of 79, Michaud went blueberry picking around Wade and never returned. The Warren's reported him missing when he did not show up for dinner that evening. Michaud was last seen carrying two red water pails, which were likely used to collect berries, neither of which were ever recovered in the search.

History has a way of repeating itself, and yet there were some residents who had no recollection of a search that occurred in Wade only years earlier. Most had forgotten. Marcelle Warren however, did not.

As they searched for Huggan, Warren couldn't help but be haunted with thoughts of Michaud. The event seemed so fresh in her mind.

Marcelle Warren, then a 54-year-old grandmother of three, marched alongside the rest of the searchers for the little Huggan girl. She fearlessly joined the line of men, who would hear her voice calling out for the child. Warren would be seen by newsmen as she hiked out of the bush, day after day, in her peaked cap, bush shirt and torn blue jeans. For Warren, the search was personal for a different reason. She was driven through the swampland by the fact that her uncle, Pierre Michaud, had suffered the same fate only seven years prior: "I know what it's like to have someone lost in the bush," she was quoted saying.[60]

When interviewed by Bob Metcalfe of *The Winnipeg Tribune*, Warren said, "Somewhere in the bush, I have always believed I would stumble across the remains of my uncle."

But she never did.

JOIN IN SEARCH: Mrs. Mary Tourand (left) and Mrs. George Warren.

* Winnipeg Tribune, July 10, 1953

After my write-up on Huggan, I felt compelled to include a section on Pierre Michaud. Even if the information was scarce, it was still important to include what very little was known about the man. I could not overlook the fact that Michaud was last seen entering the same location as Huggan would years later — a detail that left me with a feeling of unease.

No one seems to know more about Pierre Michaud than Patricia Gendreau, an archivist for the Enfant Jesus Heritage Site and member of the Richer Historical Committee. I tracked down Gendreau to confirm a few details about what was known of the mysterious man, who seemed generous and loved by his community, yet had somehow been forgotten about. Gendreau summarized the man's story:

> Although he appreciated being with family, he longed for his country of origin. One day he went to pick blueberries and never returned home. Only an empty pail lying near the railroad tracks were found; his wallet was left in his room. Pierre had disappeared. In spite of the many search parties lasting a month, no trace was found.[61]

I could not confirm the discovery of a pail found near the railroad tracks, but in an eerie turn of events, during the hunt for Huggan, searchers would find a berry bucket they believed could have belonged to Michaud. Perhaps this was the pail that Gendreau was referring to. The rusted bucket was found in a water-filled hole beneath the stump of a downed tree. Searchers say it had almost completely disintegrated. The discovery foreshadowed a grim conclusion in the tireless search to find Geraldine Huggan.

Larry Syring, a German immigrant pulp cutter from the Wade district who Thursday found a rusty and aged berry-picking can believed to have been one carried by an uncle of Mrs. George Warren of Wade who disappeared in the same country without a trace seven years ago. Syring is leading a pack of searchers in the area on daily patrols through the dense forest.

* The Winnipeg Tribune, July 10, 1953

The initial search in 1946 was led by Constable Albert Edward Magill of the OPP with a search party of about 25 men that grew from there. At the time, searchers were hopeful they would find the man alive, as there were enough berries and wild edibles in the woods during that time of year that one could survive on. But searchers remained at a disadvantage. They did not know the exact location that Michaud had entered the woods from. Marcelle Warren was one of the searchers that went after her uncle. By all accounts, Warren had no qualms about being in the bush. She was active every day of the search for her uncle, as well as Huggan. When her uncle went missing, the search was nowhere near as large as it was for the little girl. Police only searched for Michaud for one week and then called it quits. The Warrens put their lives on hold for a full month and tromped through the bushland around Wade for any sign of Michaud, but found nothing.

What is it about this part of Wade that swallows people up? I found it especially odd that such a tiny point on the map could be the location of two very similar disappearances within a few years of each other. Even more head-scratching was the discovery of Michaud's berry bucket by searchers while they looked for Huggan. It's almost as if the forest gave up the taunting clue seven years later to the searchers. It was as if the wilderness was mocking them.

Pierre Michaud is remembered as a calm and hardworking person. He loved his farm and enjoyed his pipe and Virginia tobacco.

Unlike other missing people, we do have one artifact left to preserve the memory of this man. A commemorative monument stands to honour Pierre and Hélène Michaud in the Richer Cemetery. Strangely though, the date inscribed on the monument is incorrectly stated as 1948, when he clearly went missing in 1946. The newspapers also call him M.V. Michaud. I'm unaware of any alias starting with M.V., but the discrepancy of his name and the year of his vanishing is another perfect example of improper data collection and reporting.

I consider myself fortunate to have found two photographs that showed the face of Pierre Michaud, one of which I am including here from the Dawson Trail Museum in Winnipeg.

Since the case was never resolved, by police standards that means Michaud is still considered a missing person, yet no law enforcement agency is looking for his remains. He is not on the OPP, RCMP or Winnipeg Police Service database, or any other missing persons list that I could get my hands on. The question is, why not? Without a widow, children or extended family left behind, there is no one to put pressure on authorities. If human remains or Michaud's belongings were ever to be discovered, there would be no way to confirm that they are linked to a missing person case. They would simply be filed away, never to be identified, and a further frustration for a forensic anthropologist.

Constable Magill would have had to fill out the necessary police report detailing his involvement in the search, but this documentation is nowhere to be found. My requests to the relevant departments have confirmed that no files exist. FOIA agents tell me that the OPP were not involved in the search, and yet Magill clearly was. I appealed the FOIA decision and escalated the request, but after searching various police databases, no record of Michaud was recovered. His files were either destroyed, misplaced or mislabeled. My attempts to interview Constable Magill were in vain after I learned he had passed away in March 1999.

Michaud's name is excluded from any visible missing persons list, which is a major concern for me. However, it is this fact that makes it possible for the police to safely ignore this one.

8

George Weeden and Merle Newcombe

"They simply vanished from the face of the earth."
—Bill E. McLeod

A legend grows in the Northwoods, far from any semblance of civilization. The disappearance of George Weeden and Merle Newcombe is still whispered about on nearby First Nation reserves and the tiny hamlets that skirt the Chapleau Crown Game Preserve. It is unique to the others discussed here because of the frightening fact that it involves two people who went missing at the same time. Their short profile on the Internet was not unlike dozens of others, and so I can see how it would be passed over by the public. On paper, they were just another set of missing hunters in Ontario's vast wilderness, but as it turned out, there was much more to the story that was not readily available to the public.

Much of what we know about George Weeden and Merle Newcombe we owe to Bill McLeod, a retired professor from Cambrian College in Sudbury. McLeod was born and raised in Chapleau, Ontario, where the mysterious disappearance occurred, and has done years of research and interviews to uncover what he could of the more than 60-year-old puzzle. McLeod was a local and had strong connections to those involved, and was even given an opportunity to search for the men when he was in grade 13. McLeod went on to pen a book, *The Chapleau Game Preserve: History, Murder and Other Tales,* which describes the incident. The details of this story were broken up in a series of police reports, which came back heavily redacted having some pages severed, as one would expect.

George Weeden was a 63-year-old bachelor and worked as a Canadian Pacific Rail (CPR) yard engineer. His age and birth date are incorrectly printed on the police websites (and do not match the police report). Merle Newcombe was 50 and had worked as a CPR trainman. The men were long-time friends and were very familiar with the area. Newcombe's family had owned and operated a lodge 75 feet north of the train tracks on the very lake that they were at, located at Mile 107 on the CPR line, a track that cuts through Ontario's bush country before making its way out to the prairies. There are no roads or paths into the area, and the only way to access it is by float plane or the VIA Rail Budd Car from Sudbury to White River, an 8-hour and 50-minute trip. Suffice to say that the area is remote and at any point visitors could get the impression that they are lost. The location is approximately 135 kilometres northwest of Chapleau, near the tiny village of Amyot. From Amyot, it was a short walk to the isolated tourist resort referred to as Newcombe's camp or sometimes the "Honeymoon Camp", which the men used as their base for the hunt. This camp is like hundreds of other fishing resorts that are sprinkled throughout Ontario. The property has individual rental cabins and docks for visitors to launch their boats from, and unless you knew about it, you'd probably never find it. On that day, George Weeden and Merle Newcombe were moose hunting along the lonely stretch of tracks that were surrounded by bush and lakes.

On October 22, 1959, Jean Newcombe informed police that, while visiting family with their daughter, Harriet in Fort William (now Thunder Bay), her husband had called to say that he and George Weeden were going hunting at the camp and wanted her to join. To Weeden and Newcombe, October 22 was just an ordinary day to go moose hunting, and the pair had only scheduled to be out for a few days.

Jean and Harriet declined to join them as they had made plans to travel to Montreal with her sister and brother-in-law. Newcombe had arranged to meet with his wife, Jean on October 26 at Chapleau station for him to collect Harriet, while Jean continued her trip to Montreal by rail. George Weeden was expected to be at work on October 27.

Something sinister must have happened on the morning of October 23 that prevented Newcombe from keeping this rendezvous and Weeden from returning to work. When Newcombe didn't show up at the train station, Jean made other plans for their daughter to be looked after by a neighbour and continued her trip to Montreal. Jean telephoned the apartment twice and received no answer from her husband. Newcombe had been late leaving the bush on previous occasions and so it wasn't so odd to his wife at the time, she figured perhaps they had shot a moose. It wasn't until October 28 that Jean began to feel that something was terribly wrong. With both men absent from their prearranged engagements, Jean and her daughter returned home. McLeod uncovers a key detail in the early stages of the investigation that stood out to me. Upon her return, Jean discovered that her husband's bedroll for camping was still in their apartment. This meant that he had no intention of sleeping in the bush during their trip. If Newcombe wasn't at the cabin, then she knew something wasn't right.

With this in mind, Jean and Harriet raced to the Budd Car, and arrived in Amyot at 2:30 a.m. the next morning. They walked into Newcombe's camp hoping the men would still be there snoozing in their bunks, but instead found it completely deserted. They noted that their rifles: a Savage 250-3000 and a .43 German Mauser, were missing, hinting that they had left the camp and did not return. The pair woke up other residents in the area, who confirmed that the missing men were last seen on Friday, October 23, almost a week earlier. Weeden and Newcombe were last spotted between mile marker 106 and 107 on the CPR line. A storm ripped through the area on Saturday, which caused Mrs. Newcombe and residents of Amyot cause for concern.

The OPP has them missing since October 29, but that was actually the date that the police sprang into action. As the story plays out, we can see that they vanished days prior.

It wasn't until the wee hours of October 29 that police got involved. Constable Augustine Robert "Bob" King of the White River detachment received a wire communication, at 5:45 a.m. from superintendent V.E. Everett saying, "…would appreciate you taking some action at once" on a report of the two missing hunters. Without any road access, Constable Bob King departed the first eastbound train at 8:00 a.m. to get a statement from Jean Newcombe. What follows is a thorough report of the condition of the camp and a possible timeline of what occurred.

Upon entering the camp, Constable King observed that the hunters had likely eaten dinner on the night of the twenty-second, then packed a lunch for their excursion on Friday morning. There was no indication that the men, or anyone else for that matter, had returned to the camp recently. Based on a grocery list of inventory, King surmised that only a single day's worth of food had been missing. This included four eggs, bacon, one loaf of bread (likely used for Friday's lunch), and two tins of beans. The remains of this breakfast were reported to be left in a skillet inside the cabin. Other than this, everything was accounted for; the camp was as it should be, and no rental boats were missing.

King discovered that the last people to see Weeden and Newcombe were two Indigenous trappers from Tripoli, Clem Nabigon and his 17-year-old son Herb. When interviewed, the trappers revealed that they had met the hunters around 11:30 a.m. on Friday, October 23, and conversed with them for about 15-20 minutes at or near Mile 106. After speaking, the trappers went west for five minutes, set a beaver trap on the north side of the railroad track, then headed back east, the way they came. They walked for 3 miles to the town of Tripoli Lake and did not see Weeden or Newcombe as they passed.

To further complete the timeline, Constable King interviewed railway employee Reg Bromley who had been on train number 964 on that very morning they were said to disappear. As the train passed Newcombe's camp, the employee stated that he saw both Weeden and Newcombe at the main lodge and both waved to him. This was around 8:45 a.m. While on site, King, along with locals Wilfred Labelle, and Clem and Herb Nabigon, searched the bush both north and south of the railroad tracks. His notes tell that the bush was wet with snow, however no footprints were reported. If there were footprints to be found in the area, they would have belonged to Harriet and Jean who were there the previous night. On the North side was a precarious 30-foot embankment that led into Summit Lake. King did not state that there were any signs or markings on the ground that would indicate that the men had fallen in, and if there were, they would likely have faded as the days went on. A plane from Wawa was called in and searched from above for an hour and a half. King stayed in the area until 5:00 p.m. and then called it quits due to the coming darkness. He would recruit another 10 men to begin a new search the next day.

With a full day of searching ahead of them, the 13 men divided their efforts between the north and south side of the CPR tracks. At 6:15 a.m., Constable King set out with Conservation Officer E.A. Pozzo, Department of Lands and Forests, and another man, and stated they covered a search area of 12 miles north of the track. Consider this effort for a moment — trekking 12 miles through the wet forest without the help of vehicles, roads or trails would take tenacity and dedication. To accomplish this task in one day would be an immense challenge. It would have been a gruelling bushwhack 12 miles north and 12 miles back through unforgiving country. Why Constable King set his initial search radius so far out is unknown, but if his notes are accurate, this struck me as quite impressive.

The search was miserable. Rain fell all afternoon as searchers trudged through the last October snowfall. The perpetual dampness of late fall chilled them to their bones. They shivered their way back by 4:30 p.m. without turning over a single clue.

The morning of October 31 began with another search, this time comprised of 14 men that set foot in the tangled, soggy forest at 8:50 a.m. Some of these men were Lands and Forests officers that would focus on the north side of the tracks and check the nearest bodies of water for any sign of the missing hunters. Again, the men returned in the evening, wet, cold and frustrated that not a shred of evidence was located. The terrain, which they described as, "nothing but endless lakes, swamps, muskeg and hills — really rough country," was wearing on them.

The search resumed at sunrise with 44 men that worked a full shift from 7:00 a.m. to 5:00 p.m., searching for the missing hunters. Four parties searched from mile marker 104 to 107, each group led by an experienced bushman. Ben Kent piloted a helicopter from King City, accompanied by Constable L.J. Germain, who flew overhead for four hours. When possible, he'd set down in remote camps, where Germain could hop out and search. However, still no trail, track or indication of the missing men was found.

Constable King got an early start on November 2, arriving at Mile 107 at 3:00 a.m. Twenty-nine men started for the bush at 7:15 a.m. under the guidance of a tourist operator, an Indigenous guide, and a trapper. King had praised the work of the tourist operator, who may have had the most knowledge of the area and was reported to have a "…tireless passion to check every possibility." Every camp and trapper's cabin in the area was searched. White River Air Services deployed another aircraft to no avail. Searchers were now equipped with walkie talkies and a central radio unit that would only make their efforts more thorough.

On November 3, 28 men showed up with boots laced and ready to go. Summit Lake was dragged without results. In the days that followed, snow fell steadily in the North. The search was thorough, covering more than 40 square miles in less than five days. Police often retraced the ground surrounding mile markers 105, 106, and 107. Soon, the search party numbers would drop, due to weather, fatigue, missed employment and the feeling of discouragement that seemed to permeate the North woods.

The *Sudbury Star* reported on the tireless efforts by volunteer searchers who became "…nearly lame" from plodding through rough country. One volunteer, Mr. A. Small, is quoted saying, "We've combed the country for miles in every direction and found nothing — absolutely nothing."[62]

Nearly a week into the search, locals, including Constable King, were wondering why the RCMP had not been involved. Reeve Leo Racicot was particularly vocal about the lack of cooperation from the provincial police. Racicot was a retired CPR conductor, elected mayor and likely one of the oldest search volunteers at the time. It only seems fitting that many CPR workers, retired or active, would come together like a brotherhood. In an area so dense and extensive, there was a need for all able-bodied men, especially police officials with resources for such things. Not all agreed, however, as OPP inspector Tom Crawford, who was in touch with the RCMP, stated in an issue of the *Sudbury Star*. Crawford informed all involved that the RCMP would be sending a single rescue plane into the area as soon as weather permitted, and then added that the search should be carried out by those familiar with the surrounding bush, and would not necessarily have to be police officers. I would have liked to see the look on the searchers' faces once they heard this point of view after returning from a long day of bushwhacking.

In the days that followed, Constable King would return with a new batch of men. Soon, volunteers would become scarce, and he would need to pay searchers by the hour. Ten men were hired from the Heron Bay Indian Mission, who joined the manhunt. Their first order of business would be the dragging of Summit Lake and scouring the area south of the train tracks. Scientifically speaking, when a body enters the water, it will sink immediately. That means a body would have been found very close to where they entered. If King and the searchers knew of this fact, it could have made their search area much smaller. As searchers pulled in hook after hook, nothing but weeds and sticks were recovered.

While they dragged the freezing waters, ravens were sighted roughly 2 miles south of where the hunters were last seen. Searchers were hoping the birds turned up something, but nothing of interest was found.

Still, King was not giving up. Somehow, in the late days of the search, he was able to coax 50 men to head out the next day, on November 5, under the greying sky and falling snow. By noon, a storm would develop and thwart the search party's efforts once again. By the eighth day, the snow was piled a foot deep. Constable King was accompanied by two additional officers, Corporal J. McDonald and Constable J.F. Moore, but with winter closing in on them and the lakes starting to freeze, there wasn't much more that could be done. On November 6, Inspector Crawford formally ended the search.

McLeod illustrates for us just how puzzling this search was:

> ...not one clue had turned up: no remains of fires, no signs of a struggle, no spent shells, no abandoned guns, no blaze marks, no missing boats, no boot prints in the snow, no clothing. Nothing.[63]

The falling snow would have probably eliminated all boot prints to and from the cabin that Newcombe and Weeden would have made, so all searches were based on the eyewitness interviews that Constable King was able to get.

When Bill McLeod was looking into the case decades later, he was able to interview some men who participated in the search. One such man was Reeve Earl Freeborn, who stated that the party had done everything they possibly could to uncover any sign that Weeden and Newcombe had been there. He admitted they were, "tearing apart brush piles and doing everything that could possibly be done to uncover a clue."[64]

After six long winter months, Constable King was eager to resume the search. He patrolled to mile marker 106 and 107 on April 27 and saw the lakes were still ice packed. King reported that he made two more patrols in the Amyot area in the spring of 1960 on May 13 and 14. King and Constable L.J. Germain patrolled mileage 107 and 106, as well as the shore of Summit Lake for about three hours. On the second day, they patrolled mileage 104.5, the south and west shore of Chisholm River. They then bushwhacked west from the river then north, exiting the bush on the east shore of Friendly Lake. Based on observations from these patrols, King planned another organized search, but it was delayed by two snowstorms.

With the assistance of Germain, both officers set out to investigate a small lean-to that was sighted on the south side of one of a dozen rivers in the area. There seem to be a shared belief that the men would be found in or near Summit Lake. Some searchers theorized that they fell down the steep, hazardous embankment that rose up towards the tracks. Perhaps the men had slipped down and eventually drowned when they couldn't get up. King reported there to be 5 inches of ice still on the lakes in mid-May, so if the bodies of the men were there, they wouldn't surface until the thaw. In some areas, even in early spring, the snow in the bush was still knee-deep. Both officers searched the precarious shores of Summit Lake and Merchant Lake, but no clues were found.

After ice out, searchers canoed the surrounding Summit Lake, Friendly Lake, Newcombe Lake, Merchant Lake and Echo Lake. King had also planned to search a marshy area south of the tracks, at marker 106, that could swallow up a person should they wander into it. No notes indicate if he ever explored this area, though. They returned from the forest late on the evening of May 22 without a single clue. At this point, the officers involved believed that drowning was unlikely. In McLeod's investigation, he discovered a series of curious reports drawn up by the OPP (even at this point I see no indication that the RCMP ever became involved). The reports I recovered were heavily redacted and censored.

Constable King and Germain set up a basecamp at the location on June 3 of 1960. They were determined to solve the mystery of the missing hunters and went so far as to set up sleeping quarters and cooking facilities. This rejuvenated search lasted 10 days, in which eight lakes were checked. From 7:00 a.m. to 5:00 p.m., a search party of 10 men bushwhacked the areas surrounding these lakes, northeast of Summit Lake and the woods between mileage 105-106 on the north side. King's notes list three theories that kept crossing his mind:

    1) Actually lost or met with an accident in the bush?
    2) Possibility of foul play?
    3) Took flight?

This is where things really get interesting. Bob King had received a rather eerie tip on June 11 of 1960. While walking out along the tracks, he had a conversation with someone whose name was omitted but claimed that Officer McLaughlin of the Marathon Police Department had been told by another mystery individual that the two missing hunters would be found inside a beaver dam. This was the first real tip I was able to come across, and since it was passed down to Bob King from a line of people, we can't be sure how valid the tip was. King would later confirm the report with Constable McLaughlin. According to his notes, McLaughlin and Constable Warren Gillis of the Marathon Police Department were seated in the Everest Hotel restaurant in Marathon after a hockey game. An "Indian" man [name redacted] from Mobert approached and sat himself at the same table. He tried to start a conversation with the officers but was unsuccessful. He made a second attempt, only this time saying that he and another fellow from Longlac knew where the two missing hunters could be found. "They were not lost," said the mystery man, they were in a beaver dam.

On June 15 and 16, along with Staff Sergeant Bonnycastle, Constable King interviewed this mystery man about his statement that he said "while drunk" in the Everest Hotel restaurant. He denied ever making such a statement.

Still, it had to be investigated. The Department of Lands and Forests requires all trappers to submit maps of their traplines to maintain their license. King was able to obtain one of these maps that showed all the beaver houses in the area (approximately 36). It is a common mistake for people to identify beaver lodges as beaver dams, but the structures are entirely different. King was under the impression that the tip was meant to be beaver lodges or homes, and so focused in on those.

Much of the pieces have been censored in the police files and crucial pages are missing. For example, Staff Sergeant A.L. Bonnycastle made a report dated June 21 that summed up King's actions to date, however paragraph four has been completely removed because the "personal information is highly sensitive." A note at the bottom indicates it was forwarded to the District Inspector in Port Arthur and was signed by District Inspector G.E. White and Bonnycastle. The note reads: "Would you please have one of your officers at Long Lac interview [name removed] and ascertain whether or not he is in possession that would assist in locating these missing hunters. Please advise this office as soon as possible regarding your officer's interview." So, in addition to the handful of senior officers involved, there was now another detachment drawing up reports.

It appears that Constable C.T. Dinsdale of Longlac detachment was the man to conduct the interview, however his entire report was censored from the file. It is my interpretation that he was sent to interview a trapper, or perhaps someone from the Department of Lands and Forests, to acquire the map of beaver lodges. The map also showed a campsite drawn by someone who was not named. It was hidden south of Tripoli and circled in red pencil. The significance of this campsite we will likely never know.

On July 13, King carefully searched two beaver houses and two trapper camps east of Summit Lake in Tripoli, at marker 102.8, but came up empty.

Meanwhile, Constable King was slowly developing a list of persons of interest as suspicions grew that this was more than just two men lost in the bush.

On March 29, 1961, King interviewed Eric Young, a CPR engineer who suspected that Weeden and Newcombe met their end in the Chisholm Creek, otherwise foul play had probably entered the picture. Both King and Young were struck by Jean Newcombe's odd behaviour. After numerous discussions with her, Young claimed that she was more interested in the stories circling around her husband's disappearance than anything else. Young began to doubt the details of Jean Newcombe's story, saying: "She seemed to have every detail covered." King cited further instances of odd behaviour, stating that when the group of 10 searchers arrived on the first day, "Mrs. Newcombe seemed to enjoy being the centre of attention and she seemed quite happy and she sat and joked with the men." Another noteworthy incident occurred during a visit from Mrs. Newcombe where she asked King: "Why don't you come down some weekend, I'll come up from Chapleau and I know all the good fishing spots around here."[65] King made special note that she did not seem too concerned with how the search for her husband was going, but rather just wanted to be there to see what was taking place.

Young also revealed that Jean Newcombe had an ex-husband, a Mr. Harry Melynk who had been in Chapleau at the time when the hunters disappeared. The small-town rumours described Mr. and Mrs. Newcombe as having a strained relationship and neighbours would hear violent arguments inside the apartment. According to those who knew him, Newcombe had a bad temper and an unusual personality. The question of an arrangement between Jean Newcombe and Harry Melynk against her husband seemed to cross King's mind as something to look into.

Tourist lodge owner Joseph Crichton was also never satisfied that the two men were just missing.

Mrs. Newcombe's personal opinion was that Weeden and her husband may have met up with a person who was in possession of a rifle belonging to Newcombe and were killed in the confrontation. The rifle was identified as a 44-40 lever action Winchester model 1884, which was stolen on July 10, 1958. It was never recovered.

From page 37 onward in the police report, the story quickly fades. Most of the pages were removed. However, McLeod was able to fill in a lot of these gaps. This is just more proof of the inconsistencies with FOIA censorship.

Something drove Constable Bob King to return to mile marker 107 in May of 1961. He repeatedly searched the same area throughout his investigation. Perhaps there was information regarding this area that was not publicly available or in the report. Clearly he had a tip or a hunch that the men would be found here. On June 14, King searched the area around Newcombe's camp once more and discovered a patch of disturbed earth about 15 feet away. He reportedly dug 6 feet down, but only uncovered burnt garbage of "the American variety."

On September 9, the waters of Friendly Lake were dragged all day with the help of Constable T.W. Junka, and again nothing was found. With summer having come and gone, the bodies of the hunters should have surfaced if they were submerged underwater. As a body decays and bloats, the abdomen becomes visibly distended due to the build-up of intestinal gases. When enough gas inflates the cavities and skin, the body will become lighter than water and rise. Studies show that once a body is in a full stage of bloat, it is almost impossible to sink again, even with counterweights attached. The time that it will take a body to reach this pivotal stage depends on both water temperature and the amount of fat on the submerged body. Colder water will delay the bacterial chemical action inside the corpse, but inevitably, the body will always rise. In cold or near-freezing water temperatures, the resurfacing of a body can take several weeks to several months. If the men had perished somewhere on land, the buzzards and ravens would have given away the death site, but this was not the case. As the second year of the investigation was coming to a close, still not a single clue was found.

Where on earth were George Weeden and Merle Newcombe?

On January 21, 1962, Constable Bob King requested that the case be closed pending further evidence or information.

A year later, on July 3, 1963, a report came in from Robert Willoughan Sr. of White River. He claimed that three weeks ago, while he was in the men's beverage room of the Green Gables Hotel, he heard a man from Mobert [name redacted] say, "in the indian language" to another Indian that he had killed George Weeden and Merle Newcombe. Willoughan had worked with Indigenous people for 35 years and was able to understand their language.

It seemed that was the end of the story, but then a bizarre discovery was made in the fall of 1968. Two men, Walter Telik and Hamil Robinson, were staying at Newcombe's Camp and prospecting in the area where the men were last seen. One of them discovered Merle Newcombe's wallet under one of the mattresses. It contained $2.00 and some personal papers. The wallet was not considered suspicious at the time, but it did tell a little more of what happened that day. It's very possible that Newcombe stashed the wallet just before the pair had gone out after breakfast. It indicated that they had likely planned a quick scout near the tracks and left the cabin on their own accord.

Then, on October 14, Constable M.J. Ross stated in his report that he received a call from Jean Newcombe. A week prior, she was told by a fortune-teller at the

Fran Restaurant in Toronto that one of the men would be found buried in a "leaning building" on or near the Newcombe property. The only "leaning building" on the property that Jean could think of was a discontinued outhouse that hadn't been used in years. Accompanied by Jean, Constable Ross and Corporal Farrell located the outhouse on the property, removed it, and dug down.

When McLeod interviewed Ross, he recalled with a laugh that Ferrell had pulled rank and ordered him the task of "digging out the shithouse" while Ferrell stood nearby with a grin.

During the excavation, they located bits of burned wood and brittle bone which they suspected may have also been burned. Samples were tested by pathologist Frederick A. Jaffe at the Centre for Forensic Sciences in Toronto.

Two specimens were analyzed, the first being a black, earth-like substance that may have included human hair, and the second being approximately 100 fragments of bone matter, which would crumble when handled. Jaffe concluded that the fragility of the bones was due to weathering and that there was no evidence of burning or a petroleum accelerant. Neither specimen had the indication of human matter. The report goes on to state that, "Their origin could not be determined with certainty but the presences of saw cuts and the appearance of grooving on one articular surface strongly suggests an animal origin of these specimens."

The term "saw cuts" sticks out, but it's clear that Jaffe is referring to the sawing by animal teeth or perhaps an animal butchered by a hunter. Still, the fact that the lab could not determine with certainty is a troubling thought.

The fortune-teller who hinted at all this had the cops in a tizzy and was sought out for an interview. Officers made a trip to Toronto, to a number of restaurants, but could not locate them. It was believed that they may have been a person of interest, but the trail immediately went cold.

The business of the fortune-teller is only one of the odd leads in the case of George Weeden and Merle Newcombe. While compiling information for his book, Bill McLeod received a phone call from Jean Newcombe herself. Jean revealed a story to McLeod that as far as I could tell was not on record anywhere else (unless it was redacted from the police reports).

She states that, while in a department store in Fort William, she had been trying on a new dress. Suddenly she felt "a powerful blow to her forehead" and had a vision of her husband, Merle, being shot in the face. It is believed that Jean had an interest in psychic phenomenon and the supernatural, but it's not known if she ever had visions like this on previous occasions. Furthermore, Jean tells a story of being approached by a man at the White River train station sometime in the mid-1990s. The man said that he knew what happened to her husband and was prepared to tell her, probably now that some considerable time had passed. Jean listened with interest but felt that his statement should be given in the presence of an OPP officer. The meeting was arranged and a compelling story was told.

While waiting on the platform, the mystery man told a very convincing story. He said that George Weeden and Merle Newcombe were walking down the tracks when they met a man and his son. Apparently, the father of the pair was holding a gun that belonged to Newcombe — the gun that had been stolen sometime earlier. When Newcombe confronted the man about the gun, both of them were shot (possibly in the face, as Jean's vision foretold). The father and son then disposed of the bodies in one of the nearby lakes. Jean said that the lake in question was dragged by police, but nothing was found. The mystery man said that he was related to the shooter by marriage, and he had since died; the son of the shooter had died in a railway accident not long after the disappearance. The alleged murderer had threatened to kill any members of his family who would reveal the secret, but since he was now dead, the mystery relative came forward.

However, neither McLeod nor myself were able to confirm if the meeting between the mystery man, officer and Jean Newcombe ever took place because it was not in the police files. Neither the officer or the man's name could be recalled by Jean, who had suffered a head injury years later. On account of her memory loss, the statement could not be followed up on or confirmed. Furthermore, none of the officers McLeod interviewed had heard of the story before, or at least wouldn't admit to it. McLeod did speak with an officer that knew of the son getting in the train accident, but he ended up surviving. The officer considered confronting the injured boy to give him a chance to clear his conscience about Weeden and Newcombe in case he died from his injuries, but he never followed through and had regretted it ever since.

Either this story is a fabrication, or it was hidden from the public and media. If the police thought there was any validity to this story, you'd think they'd interview family members of the father and son pair that were reportedly involved. Why not make an arrest at the time and bring the two in for questioning?

Officers — especially King — seemed to be convinced that a crime took place. In fact, it's interesting to note that the investigation was filed on a *Crime* report sheet the entire time, instead of a *Missing Person* one. The police seemed to have a hunch that this was a case of homicide, but there was no evidence gathered to suggest that a homicide occurred. In fact, there was no evidence found, other than the remains of their breakfast, that Weeden and Newcombe were in the area at all. The odd thing is that if police were treating this as a murder investigation, usually the last people to see the victims alive would be heavily scrutinized, but that doesn't appear to be the case here. As far as I could tell, the two trappers were only interviewed twice by police, were part of the initial search team and no follow-up with their family has ever been done. Are police expecting family members to approach them out of the blue with their statements?

One thing we can say for sure is that Weeden and Newcombe did not just get lost in the bush and perish. Newcombe grew up at the camp and had a lifetime of experience, he was a competent and skilled outdoorsman. He once got turned around in the bush before and was able to take care of himself and walk out the next day. At one point, Newcombe had flown aircraft for the Department of Lands and Forests. During his investigation, King uncovered a map that Merle Newcombe had drawn of the area around mileage 105 from memory. It included bush and waterways and was, "In very much detail and would only be drawn by someone thoroughly familiar with his subject."[66]

George Weeden, on the other hand, could barely walk and did most of his hunting from the railroad tracks, moving very little. He suffered a broken back and severe injuries in a head on collision between two steam engines in 1941. This is part of the mystery that is so perplexing. How could the men vanish when they couldn't go anywhere? Both men smoked and would have carried matches with them at all times, so they had the ability to make fire should they have gotten lost.

Are we being led to believe that George Weeden and Merle Newcombe were murdered over a single stolen gun? If this was the angle police were driving at, they sure weren't investigating it as such.

Let's consider the possibilities of both foul play and misadventure of this disappearance.

I think after reading the statement from the mystery man at the White River station that most of us were jumping up and down shouting "Murder!" After all, the motives were clear, the opportunity was near perfect, the man's reason for coming forward made sense, and this fit nicely with Jean Newcombe's department store vision. We'd assume that this confession of murder was the answer we had been looking for all these decades. However, there are several problems with this theory.

First, we aren't sure that the story of the White River mystery man was even true at all. His statement was never confirmed (by police or Newcombe's wife) and his identity has never been revealed. Furthermore, Jean could not recall the story later (because of an injury) and so a follow-up interview regarding this strange meeting was not possible. With all that said, murder still seems plausible, but there are many reasons why it may not be the cause of the men's disappearance.

To murder two men sounds neat and tidy on paper, but the actual technicalities make this theory next to impossible to pull off. Back then, before the construction of roads, trains were relied upon to get from point A to point B. There were more of them passing by the area, leaving the murderer(s) precious little opportunity to get into an altercation and commit the act. If the two trappers were responsible for killing Weeden and Newcombe, then they would have had less than 20 minutes to hide the crime. During that 20 minutes, two CPR section men had rode through on a jigger and saw no sign of the men or a crime.

All passengers and work men who would be on these trains would be aware of Newcombe's camp. This was a resort business seen from the train, and to murder a man in his own backyard would not be wise of anyone.

Furthermore, to kill two men over a stolen rifle seems a tad unrealistic, especially since both the trappers and Newcombe were locals. I'm sure they could have settled the matter right then and there without violence, and probably without police involvement. He could handle himself. A number of coworkers stated that, Newcombe would not panic no matter what the situation was. If Weeden and Newcombe were shot, there should have been evidence of the crime, yet nothing was found. There was no blood, no spent shells, no drag marks, no clothing, no signs of their packed lunch or other accessories that the men carried. Considering that some time had passed before the search party started, the blood and footprints would likely have disappeared, but the drag marks of two large men and other evidence should have been seen by railway workers, hunters and locals. Not to mention the buzzards, which would have scavenged even the smallest traces of the bodies. George Weeden wore glasses. If he was shot in the face (as Jean Newcombe's vision foretold), you'd think there would be fragments of them somewhere. For the murderer to scour the railroad tracks picking up skull, brain and fragments of glasses to conceal the crime seems hard to believe, especially within a less than 20-minute time window before the section men passed by or another train came barreling through.

To move two full-grown men as dead weight would be difficult. Even if they were average height and weight, say 5-feet 11-inches, 175 pounds, this would have been an undertaking.

Another problem with the murder scenario is that no one reported gunshots in the area. During hunting season, there are many men and women out in the bush, most of them staying at hunt camps like Newcombe's, but no gunshots were reported. Also, both Newcombe and Weeden had guns. If one of them was shot, the other would have a second or two to fire back in self-defence.

The murderer(s) would have had to move quickly, knowing that the next train car could pass by at any moment. Where do you hide a body in the middle of nowhere without the aid of shovels, tarps, or any other means for nefarious activity? If a murder took place, it would have had to have been spontaneous. The trappers were not prepared to cover up a murder. Searchers repeatedly dragged lakes and tore apart brush piles, so something hidden should have been found. If the trappers rolled the bodies down into the surrounding lakes, there should have been some evidence of this. How could they collect the hunter's belongings and dispose of them without being seen? Guns, hats, glasses, ammunition and other belongings, are all likely to fall off when moving a body. Any guns left in the area would almost certainly be discovered.

Lastly, if the trappers were suspects, then wouldn't police check their weapons and clothing for evidence? It makes no sense to me that if the two trappers were the main suspects in this case and the last people to see the two hunters alive, then why weren't they treated as such? Why were they allowed to participate in the search?

The accident theory is one that first entered the mind of the searchers. With no guard rails around the tracks, it's possible that the men could have fallen into the nearby water and drowned. They couldn't have gone far, based on Weeden's condition, and so they should have been around the mile markers that were searched extensively. If they slipped down, it's possible that their calls for help would have been heard by the two trappers on their way back home. The two men could have also fired off a few gun shots while they treaded water. And again, if they did fall into the lake, their bodies would have been found.

In both cases, scavenging animals would have given away the crime scene in the early days of the search, or in the coming spring. The fact that literally nothing of the two missing hunters ever surfaced is completely baffling and the reason this case lands itself in this book. Not finding clues of the men at all or what happened that day is verging on the paranormal.

The mystery will likely never be solved. If such an extensive search turned up nothing back then, chances are slim that any evidence remains today for us to find. Many of the men involved are sadly no longer around and cannot be interviewed. Constable Bob King retired to Nova Scotia and has since died. The two men who found the wallet are both deceased. Trapper Clem Nabigon died long ago in 1982, and his son Herb passed away in 2016. He was interviewed by Pat Hewett for an article for *The Canadian Press* but did not have much to add to the mystery. Through some investigating, I was able to confirm that Herb Nabigon was the son that the White River mystery man was referring to who had the train accident at the age of 20. Many stated that he had died, but he survived the ordeal, at the cost of his right arm.

Sometime around 2014, Michael Neiger, a retired Michigan State Trooper and lead investigator of Michigan Backcountry Search and Rescue (MibSAR), took an interest in the Weeden and Newcombe disappearance. He organized and deployed a search party in July of 2014 to see Newcombe's camp for himself and if anything of interest would be found. His online write-up of the search gives us the gist of his plan:

> ...use combo of bush-road driving, mountain bikes, canoes, and ground pounding to access our very remote area of operation in the Newcombe Lake area; (July) 7th to 11th, skin diving, underwater metal detecting, above-ground metal detecting, sifting, clandestine buried-body probing, free recon, corridor searches, and wide-area grid searching in bush; 12th return to Sault; 13th return home.

Sadly, Neiger gave up the search because of lack of co-operation from the police.

It's beyond frustrating to me when there is a situation in which police have exhausted all leads and a case eventually turns cold — or rather damn near freezing — and yet they still are unwilling to collaborate or cooperate with others on the case. I appealed the FOIA decision in 2020 to get the full unredacted report, citing several inconsistencies with their decisions. Nearly a year later, my appeal was denied and accompanied by the following non-answer: "[The] OPP maintain their exemptions as applied." It took 11 months to get those six words, and it's not even the beginning of an explanation.

There is something preventing what could be a fruitful collaboration, and whether that is a case of control or practices, I have no idea. If it's simply a matter of time and resources, then why not use someone else's? In this case, I am referring to the public and groups like MibSAR.

After more than 60 years, a complete profile on the men still does not exist. Merle's name is still spelled wrong on the police file and missing persons list. Details of the two men such as their height, weight and what they were wearing are still absent, which came as a shock to me given the number of times that Jean Newcombe was interviewed by police. The OPP were also unable to confirm Weeden's exact birth date. Apparently Weeden had an ex-wife and an electrical shop in Detroit, Michigan. He was rumoured to have a brother, James who was employed by the CPR in Thunder Bay.

To this day, the story of George Weeden and Merle Newcombe is one of Ontario's most enduring and baffling mysteries. The remote wilderness in which it is set is lush and lonely, with a rust-coloured railroad running through it, winding around a small hill and out of sight. Like the railroad, I wonder if this story will ever have an ending. Above the seldom used entrance of the cabin where the pair spent their final meal together, a homemade sign of driftwood hangs with an open greeting to any traveller who just might happen to pass by: "Welcome to Newcombeville. It's a long, long story…"

9

Agnes May Appleyard

Ralph Godfrey awoke at 4:30 a.m. on the morning of April 27, 1986. He creaked his way through the old farmhouse, passing by the living room on his way to the washroom. The moon, three days since full, cast a ghostly gloom into the sitting area, barely illuminating a figure in the dark.

"Good morning…" Godfrey uttered into the blackness.

The figure responded from the large chair. Although she had not flicked on the lamp, Godfrey knew that this was Agnes May Appleyard, his 72-year-old neighbour. Godfrey continued with his business and returned to bed. He knew better than to get involved, as Appleyard had dropped in on him before. Sometimes she'd arrive at midnight or in the early morning hours. No matter the weather, Appleyard could show up. Godfrey had seen her arrive in the middle of a snowstorm that was so bad he wouldn't let his dog out.[67] She would visit three or four times a month and then return to her home in the morning, after she called one of her sons for a ride. These were not poorly timed social calls. Appleyard was hiding, and this would be the last time Godfrey would see her alive.

According to police, Agnes May Appleyard (who preferred to be called May) disappeared from her front yard in Emsdale on April 27, 1986. There aren't many more details than that. It's one of those stories that is full of gaping holes and rumours. In her case, there is only speculation as to where she could be now. Appleyard's body has never been found — it's as if she dissolved into the soil that surrounded her isolated home, located 34 kilometres north of Huntsville. It is because of this irrefutable fact that she will remain a missing person.

I had come across her name, like so many others, on the *Canada's Missing* website. Her name was part of a collection of over 1,000 strangers that ran down the page like some heartbreaking "to-find" list. A single, inaccurate sentence summed up her life and the details of her disappearance. Sifting through what crumbs of data I could recover, I realized that there was more to the story than was initially released. Only after a lot of persistence did a more complete version come to light. And it was a very ugly one.

By all accounts, May Appleyard was a lovely woman and a hardworking mother and grandmother. She inherited the homestead in Emsdale from her parents and lived in the area all her life. Newspapers of the time would refer to it as a "shack." In fact, it was an 18-by-20-foot cabin, with a total of three rooms, one door and a small, attached porch. The property was isolated and the road leading in was described as "impassable" unless you had a four-wheel-drive vehicle. The nearest neighbour was the Godfrey's, 2.5 kilometres away.

There was no hydro, no telephone, no indoor plumbing and whatever comforts they enjoyed were achieved by hand. Appleyard and the children used to fetch buckets of water from a spring about 100 yards away. It was a hard, yet simple lifestyle carried out in the seclusion of the dense forest, where they received no visitors or attention from the outside world. Until the day she vanished.

She lived with her husband, 82-year-old Sydney Arthur Appleyard (sometimes spelled Sidney), who had been a very hard bush-worker. He was of slim build and reported to be funny and generous, unless he had been drinking. According to multiple sources, Sydney Appleyard drank a lot… and when he drank, he turned into a different person.

On the day of her disappearance, May Appleyard was described as having grey shoulder-length hair, was wearing a white shirt, a skirt with a floral pattern, a green woollen tam, and black boots. Since clothing can sometimes be preserved in certain environments, the details of what people were wearing becomes more important over the years.

Knowing that police were likely withholding valuable pieces of the story, I submitted a request for more information on the case but was denied access, stating that the release of any files was in breach of a criminal investigation. In fact, the exact wording was, "Currently under investigation." Needless to say, I had my doubts that was true. There had been no mention of Appleyard's disappearance since the 1990s. Police did not release information, a press release, or participate in media interviews or social media posts. As far as I could tell, I was the only one looking.

A few years after I was denied the police report, I found myself cruising down Ravenscliffe Road under the fractured shadows of the maple leaves that flashed along the hood of my car. The route to Emsdale was paved with hills and I struggled to keep my speed at 60 kilometres per hour. The patchy rural highway led me through a small beach village that I admittedly would much rather have been the draw for my trip here. It was mid-summer and my surroundings were rich, making the beach cottages more inviting as they entered my rear-view. Once the road narrowed and the tree's canopy began to darken my path, I seemed to be transitioning into some strange out-of-the-way place. I was wondering if I was even on the map anymore as I passed by huge weedy lots with barriers marked 'Private Road', 'No Trespassing', or 'Do Not Enter.' At every turn, I was getting the feeling that this place was trying to keep me out.

The houses were so inconsistent that I made special note of it — some giant log dwellings, easily appraised at over a million dollars, neighbouring some clearly run-down homes. Their roofs were sliding off, their garages overtaken by the surrounding forests. I can't recall another place that had such diversity in such close proximity. Emsdale is not all that far from major cities, but it has the sense of being remote and cut off from the outside world. I am used to being in these types of places, but at the risk of sounding a bit paranoid, I sensed the eyes of the local population on me — a stranger who didn't belong. Their glare was so piercing I feared they'd pop my tires and I'd be stranded on these backroads.

The speed limit was slower than I would have liked, but it gave me a chance to observe the dwellings and unmarked trails that darted by my windows. Still, I found myself speeding through the town, not sure if I was eager to get to my destination or eager to leave. Finally, I came to a road very near to my predetermined waypoint on the GPS and pulled over to check my maps. In the sky above me, I pictured a helicopter whizzing by as they searched for any signs of Appleyard.

As the story goes, Appleyard's son Stanley arrived at the homestead on April 26, between 9:30 and 10:00 a.m., to take his parents grocery shopping and to cash his mother's Old Age Security Pension cheque in the nearby town of Kearney. Stanley dropped off his parents back at the house around 11:00 or 11:30 a.m. and helped carry in the groceries. Along with the usual assortment of food, Sydney Appleyard had purchased a 12-pack of beer.

We can only speculate how ugly things had become, because Appleyard left her husband in the middle of the night and walked the 2.5 kilometres to her nearest neighbour, Ralph Godfrey. Godfrey noticed that Appleyard would show up to seek refuge around the time her husband was able to stock up his alcohol supply. It happened with such frequency that the Godfrey's would leave blankets out in anticipation of her arrival. Godfrey told her that the house was never locked and that she could sleep on the couch anytime she liked.

The final morning Godfrey discovered her downstairs in his living room, she was said to make a call around 6:00 a.m. to her oldest son Elmer to come get her. Elmer and his wife Irene showed up soon after and met them in the yard. Appleyard climbed into the pick-up truck and asked to be taken to their place in Emsdale. As they headed towards town, however, Appleyard asked that they go back to the homestead to get her purse.

Elmer drove the muddy backroad that would lead them to the homestead. According to Irene, when they arrived, May Appleyard searched for her purse but could not locate it. Her husband, Sydney, who was still drunk from the previous night, stood up and attempted to give her a kick as she entered the bedroom to search. The kick, however, did not connect and Appleyard failed to notice. Sydney had always accused his wife of running around with other men and this morning was no different. He would often accuse her of being with Ralph Godfrey or another neighbour, Martin Austin. These arguments were commonplace for the couple, in which Sydney would accuse her of sleeping around with almost anyone, including her grandchildren. Godfrey was aware of the accusations by her husband and on the occasion when he would drive Appleyard back home, he made sure to let her out at the last corner so the old man wouldn't see and create more problems.

Appleyard asked for her purse, and her husband gave it to her. After she looked inside, she asked where the money was from her Old Age security cheque. Sydney Appleyard pulled the brown envelope from his pocket, barked "Here's your damn money," and threw it at her. Appleyard counted the money in front of everyone, then returned to the bedroom with an IGA grocery bag to gather clothing, intending to stay with her son and daughter-in-law. A minute or two later, Appleyard returned to the main room and decided she would stay home.

Irene admitted they stuck around for a couple of hours, all while Sydney Appleyard was sipping Black Label beer in his chair. After a couple of hours passed, they asked Appleyard if she wanted to leave, and she politely declined. Irene asked that her mother-in-law phone them from the Godfreys if she needed them to come back. Elmer and Irene estimated that they left the property around 9:30 a.m., seeing the couple in the front yard. They would be the last two people to see May Appleyard alive.

Later that day, between 2:00 or 3:00 p.m. on April 27, Stanley returned with a gallon of coal oil that he had forgotten to unload during the previous day's grocery trip. He parked up the road, due to the driveway of the homestead being impassable. Stanley noticed another set of tire tracks in the mud, both coming and going from the Appleyard residence. He would later assume that they were Elmer's tracks because Elmer had a vehicle equipped to navigate the terrain. Stanley reported to see his father sleeping, and after yelling for him and only receiving a groan, his son assumed he was drunk. He had a hard time waking his father, which was not normal, even when he had been drinking. His mother was nowhere to be found. Stan indicated that there were no signs of a struggle or violence in or around the home, but that he had found a plate on the step with fried eggs on it. When his father finally came to, Stan Appleyard asked him where his mother was, and the reply came back that he did not know. Stan then returned home and phoned his wife Jo-Anne to see if she was with his mother, but she had not seen May Appleyard since a few days prior.[68]

According to the timeline provided, Elmer and Irene Appleyard left their mother around 9:30 a.m., so she should have been there.

After making some calls, Stan came upon his brother Elmer and one of his sons fishing near his Emsdale home. Stan informed Elmer that he was at the homestead earlier that day to drop off the oil, and their mother was nowhere to be found. According to Stan, Elmer did not react to this with either surprise or concern. Instead, Elmer continued to fish and then after about 15 minutes, got up and left.

Irene claimed that she and Elmer returned the next day, the twenty-eighth, at 9:30 or 10:00 a.m. Again, there was no sign of May Appleyard. Why Elmer did not return on the twenty-seventh, once Stan told him she was missing, is unknown. Irene asked Sydney where his wife was, and he replied that she was probably at the Godfrey's. Irene thought it strange because if Appleyard went to the Godfrey's she would have called, like she had asked her to the day before. However, neither Elmer nor his father seemed concerned; instead, Sydney asked his son to go into town to buy more beer instead of searching for his wife.

During the investigation, in which the siblings were interviewed by police, each confessed to understanding that buying alcohol for their father was to be avoided at all costs because it would get him into an ugly, abusive mood, yet for some reason Elmer did so on April 28, while Irene stayed at the home with her father-in-law.

Elmer reportedly drove to Kearney for beer, which his father paid for. Afterwards, Irene and Elmer returned to their home, approximately 8 miles away. Oddly, they never thought to stop in at the Godfrey's house on their way out to check on Appleyard's wellbeing. Knowing it was only 2.5 kilometres down the road, myself, the police, and the defence attorney all found this strange.

Once home, Irene claimed she telephoned a few of the Appleyard children — namely Edith, Ivy and her sister Helen — but she did not telephone the Godfreys to check there first, her reason being that she did not know the phone number. An article from the *Parry Sound North Star* indicated that after not hearing from their mother for another few hours, Elmer called the OPP to report her missing.

Burks Falls Police Department received the call of a missing person at approximately 2:35 p.m. on April 28, 1986. Sergeant Gray and Constable John D. Newstead responded to the call. Gray was familiar with Appleyard and had known her to stay at Helen Rand's residence on Star Lake Road, so it was a logical place to check first. Finding nothing, the officers proceeded to the homestead off Fern Glen Road.

Ivy Appleyard, daughter of the missing, drove out to Fern Glen Road and was the first to reach the homestead. Up the road behind her, she heard a half-dozen other car doors slam, and she saw that her sister Edith, brother-in-law Elmer Fisher of Huntsville, Helen Rand, and Constable John Newstead had arrived just after her.

Ivy claimed to be the first to enter the house and found her father alone. She asked him flat out where her mother was, and her father guessed that she was likely at the Fisher's house. Ivy knew this couldn't be true since the Fisher's were a few steps behind her, primed with the same questions that she had.

"Where the hell is she?" Ivy demanded.

Something must have snapped inside Sydney Appleyard at this point and he shot straight out of his chair. He pointed his finger towards the swamp and confessed, "She's over there, they shot her."

Ivy told him to sit down, to which she asked him again. Her father jumped up once more with the same response, his weathered finger trembling towards the swamp. At this point, the others entered the scene, including Elmer and Irene Appleyard.

Ivy then asked for her mother's purse. Her father took her out to the woodpile and produced it from under a foot or so of chopped logs. Then he returned to the bedroom and brought out the brown envelope of money. The items were handed to police and the search began.

The business of the purse being buried in the wood bin could go either way. While it appeared to be hidden under logs, Appleyard was a smart lady and neighbours would tell me that she always kept her purse and a thick sweater in the wood bin, in case she needed to escape her husband in the middle of the night.

Outside the home, Newstead began organizing the search, while the family members stood around. Sydney, Elmer and Irene Appleyard formed a circle, with Irene's back to Ivy Appleyard, approximately 6 to 8 feet away. They were having what seemed like a private conversation, during which Ivy overheard her father say, "I've got to go to jail. I've killed my wife." Elmer reportedly snapped back, something about his father being stupid followed by what could have either been a statement or a question: "There's no body. Where's the body? There's got to be a body." At this point in time, Elmer noticed his sister was eavesdropping on their conversation and turned his attention towards her: "Ain't that right, mouthy?" Ivy responded with, "Anything you say."

The search began soon after. Newstead wasted no time and was able to recruit 35 civilian searchers (that included family members), 18 police officers and a search coordinator who would keep ground crews in an organized grid.

They searched neighbouring properties, fields, pine forests and nearby swamps. Newstead requested an OPP helicopter from Brampton, which arrived at 5:30 p.m. Searchers split into groups to cover a wider area. An experienced local was invaluable for these types of operations, a person unfamiliar with the land could get lost in minutes. Growing up on the homestead, Elmer Appleyard was said to be the most familiar with the lay of the land and so would lead a party of searchers through the forest. He hunted and collected wood from the surrounding bush and knew all trails, hazards and hiding places that the land had to offer. Ten volunteers followed behind him, obeying the commands he would holler back over his shoulder. Stanley and the other siblings all took part, along with neighbours. Sydney Appleyard did not want to join the search, however, saying things like, "I'm not wading around. She's not God damn in there." He was no doubt referring to the swamp that he had pointed out earlier. There were reports of him drinking alcohol during the search, possibly corroborating the story of Elmer buying beer. Cans were found discarded throughout the woods.

Two dog teams arrived to aid the men, one from Barrie and one from South Porcupine. Police covered the land between the Appleyard house and the Godfrey residence extensively, but found nothing. Grid searches were conducted on either side of the access road, where dogs aggressively sniffed the newly thawed ground. Visibility in this area was reported to be "very good."

Newstead scanned the timber overhead from the helicopter on April 28, 29, and 30 in a northwest diagonal grid pattern, then a parallel pattern and any other way one could think of. Being April, the trees had yet to sprout their leaves and Newstead described the visibility as "excellent," especially in and around the maple forest. The chopper swept over the main property and outlying area, expanding roughly 2 miles past the homestead. The swampy area behind the house to the west was visibly clear, yet difficult and tiring for ground teams to walk through. About 250 yards of the swamp was searched, but no sign of Appleyard or her clothing were found. A second swamp to the northeast was searched shoulder to shoulder, yielding no results.

To aid the men, Constable Gary Alexander, who had considerable search and rescue experience, was transferred to the detachment on May 5. The search carried on into the first two weeks of May, with lead investigator Newstead along with Officer Norton Rhiness. Newstead took to the air once more on May 12 and 13, but again no sign of the missing woman was found. Police removed three to four cords of wood from the woodshed and dug up the dirt floor, an area of approximately 10 by 20 feet.

Local busses, trains, airports, taxicab services, and stores were alerted, in the hope that Appleyard was seen skipping town. The police helicopter only reported to find a moose carcass, but nothing related to Appleyard or to indicate that a crime had been committed.

Searchers calculated that roughly 100 acres was combed either by air or by foot. It wouldn't be long before the official search was called off and the adult children and their families would continue to search for over three months without police support. Elmer and his wife Irene supposedly never gave up searching.

Newstead made special note of shovels, a rake and a wheelbarrow near the Appleyard house that may have been used recently. Initially, the disappearance was being treated as a missing person case, but upon the second day of the search, Newstead had his suspicions that he was in the middle of a homicide. Newstead was unable to convince his superiors of this, which is why he could not test the garden tools or pursue other avenues of the investigation. The official search came to an end, and in the later years, two psychic mediums were hired to work on the case, but neither were able to determine the location of May Appleyard.

But the case was far from closed. There was no evidence to suggest that Appleyard had left the property on her own. It wasn't long before the newspapers started referring to Appleyard as a "dead woman." Newstead continued to develop a theory with the help of return visits to the area and various family members that approached him after the fact. Police targeted her husband as the prime suspect in her disappearance, but as of yet had no physical evidence.

A year after her disappearance, almost to the day, Elmer Appleyard telephoned the Burks Falls Police and reported that he had found a human skull in the swamp, roughly half a kilometre from the homestead. Constable Alexander responded to the call and followed Elmer to the location. The skull stared back vacantly as they approached. It rested on plant matter and was missing teeth and the lower jaw, eliminating any chance of identification from dental records. The skull had no visible trauma. Instantly, Alexander surmised that the skull could not have been there for longer than a day and that it had obviously been planted. "There's no doubt in my mind that was May's skull."[69] Green vegetation was observed underneath and there was no sign of weathering from the elements.

Son-in-law Elmer Fisher would later ask Sydney Appleyard if he knew anything about the skull and he responded confidently that it did not belong to his wife. How he knew that was up for debate and I'm sure raised a few eyebrows with police. Just to pour on more suspicion, Sydney Appleyard then went on to ask, "Was there a bullet hole in it?"

Newstead had his own theory about what might have happened. Apparently on a return visit, there was blood found on the kitchen floor near the wood stove. There were also some clothes that belonged to Appleyard and a quilt inside the home that looked to be stained with blood. Newstead believed that, in a fit of rage or drunkenness, Sydney Appleyard pushed his wife against the stove, killing her.[70]

Elmer Fisher confessed to finding a tuft of grey hair in the front yard that matched Appleyard and handed it over to Newstead, along with a 20-gauge shotgun that had recently been fired. All items were handed in to police, who would remain tight-lipped about whether the "hair" was hair, or the "blood" was blood.

My first question is, how could police miss a human skull, a tuft of hair, and a quilt with what could be blood on it, all on the victim's property? Were these items placed near the home after the fact, or are we meant to think that the initial search was not so thorough? How could search dogs miss the blood or hair? Her grandchildren would later tell me that they believed the search was not as thorough as it should have been and only one of two wells on the property were searched. However, the dogs joined the search after dozens of civilians had trampled the area, which could have affected the results.

In any case, it looked as though they determined that the skull did not belong to Appleyard because it would have been used in court as proof of a body, but no body, skeletal or otherwise, was recovered. It turned out there was a lot more going on here that police and newspapers failed to communicate, which haunted lead investigator John Newstead.

The clump of hair was examined by Keith Kelder of the Center for Forensic Sciences. He described it as ranging from colourless to a straw-like colour and ranging in length up to 20.5 centimetres. Eighteen hairs were sampled, along with the roots, which he determined had been "forcibly removed from the scalp by some means." Some of the samples contained blood, but Kelder was unable to determine who the blood was from. However, his conclusion was that the hairs were 100% human, either removed with violence or by aggressive brushing. Why these samples were not checked against a sample of Appleyard's hair is unknown.

Officer Newstead was displeased with how the case was handled from the get-go, and it bothered him for years after. He insisted on help from Officer Rhiness, who I'm told "had a steel trap of a mind," and was very good at his job. Throughout his career, he would be credited with solving many crimes in the province.

As for the human skull, Newstead sent it to Toronto for analysis. The results eventually came back as "the skull of an Indian," according to whoever examined it. This is why it was believed to be unrelated to the case, but Newstead wasn't buying it. It was believed that the coroner who examined it was Charles Smith, who had a reputation among police officers throughout the province for doing a shoddy job. Officer Newstead had dealt with Smith in the past, and he believed that every time Smith did not want to work a specific case, he would identify the remains as "Indian" and the case would go away pretty quickly.

In later years, the Ontario government ordered a public inquiry into Smith's career. Led by Justice Stephen Goudge, the inquiry concluded that Smith "actively misled" his superiors, "made false and misleading statements" in court and exaggerated his expertise in trials.[71] Goudge wrote that: "Smith lacked basic knowledge about forensic pathology." After being exposed, Smith admitted that he was not qualified to be performing autopsies, "Dr. Smith received no formal training in forensic pathology during his medical education, nor was he an accredited forensic pathologist. What he knew about forensic pathology was self-taught through experience doing coroner's cases."[72] Due to Smith's lack of training and qualifications, there was a good chance that this could have been May Appleyard's skull. The coroner's report only soured Newstead even more, and he would sarcastically refer to it as the "Indian artifact" when working on the case.

At this point in the investigation, it is unclear if Constable Newstead was able to convince superior officers Rhiness or Gray to escalate this to a murder investigation. Newstead returned to the property sometime in 1987. Evidently, his findings were enough to indicate that a homicide could have taken place in the home and he must have bent the ears of his superiors. Whatever Newstead's findings, he was able to charge Sydney Appleyard with second-degree murder.

Even without a body or a crime scene, Ontario Supreme Court Justice Jean MacFarland ruled that there was enough evidence to bring the case to court. *The Huntsville Forester* printed this update on the matter:

> A Perry Township man is being held at Perry Sound jail until a bail hearing has been set after he was charged with second degree murder September 6. Sidney Appleyard, 82, was charged in the murder of his wife, Agnes May Appleyard who has been missing from her Emsdale residence since late April 1986. Her body was never found.[73]

The Appleyard case went to trial in March of 1989 under the eye of Judge L.S. Geiger. In August of that same year, Sydney Appleyard would file an application for an Order of Certiorari Quashing to Judge MacFarland, meaning that Mr. Appleyard requested a higher court to dispute the decision of a lower court (proceeded by Judge Geiger) in the count of second-degree murder. The Osgoode Hall Report in *The Globe and Mail* stated that this application was dismissed.

The trial would expose the disturbing truth of what really went on in that isolated homestead that was tucked away in Ontario's backwoods. There had been a history of spousal abuse being dealt by Sydney Appleyard. In a small community, dotted with shacks and cabins and spaced out between massive weedy lots and thick forests, this type of behaviour went on unseen for years.

One of his sons later testified that his father was usually very nice, unless he had been drinking — then he would become verbally and physically abusive. According to the newspapers at the time, when Mr. Appleyard got drunk, his wife would take the children and walk off until he sobered up. Sometimes hanging around in the yard, sometimes hiding in the cellar or woodshed or taking that long walk to the neighbour's house. It happened often and usually lasted all night. When his son Elmer got drunk, he told stories about some of the horrible things his father did; one of them was setting fire to a barn in the area with the animals still inside.

Family and neighbours would witness the brutality from "old man" Appleyard the entire time they lived there. Nearly every time May Appleyard visited her children, she arrived battered and bruised.

Many grandchildren recalled witnessing the abuse of Appleyard on their visits to the homestead. There were times when her husband would punch, kick and drag her around by her hair. The abuse would stick with them for the rest of their lives. Irene told of a story where her father-in-law grabbed a knife and held it to Appleyard's neck while pushing her against the cupboard. On their fiftieth wedding anniversary, Sydney Appleyard reportedly hit his wife in the face with a beer bottle.

One granddaughter remembered a traumatic visit to the homestead in which she tagged along with Appleyard to draw fresh water from the spring. As Appleyard scooped the water from the icy pool, her husband came storming down the trail in a drunken rage, grabbed her grandma by the hair and shoved her head into the water, holding her there for what seemed like a lifetime. When he pulled her head back, he said, "Next time I won't pull you up." Drowning attempts like these have been corroborated by neighbours.

On another occasion, Appleyard was sent out to the shed to get wood. When she returned, her husband stood on the porch and would throw the blocks of wood back at her while screaming profanities. Another terrifying encounter recalled by a granddaughter was when Sydney Appleyard began shooting at her and his wife.

She remembered having to hide from the bullets under the cover of the ferns in front of the house until her grandfather gave up and went inside.

Appleyard's doctor testified that he treated her numerous times for broken ribs. In May 1985, Ivy and Elmer Appleyard dropped in on their mother to find her sick and in bed. Her leg was terribly swollen and hot, and she was unable to move it. Elmer left and returned with an ambulance. As soon as Sydney Appleyard saw the two paramedics, he went ballistic, cursing and swearing that they were not coming into his house. He then accused them both of sleeping with his wife. Ivy noticed a large round bruise on her mother's forehead and on her way out discovered a hammer sitting near the door. A paramedic revealed during the trial that he believed Appleyard had been "assaulted with a hammer on more than one occasion." Appleyard returned home with her leg in a cast.

A year later, Appleyard was missing, and everyone seemed to have a pretty good idea of what had happened. While I slowly uncovered the tragic story of abuse, it seemed like a very clear-cut murder case, but I couldn't wrap my head around the fact that there was no crime scene or enough evidence of a murder.

Through interviews, I learned that family members were concerned that one braided rug had been missing from the home and was not located during the search. Whether this has anything to do with Appleyard or not remains to be seen.

Besides the cry of murder, there were different ideas floating around of what else could have become of May Appleyard. A neighbour told me that in the early morning, before her disappearance, she actually sought shelter at a different neighbour's house and called her son Elmer. This neighbour asked her to wait for Elmer to pick her up in his car, but Appleyard insisted on walking home alone before sunrise. But according to Elmer, he would later say that he drove her home and would have been the last person to see her alive.

Appleyard was very shy and would never have taken a ride from a stranger, even if it meant getting away from her husband. There is also a lot of talk of sinkholes in the area. I first thought this was a baseless theory, but as I spoke to more people, these sinkholes were hidden throughout the surrounding woodlands and were a real threat to residents. Locals would keep to the paths and trails they were familiar with to avoid being swallowed up by them. One such hole was just past the local school, and the children would have to keep it in mind as they played hide and seek. A few residents even told me that they had lost a cow in one of them. During the search, locals reported that the police would walk up and down the road, checking the ditches, while locals swept through the bush, because they knew where all the sinkholes were and thought that Appleyard could have fallen into one of them. However, many doubt the theory since she knew the area so well and had lived there all her life.

During the trial, John Rosen, one of Sydney Appleyard's lawyers, argued that there was no body and no signs of struggle within the home, which means the findings of Newstead and searchers were either not admissible in court or completely ignored. He also put forth the idea of an 80-some-year-old man disposing of a body and cleaning up a crime scene. Would it even be possible? Rosen told of an incident where two ambulance attendants that were once called to the house could not lift her because she was too heavy. Irene also made the same claim, but I don't know how true this statement could be. The police list Appleyard's weight at 130 pounds with a height of 5-feet 11-inches. In the photographs of Appleyard I've seen, she doesn't appear all that heavy either, so something doesn't add up, and yet this testimony was mentioned in court. With all that said, moving any type of dead weight would be extremely difficult for a younger man, let alone a man of 80 years, who was reported to have arthritis, and who would have been drunk at the time.

The police and the crown prosecutor were faced with the same question we are: would it be possible for her 82-year-old husband to commit murder and dispose of the remains while intoxicated?

The case went back to trial in May 1990, but failed to produce an answer to the question everyone wanted to know: Where on earth was May Appleyard? Instead, it took just over an hour for the jury to fully acquit Sydney Appleyard of second-degree murder. The evidence demonstrated that for four decades, Mr. Appleyard had beaten and verbally abused his wife while he was under the influence of alcohol but showed no evidence that he had killed her. One of the cold hard facts of the case was stated by Justice Steale directly: "The mere fact that you find that Sid was a bad man or a very bad man doesn't show he's guilty of killing his wife."[74]

Sydney Appleyard still declared his innocence long after the trial was over, and some family members defend him, saying he never would have intentionally murdered her. The consensus was, if that was the case, he would have done it years before. Apparently, Stan and his wife sat him down during the investigation and asked him for his version of what had happened. He said he didn't remember anything. He was sleeping and when he woke up, she wasn't there. After interviewing a dozen or so family members, they seem to be split down the middle on Sydney's guilt. Naturally, the kids were always defensive of their father, even though they didn't get along very well. As a handful of them took the stand, they struggled to admit the abuse their father had dished out. Then there are those that believe that Sydney Appleyard did kill his wife, but that it was an accident. After May Appleyard returned from the Godfrey's, she cooked breakfast for her husband, who then pushed her and she fell, hitting the stove on the way down, and that he doesn't remember doing it — an idea that corroborates Newstead's theory.

As I spoke to those involved, this one theory kept popping up. They believed that Elmer and Irene arrived at the house and found Mr. Appleyard asleep and his wife dead near the wood stove. They then covered up the crime for the old man and removed May Appleyard from the area, which is when Stan would have arrived at the homestead.

Officer Newstead felt this was a possibility and apparently had an eyewitness to corroborate it. He was told by another family member that Elmer and Irene left with May Appleyard in the backseat of their car. Attempts to track down this witness have failed so far, but as with all missing persons cases, the investigation is ongoing.

Many family members believe that Elmer would not be capable of such a gruesome thing as covering up the murder of his own mother, but Irene was a different story. No one I interviewed had a nice word to say about Irene, and apparently Elmer would do anything she asked of him. To police, Elmer and Irene Appleyard seemed like people of interest, at least for a little while. He was seen driving to Kearney on the morning his mother vanished. Some neighbours tell me he drove to the dump. I had no way of confirming this, but they believed police had searched through Elmer's trash and his property, but again found nothing.

Meanwhile, Sydney Appleyard made no attempt to appear innocent during the search or the trial. He threatened to kill his wife on multiple occasions in the past. He was heard saying, "I've got to kill you, you old son of a bitch before I can go on living."
Appleyard would reply, "They'll find me and you'll hang."
According to their children, Sydney would grumble back, "Not where you'll God damn well go and they won't find you."
After she disappeared, Sydney would utter things like, "I guess I killed her" and "I fooled them."[75] Was Sydney covering for one of his kids or are his kids covering for Sydney?

The Appleyard case is unsettling because she vanished without a trace from her very own home. What little clues they found could not conclusively be tied to her disappearance. Maybe now, with scientific advancements in DNA technology, we will learn who that skull belonged to. That is, if we can find it…

After it was tested, the skull was shipped back to the property vault at the Burks Falls detachment, where it stayed in a paper bag until sometime later. In 2016, Newstead was called to discuss the possibility of reopening the case, but when police went to retrieve the case files from the evidence locker, everything belonging to Officer Newstead had inexplicably vanished. This included Newstead's black notebooks, which he would have recorded his daily activities on and would have been invaluable to the investigation. How could years of police work, interviews, evidence and a human skull go missing?

Needless to say, the case could not be reopened, at least not properly, leaving Newstead storming off, even more frustrated.

Sources tell me that the skull is likely sitting in a banker box in an unknown police detachment. Newstead's family thought it was sent to Orillia — perhaps there it waits with a faded, yellowing label marked "Indian," or quite possibly that label has been long peeled away, leaving a nameless head, rattling around in some storage locker. Make no mistake, this in no way means that the skull would be added to the list of unidentified human remains. If no one asks and no one is looking, why should anyone care?

The time in which Appleyard would have had to murder his wife, dispose of her, and cover up the evidence and crime scene would have been minimal. According to Irene, her and Elmer left Appleyard mid-morning on Sunday, April 27. Her son Stanley showed up between 2:00 or 3:00 p.m. that same day to drop off the oil. Appleyard was nowhere to be found, leading us to believe that it was within this window that something happened to her. That would have been a maximum five- to six-hour window.

It's possible that someone out there knows more than they are willing to tell. If Sydney Appleyard had assistance from another individual, they would have had to speed over there in a hurry and hide her body in a place they knew police wouldn't look. That is, of course, unless Irene and Elmer are lying. Interestingly, Irene admitted to lying on her statement to the police, and changed her story a number of times while under oath.

During the trial, defence attorney Jim Anderson revealed that May Appleyard did not get along with Irene and there had been an argument between the two before she went missing. It was said that they went back and forth over the cutting of trees on Appleyard's property and the collecting of firewood. Irene denied the idea that either she or her husband Elmer ever butted heads with Appleyard on the issue, however other family members did corroborate the idea. Anderson asked Irene about the firewood dispute seven times while she was on the witness stand, but she denied it. However, when Anderson asked the question an eighth time, her answer changed. "Well, certain wood maybe they didn't want cut, they generally give us another spot if, like, they didn't want wood cut down, the maple bush or something, they would generally give us another piece to cut on."[76] While the search for Appleyard was going on, Irene and Elmer returned to the homestead to cut and process a poplar tree for firewood.

Are we being led to believe that May Appleyard was killed over a dispute of firewood?

Anderson quickly builds a case around Irene and Elmer and accuses her on the witness stand, saying, "I suggest to you, Mrs. Appleyard, that you and your husband had an argument with May Appleyard… on the day she went missing?" Irene denied it twice, to which Anderson continued, "And I suggest that however it happened, however she died, you used your truck to remove the body from the house?"

The more Anderson's questioning continued, the more Irene's responses deteriorated. Irene tells a story of taking Sydney Appleyard to the hospital for "his nerves" when he was staying with them for a few days in Emsdale, however only minutes later, confessed that she did not take him to the hospital and that he was actually staying at his daughter's house in Huntsville and not her residence.

But there was one problem with Anderson's theory, that being the use of a four-wheel-drive vehicle that would have been required to access the homestead to load the body and drive back out. Stanley confirmed seeing tire tracks upon his visit to the house in the early afternoon. Neither police, family members or ambulance drivers could access the home from the driveway that was just less than half a mile away and instead would have to park up the road. Elmer and Irene drove a half-ton, two-wheel-drive, open-back pickup truck, which could not navigate the chewed path that led to the homestead, especially if conditions were muddy.

The answer to this problem came from Officer Newstead himself. Sydney did not own a four-wheel-drive vehicle, but Elmer was known to drive a white Lada owned by someone known only as "Mr. Clark." The Lada is a tough little car with reinforced suspension. Newstead confirmed that Elmer's Lada had been at the property before April 28, which means Irene was not being truthful about picking up Appleyard in the truck. The story of the Lada also coincides with the story told to Newstead by the witness who saw Elmer, Irene and May Appleyard leave in a car, not a truck.

From my knowledge, the Lada was not taken in as evidence, so this could be the missing piece of the puzzle. This was the only vehicle capable of off-road terrain. Just like the Lada commercial says: "To take on loads, and the roughest of roads" — a selling point for those who live remotely, only in this case the load in question refers to a 72-year-old woman.

Until someone comes forward with more information, this case will remain unsolved. Newstead's witness is still out there, but to my knowledge has yet to come forward. May Appleyard could be anywhere. Emsdale has no shortage of washed-out backroads, swamps, lakes, sunken shacks and sinkholes.

I was able to locate Mr. Appleyard at St. Mark's Cemetery. He died on January 13, 2000 but was only given a head and foot marker instead of a tombstone. Elmer and Irene are buried there too, taking whatever truth they had with them. With Sydney Appleyard long gone, police only need the remains to close the case.

Even though Sydney Appleyard treated his wife poorly, we need to keep Justice Steale's words in mind, that just because he was a bad man, we can't automatically assume he was a murderer too. It's bad enough that we don't know what happened to May Appleyard that day, but the worst part is not being able to bring her home to her family, who are still seeking answers.

This is where her story ends, not because it is an ending, but because the ending hasn't been written. I could not find any further details on the case, but they are out there somewhere. For over three years, I have been having a back and forth with the Ontario Court Services and the Archives of Ontario to try and locate more records. Some have come through, but many documents are still missing. They could exist somewhere, catalogued under a different name, but if the record-keepers themselves can't locate them, what chance do we have? I have attempted to contact Jim Anderson, the now retired defence attorney for Sydney Appleyard, but he has not returned my calls. I connected with criminal defence attorney John Rosen, who was a part of the case in 1989. He has no memory of the case and had no surviving records for that time period.

Is this case "currently being investigated" as police claim it is or is it sitting in a filing cabinet somewhere? We can't confirm the last time someone looked at this case or if those lost files were ever recovered. Most of the family members, including Elmer and Irene, are long dead, but remaining family members and neighbours are still seeking truth and justice for May Appleyard.

Perhaps someone out there could help find her remains. The locals tell me of a bottomless bog in the area that has been used as an unofficial dumping ground by locals, but until someone comes forward with new information, the police are hesitant to entertain such ideas. We can speculate that Sydney may have done some cleverly devilish things to dispose of her, but it won't bring us any closer to the truth.

I was roughly 1 kilometre away from her last known location. The lot number, which was given by the OPP, was my destination; however, I still had trouble locating it. To locate the property to see what remained of this couple's home, I had to do some painstaking research into the area. It turned out to be more tedious than I thought. I counted myself lucky that I wasn't in the market for a home or land in Emsdale, because the search would have completely turned me off. The systems in place to find such information are only available at one office located in Perry Sound. There is no web or phone assistance. The in-person computer terminal (which is not free to use) was nowhere near the actual property I was searching for. While I combed through some maps, their software lists the road they used to live on as Appleyard's Road. I would only find out later that police had the address wrong on the case file, which sent me on a wild goose chase.

The jarring sound of my tires spitting out stones was a sign that I was nearly there. The roads around Concession 2 are gravel, and in some spots the potholes were as large as kiddie pools, and I had to swerve several times. One section of the road was washed away, and I was worried I would pop a tire or get my car stuck in one of the deep gouges cut by rain and run-off. I revved my accelerator hard to climb up a section that at its best was about 35% drivable road. The lots looked giant and bushy, most of them butting up against thick woods, blurring the boundaries. The driveways were long and winded into the dark bush that human eyes couldn't penetrate. Here was a place dotted with lakes large and small, wetlands and extensive quiet stretches of road that seemed to all end at a mystery. If a crime was committed, there was a wealth of hiding places. Two steps off the road and you wouldn't be able to see me. Straight away it was easy to see how secrets could remain hidden here and how futile the searchers' job was. It was the proverbial haystack and would be damn near impossible to locate a lost person or any kind of human remains. In the eighties, it would have been even less developed than it is today.

I got out of the car and parked along one of a hundred isolated roads. The forest was thick on either side and I imagined how this was likely a very active hunting community. I didn't feel good here. I felt like I should leave, and so I made a careful check of my surroundings. At the same time, I was glad I went to the location where I could see what she saw and breathe the same air. In a way, I felt I was visiting Appleyard herself, even if she was no longer in the area. After all, her last known location was steps away and without a grave marker, the wilderness around me was the next best thing.

A complete profile on May Appleyard does not exist. At 72 years old there is only a single sentence on the police database that grounds her as once being a resident of our world. Police and various missing persons websites still don't know her race or her medical condition or history. I never understood how you could search for a missing person without knowing their race. Even after policed conducted multiple interviews with the family, this fact was never brought up. It is the investigator's job to compile an accurate and detailed description. False information or a void of information altogether can lead to identity mismatches, which wastes time and resources. Not only this, but it can also bring a false hope to family members. Through one family member I spoke to, I was able to confirm that May Appleyard is Caucasian.

There is no indication that the police have recovered the lost case files or are investigating the case, however, family revealed that an investigator had interviewed one of Appleyard's adult daughters in 2020, saying they may have had a "breakthrough" in the case. Apparently, familial DNA was collected. Is it possible that police have located the lost skull?

Not all memories of May Appleyard are tainted with sadness, however. Her grandchildren still remember her kind and loving nature. She is remembered giving candy out to the kids and making homemade bread, which I'm told was out of this world. I can only imagine the smell as it wafted down to the creek and over that quiet, isolated road.

After going over the story in my head again and again, I figured it was time I should leave the area. The bad vibes I had felt initially only grew with each passing minute. I stared into the woods and said a quiet prayer for Appleyard. I let her know that I was here to visit and what had brought me to this point. Then I quickly jumped in my car, prayed again that it would start, and when it did, sped off like a bat out of hell.

I initially thought the discomfort I was feeling was paranoia or even fear, but hindsight has taught me differently. Maybe my gut was trying to tell me something — not to leave, but to look. Maybe it was telling me that I was in the right place after all. We may never learn what happened to May Appleyard, but by sharing her story we can ensure that she is not forgotten. I only wish I had more of the story to tell.

Tim Marczenko

*Courtesy of Phyllis Rand

10

When No One Is Looking

"Our dead are never dead to us, until we have forgotten them."
—Mary Ann Evans

When a missing person is found or a skeleton is identified, it can give the illusion that the case is solved. Those we have recovered are either buried or burned and given a final resting place — their story comes to a neat and tidy finish... or at least that's the idea.

The truth is that a mystery can still persist years after a case becomes closed. I have uncovered a handful of bizarre deaths that have, at one point or another, been resolved, yet the situation surrounding the demise or disappearance of these individuals remains unexplained. Each case began with a series of puzzling questions, but once the body was recovered, it was as if those questions weren't worth answering, as if it no longer mattered. Burying those we have found brings forth a finality and a feeling that we can safely move on and forget. However, there is a piece of the puzzle lacking from the final hours of these people's lives. These occurrences are numerous and prove the disturbing notion that solved cases do not mean we have all the answers.

Charles Bertram Smith

In 1925, the *Sudbury Star* reported the discovery of a body at 11:00 a.m. on Tuesday, July 7. The body of Charles Bertram Smith, or "Bert" to his friends, was found in three feet of water in Root River. Mr. Smith was a loved and respected druggist from the northern town of Sault Ste. Marie (known as the "Soo" to Canadians). While the man's remains were eventually found, his disappearance was too bizarre to dismiss as simple misadventure. Something weird happened to this ordinary man, and the investigators appeared not to spend much time or resources to uncover the cause of his mysterious end.

The body was discovered by "Soo" Mayor James Dawson, who was part of a search party for the man. Prior to his death, Charles Smith was reported to drive his wife, Jane Paisley, from their home on Pim Street (sometimes reported as Pine Street) south to Queen Street near the St. Mary River. On their return trip home, he told his wife he would like to "use the car" again and left her around noon. That was the last he was seen alive; he was missing for three days. His wife noticed him missing when he failed to return after the lunch hour. Formally from Orangeville,

Jane drove back to her hometown on the Sunday in case her husband had found his way back there. She returned the same afternoon with nothing to report.

Local resident and farmer, John Abercrombie, spotted Smith's car on top of Warner's sand hill on the night he failed to return home. He thought it was an odd place to find a parked car, and so mentioned it to a neighbour. Word eventually got back to Chief H.B. Graham, but not until two days later, on the Monday. Chief Graham visited the car and organized a search for Smith that comprised of more than 50 local residents and the fire department.

When searchers arrived at the car, they quickly noticed that Charles Smith was not inside and so proceeded to fan out about 10 feet apart between the Algoma Central Railway tracks and Peever Road, working east. The search was extensive and covered a wide area. Groups of men drove up and down the surrounding roads for any sign of the man.

After approximately 20 to 25 minutes of searching the vicinity of the car, ground teams entered the thick bush on either side of the abandoned vehicle. Mayor Dawson was at the forefront of the group that headed east, where the bush came to a point at a bend in the river. It was Dawson who would make the grim discovery. The body of Charles Smith laid at the bottom of a clay incline. Interestingly, Smith had one hand gripped to a short branch of a tree that was overhanging the bank. His hat was found floating 15 feet down stream. Smith was lifted out of the water and looked over by coroner, A.S. McCaig. The consensus was that he drowned. The coroner described the body as being in water for two to three days. After the grim discovery, officer G.S. Harbottle solemnly withdrew his revolver and fired two shots into the air, signalling to all that the search had ended.

I was immediately bothered by some of the details of this incident. Why would Charles Smith leave his car parked at the side of a desolate country road to go traipsing through the thick bush? The report stated that he walked between a quarter mile and a mile and a half through the bush, past the place his car was left on the right side of the road. That means he left his car and then circled back around to pass it once more. The path he took eliminates the idea that he had gotten lost. At first glance, one could explain his actions by claiming he pulled off to the shoulder to relieve himself, but a mile and a half through the bush is a difficult path just to gain privacy in an already isolated location. The car was found with plenty of gasoline in the tank, and oddly the keys were found on the ground nearby.

Was Smith looking for something? Did he see something along the road and go off after it? And why go down so close to the riverbank? No other footprints were described in the news articles and no witnesses were mentioned. At the time, the road in question was little traveled and used wholly as a tote road for suppliers and farm equipment. Perhaps equally intriguing was the medical examiner's report. Dr. Ben R. McMullin stated the cause of death as "Suffocation by immersion in shallow pond of water. Mental derangement." The word "derangement" was underlined twice. I could not find the results of an inquest or if one was ever done, but the final statements of the doctor have me puzzled. It's never explained why Smith was in the place that he was found.

Further to that, how can a man drown when one hand is firmly gripped on a tree branch that could have saved his life? Did Smith meet someone who wanted him dead? If he was alone, he could have pulled himself out of the water. If not, he could have slipped in and simply stood up — keep in mind the water would have been below his waist. The theory of suicide raises even more doubt. Drowning is not instantaneous and would be painful and near impossible without counterweights. Why would he choose this location? If he decided to end his own life, he could have taken a potent concoction of pills from his pharmacy.

Lastly, I find it odd that the medical examiner ended the report accusing Smith of "mental derangement." Clearly this is an attempt to explain away the bizarreness of the matter, but it seems to come out of nowhere and is presented as a fact. There is no evidence to suggest that mental derangement could cause this death. A man who is dead cannot receive psychiatric assessment. At the very least, it would serve as small-town gossip and at most, it would be defamatory to Smith and unwarranted to do so since he was a beloved member of his community. I am sure Smith would not appreciate being called crazy just because the circumstances of his death were out of the ordinary.

The story of Charles Bertram Smith and others like him leave us with the lingering feeling of something undone. It's an injustice to close the book on this matter just because his body was recovered. Outside of that, there was little to no information recorded and left to be found. I had reached a dead end in providing any kind of clarity to this bizarre death. All my attempts to pull records came up with no results. Even the police were not familiar with the case, or the man who was supposed to be so well-known. I had planned to visit the bend in the river where his untimely death occurred, but no map could give me clues as to the specific location. It's likely that the printed names have all been updated and changed. The Root River can be traced northward to Upper Island Lake. Currently, a golf course sits on the east side of it and its banks are lined with private property and overgrowth, making it impossible for me to fully explore. Unfortunately, without pinpointing the exact location or speaking with searchers who were there that day, I cannot trace the steps of Smith accurately enough.

Charles Bertram Smith was originally from Owen Sound. After purchasing the Pharmacy at 795 Queen Street East in Sault Ste. Marie, he relocated and operated it for 25 years. Locals described him as "Prominent." Smith was a member of the Anglican Church and took an active part in the Masonic Lodge of the city, along with Mayor Dawson. Smith had been married for 19 years. He was 50 years old when they found him.

His remains were buried along with the true story of what really transpired that day.

*Courtesy of the City of Sault Ste. Marie

James Wilbert McGregor
While combing through an endless cascade of black and white newsprint, there are times when a headline will cry out to me. The headline in this case was "Locate Body of Missing Man" that drew my eyes to a small, roughly 3-inch column printed in *The Huntsville Forester*.[77] The column went on to say that the body of Mr. McGregor of Silverbirch Avenue in Toronto had been found dead.

I was surprised not to find more details on the case of James Wilbert McGregor. When I first read the story, I figured it would be easy to find a resolution, but I was wrong. The difference between this case and some of the others in this book is that this one, at least to police, has a satisfactory ending. Unless of course you are one of the curious — then you will find it quite unsatisfactory. I apologize for the brevity of the mention of McGregor here, but it is this fact that is a constant irritation of this book.

At 73 years old, McGregor went on a hunting trip in late October of 1962 at Camp We-ne-ak with his son, William, and daughter-in-law. McGregor left the lodge alone on Tuesday, October 30 to hunt partridge in the surrounding woods. When he did not return that night, a search party was arranged, but was hampered by a severe storm. If there were clues or trails left by McGregor, they would have been washed away. On November 1, searchers found his body beside a burned-out campfire, only 3 miles from the lodge he was staying at. The consensus was that he had died of exposure. That single news article would be the last we ever heard of Mr. McGregor and this story.

No follow-up news was printed and to my knowledge no inquest was held. As I hinted at before, there is something about this story that doesn't sit right. McGregor clearly had some hunting and outdoor experience, or he wouldn't have ventured off alone. I can't understand how he could, presumably, get lost and then start a fire without being seen and still die from exposure. Even if he did not have a map and compass, could he not have returned the way he came or used his internal sense of direction to walk towards shelter? If he got turned around in an area he was unfamiliar with, then it would have been difficult to self-rescue. Perhaps he did not know how close he was to the lodge and decided to stay put for the evening, only to have the fire die out while he slept. Still, McGregor was hunting and therefore had a rifle with him. He could have fired off three rounds to notify anyone in the area that he needed help. Three gun shots are a known signal of distress.

I had submitted a request for more information on this case but was denied because the investigating police force did not keep a record of it. I've spoken about the retention period in correlation with the *Freedom of Information Act* requests and here was another example of failing to preserve documentation. No information could be found in the surrounding police detachments either (I contacted several). My feeling was that since the case was not suspected to be a homicide, whoever the investigating officer was had purged the paperwork after a body was recovered.

The details are scarce, and I cannot even pin down a hunting lodge or camp for an exact location to visit. It is not uncommon for these lodges to change ownership and names over the years. Because of this, I'm afraid the trail will go cold here, and we will never know what really happened to James Wilbert McGregor. Nothing more will ever be known about this mysterious death, and this is why this story is important. Without an understanding of what happened or a written record of the incident and response, how can we take steps to prevent it from happening again?

Alexander Charles Fenech

Alexander Fenech once shared a page in the newspaper with Agnes May Appleyard. This is odd in itself, but it's the strange death of Fenech that lands him a spot in this book. Fenech was a 20-year-old man from Ajax, Ontario. He and a friend had gone camping at the Shangri-La Park near Kearney over the Labour Day long weekend in 1988. He disappeared late on Saturday evening (September 3) or Sunday morning (September 4), which sparked a massive search of the area. The Burks Falls Police detachment of the OPP investigated the matter. Searchers deployed tracking dogs and helicopters in a large-scale effort, but still they failed to find Fenech or any trace of him.

At approximately 10:30 a.m. on Sunday, September 11, a passerby came across the body of Fenech near the shores of Sand Lake, slightly north of the campground. The body was found near a trail in "a remote bush area near the park."[78] Medical professionals concluded that Alex Fenech had been dead for three days. An autopsy completed on September 12 concluded that he died from hypothermia.

Readers might be quick to dismiss the case as a young kid who was partying with friends and maybe got lost after drinking too much. If he couldn't find his way back and perhaps passed out, there is a good chance he would succumb to hypothermia. The problem is that the timeline does not support the theory of drunkenness. He would have sobered up long before dying on the ninth. The medical examiner also would have indicated if there was alcohol in his blood, which they did not. For the record, the newspapers never brought up the theory that he may have been drunk. I only bring it up here because it is a stereotype of young people who take part in long-weekend camping trips.

Even though Fenech was no longer a missing person, there were red flags that immediately jumped out at me. First, consider the massive search for the man. The reports of the time do not state the manpower that went into the bush, but they do state multiple tracking dogs, police and helicopters. Labour Day, being a popular vacation time, should have garnered more search volunteers in the form of vacationers, campground staff and nearby cottagers in the area that weekend. Professional searchers are good at their job, and they do make note of all significant bodies of water in the area for obvious reasons. Naturally, they would have searched the trails and shores of Sand Lake and yet they did not find him. Sand Lake is a fair size lake, but its border is also dotted with dozens of cottages and at least three other summer resorts. The area is dense with wilderness, but highly populated and well-traveled, with a single-lane highway running around the lake. How was a passerby, with no connection to the search, able to find a missing man near a trail? Why would Fenech not hop on the trail and hike himself out? After all, there were no injuries preventing his mobility. It's highly probable that this area had already been searched and he ended up there later. *How* is the real question.

The second disturbing problem I have with this case is that Fenech had only been dead for three days, yet the search lasted a full week. Where was Fenech for the remainder of those days? If Fenech was alive, as the medical examiner stated, why then did he not cry out for help? This doesn't make any sense to me, yet the police did not raise any suspicions about this, at least none that were made public. Police stated numerous times that they had no reason to believe that foul play was involved, yet he was unaccounted for for seven days in the wilderness.

This is one case that boggles my mind, and I can't help but think that Fenech was robbed of a full investigation. Was he taken against his will? Is there something else going on here?

I faced the same reality that I had in my investigation of McGregor in the previous story. The police denied my request for records because they didn't exist. No information could be located from the surrounding detachments, nor could I find any other articles from various archives or libraries.

Again, my feeling is that as soon as the investigating police force announces there is no suspicion, the files are put in queue for the shredder. And like James Wilbert McGregor, I fear that nothing more will ever be known or understood about this death. It's too late to reopen a case when there is no documentation to start from, but clearly a piece of the story is missing. Without data to comb through, these questions will go unanswered. Is this why the retention period for resolved cases is practically inexistent? It seems all mention of this incident is slowly turning into vapour and there are no leads to follow up on. The friend or friends he was camping with are not mentioned by name in the article, so we cannot get their comments. The family cannot be located, so I cannot get their opinion on the matter. Even the campground has changed their name, as if to put the past behind them. What was once the Shangri-La Park is now the Granite Ridge Campground, and soon memory of the previous name will be forgotten along with those who have visited.

We've explored those not-so-rare cases that tease us as being resolved but remain a mystery to this day. If only some witness had been present to see the last moments of these individuals. We cannot determine if these cases are criminal, misadventure or something more mysterious. Without somebody there to watch, we will never know. These people have taken the answer to the grave, leaving us only with an uncomfortable feeling and the disturbing, undeniable fact that strange and tragic things happen when no one is looking…

11

Who Do You Think We Are?

*"Hallowed and Hushed be the Place of the Dead.
Step softly, bow head."*
—The Unknown Grave

There is a chance that many unsolved missing persons cases were actually solved long ago without our knowing. Our missing people may not be missing at all; in fact, they could be waiting in drawers to have their toes tagged. Literally hundreds of human remains are found in wilderness areas, waterways and ditches every year. Most of these bodies or body parts will age in basement banker boxes somewhere and never be identified.

In Canada, the number of recovered unknown bodies fluctuates every year, but the National Centre for Missing Persons and Unidentified Human Remains (NCMPUR) estimates there are over 750 unresolved cases of remains in their database. Approximately 50–100 new cases, on average, can be reported any given year. That is over 750 people who were born, lived some kind of life and then… nothing.

I have rediscovered a collection of puzzling deaths from old news clippings and police databases that I'm obligated to mention here. Some unlucky traveller was minding their own business when they walked upon a scattered collection of lost bones in the wilderness. In some cases, they are partial remains: a jawbone, a leg bone, a skull. Other times, the body is in an earlier state of decomposition, a ghastly discovery for any happy-go-lucky hiker. They report the corpse to authorities, who then enter it into their database and the public never hears about it again.

On a few occasions where a body was found, authorities only waited a short time before burying the remains and closing the case, even though they had not confirmed the identity. In the past, once a body was buried, the case was no longer investigated. We have buried an unknowable amount of missing people in unmarked graves and simply let the grass grow over.

Unsatisfactory conclusions have been pinned to the discovery of floating bodies in provincial waterways. Water damage on a human body erases many distinguishable features of a person. This fact alone has caused our older cases to remain permanently anonymous, unless by some dumb luck we are able to relocate those lost burial sites and exhume them for DNA analysis. Sometimes there is no body at all, but evidence that something foul has taken place.

The Phantom Body of Blanche River

Flowing north out of Lake Timiskaming, the Blanche River passes into the Kirkland Lake District and serves as recreation for residents of both Belle Vallée, Englehart and beyond. It is the home of a variety of fish species and traces of surrounding wildlife are frequently seen along its banks. But in July of 1936, something out-of-place was also discovered on-shore: a heap of men's clothing. The pile was found by bush-workers tromping through the area, which led them to believe that a naked man had either jumped or fallen into the river. Provincial police began dragging the Blanche River with hooks, hoping to pull into a body of the naked, nameless man. The clothes were the only clue, so we can't be positive if the individual was there for a recreational swim and drowned or some other purpose, such as suicide, which is exactly what police were thinking. It was unclear how they came to this hunch, but I have heard of some cases of suicide in which the person does remove their clothing prior. Perhaps police thought it unlikely that a man of sound mind would take their clothes off in the wilderness. There was no follow up story printed and no body was ever found. It's possible this man may have been trapped under tree branches or washed away into a larger body of water, or perhaps hidden in one of more than a dozen tributaries. Sadly, it will forever remain yet another unknown person who is lost and never found.

The Body of Lac D'Alembert

Two boys, Donald W. Evans and Ronald F.A. Burton, were fishing in Lac D'Alembert on July 29 of 1936 when they made a gruesome discovery. Floating in the water was the bloated body of a man. The location was not far from the town of Kirkland Lake, in the province of Quebec. It's been the site of more than one waterlogged discovery; in fact, there were two bodies found within two weeks of each other in 1939. The first body was identified as George Meyer when his teeth were used to aid in a positive identification. The identity of the second individual remains a mystery to this day.

The body found by these two boys was fully clothed and appeared to have been in the water for a month or so. All his clothes were described as brand new, and he wore a suit with shoes — not the typical apparel for a bush-worker. When police recovered him from the waters, they searched his pockets and found a receipt book with claim numbers written inside. Police believed that he was a prospector and had hoped to identify the man by tracing these claim numbers. An eerie addition to the story was discovered afterwards. The police recalled that they received a report from a man who had heard crying near this lake in the middle of the night. At the time, police thought the report to be directly related and may have been the man's cries for help. With no identification on him, the body was transported to the Marcoux funeral parlour and waited for a coroner to arrive and investigate. This is not the typical practice, so I have no clue why it was done here. Once a body is discovered, the coroner is called immediately. The body cannot be moved until the coroner arrives at the scene. Once there, they will decide if the remains are of forensic interest or if they show evidence of a crime. Remains are then carefully removed and transported for further examination. It is the coroner's role, in every death investigation, to find out the identity of the deceased, the date of death, where they died, how and by what means.

While police waited for any kind of official word, they requested that local citizens help by attempting to identify the body. One by one, they visited the remains and were able to get a look at his clothing — his suit, shirt, sweater and tie. There was also said to be identifiable marks on him: a broken nose, a scar on one foot and several gold teeth. After the morbid exhibition of the corpse and its items and indicators, five people confidently came to the same conclusion: this was the corpse of Elmer Lisburg, a resident of Timmins. The body had the exact amount of gold teeth, and to further the story, Lisburg was said to camp at Lac D'Alembert. After seven days, it looked like the mystery had come to a close.

Dr. J.E. Bertrand, Coroner of Macamic, Quebec, had arrived in town to begin the inquest. He confirmed that the location of the body and timing of discovery fit in with Elmer Lisburg's schedule. Lisburg left his job at Noranda Mines Limited at the end of June for vacation, and so it was concluded he must have died in early July. However, in order to corroborate the story, investigators reached out to Timmins Police. Their response turned the whole ordeal on its head.

They emphatically stated that Elmer Lisburg was alive and well and was speaking with the chief of the Timmins Police Department earlier that afternoon. Apparently, this "dead man" walked into the police station... there's a joke in there somewhere. Later that same day, it was confirmed by friends and police that Lisburg was not the name of the deceased man, and the five citizens falsely identified the body, whose face was unrecognizable.

As a strange footnote to this story, this was the second time Elmer Lisburg had been mistakenly reported to be dead. I guess the locals were not optimistic about his life expectancy. More than a week later, the local police were still puzzled by the man's identity and went over his belongings again to seek clues. His pocket handkerchief had a name written in marker on it, but it turned out to be another dead end, the owner of the handkerchief was still alive, and could not explain why the dead man had possessed it. What about the receipt book? Could that be some clue? Again, no, it belonged to someone else who also had no explanation for why the dead man was in possession of it. Who was this odd chimera-like nobody who collected items that did not belong to him? One has to wonder if his clothes also belonged to another man. Was this done as an attempt to disguise his identity? The heads of the police officers must have gone raw with all that scratching. In the days that followed, they made a last-ditch effort to send fingerprints to the RCMP, hoping to identify the man by way of a criminal record. After all, if the items in his pockets did not belong to him, maybe he was a thief. This is where the trail goes cold. At the time of this publication, no follow-up report confirmed a criminal record, and the man's identity will remain lost forever.

The Waterlogged Corpse
Another unknown man bobbed into the public eye on May 3, 1939. The corpse was badly decomposed and thought to have been trapped under the ice of Lake Timiskaming for several months.[79] At the time, there were no missing persons reported in the district, which led the police to believe that the man may have washed in from the Quebec side. Whether this was true or not, a provincial border should not stand in the way of a conclusion.

Three local boys spotted a cap poking through a crack in the ice and went over to investigate. Once they wrenched the corpse from the icy waters, Constable Art Souliere and Constable Fred Simpson responded to the scene and called in the coroner, Dr. W.C. Arnold. Upon review, the body was so badly waterlogged that they could not even determine an age of the victim, and all attempts to identify him were based on clothing alone. Just going off the body found in the previous story, you can imagine how unreliable this identification tactic is.

He wore lightweight pants, overshoes, and two sweaters. No one came forward asking about their missing son, and the body was quickly arranged for burial. The story of this poor unknown human ends here, like so many others, without a conclusion or another word printed about them in a follow-up issue of the paper. I can't fathom that these stories end this way. Would a parent ever stop looking for their son? Would a wife ever stop looking for her husband? Would a worker not care enough to wonder about his missing colleague? How can it happen that a human being is capable of being lost and forgotten? Instead of placing the body in temperature-controlled storage, it was hastily put in the ground. I checked with a municipal clerk at the City of Temiskaming Shores, and after an internal search, they could not identify any burial locations for these unknown bodies. They do not have records of a single one. Somewhere out there his bones lie in an overgrown grave, in one of over 100 cemeteries, crying out for justice.

Skull and Bones
It is believed that the remains of two separate people were found in May of 1976. The first discovery was made by a Thunder Bay area man who had been walking his dog through the wooded area around Lakehead Psychiatric Hospital. A human skull was found. A search for further remains was initiated, but no other bones were recovered. The hospital was not missing any patients at the time, and everyone was accounted for on the premises. As a result, the owner of this skull was never identified. If teeth were present in the skull, they could be used for a

positive identification by comparing them with dental records. The police would not cough up the report to confirm specific details on the bones or if other remains were ever recovered. Interestingly, for whatever reason, this skull has not been used to create a 3D rendering of the unknown person's face. Since records will not be released, I cannot find out why this hasn't been done.

On the previous weekend, two teenagers found the skeletal remains of another human in a wooded area off the expressway, to the northeast of the hospital. Police assumed that this was a possible suicide case and so checked the records for missing persons, but to this day, more than 40 years later, nothing has been found that could identify these bones. The report reads as follows:

Name: Unidentified Remains (Male, 30–50)
Details: On May 1, 1976, the skeletal remains of a male, were located in area of heavy bush north of Hwy 17 (0.5 miles east of Hodder Avenue on the Lakehead Expressway near a scenic lookout), Thunder Bay. Police reports approximate the height of the deceased to be 5-feet 8-inches, however, no anthropological analysis was carried out on the long bones, so this value is merely a non-scientific estimate. It is believed that he died approximately 10 months to five years prior to discovery.

They could not determine the race of the deceased as he was almost completely skeletonized, but they were able to tell that he had long, brown hair tied back with elastic fasteners or plastic balls. In his mouth was an acrylic upper denture. Within the lower jaw were signs of several molars and premolars that had been pulled prior to death. Whatever teeth remained showed signs of decay. Paper matches with the zodiac theme "the moon" on them and Du Maurier cigarettes were recovered from the pants. Police recovered a grey or off-white sweatshirt with a crew neck collar, a green wool sweater, a brown leather belt that measured 37 inches from the hole used to the tongue of the buckle, blue or brown denim jeans, grey socks and Brogue-type Oxford shoes that were approximately size 11. These items provide very little in the way of identification. A metal chain was located near the body giving investigators the impression that he may have hanged himself from an overhead branch.

The reason why this case is so vexing to me is the idea that even after all this time, *"no anthropological analysis was carried out on the long bones so this value is merely a non-scientific estimate."* How can we put an end to this mystery if investigators have not given the remains a fair scientific analysis? Without anthropological data on the deceased, can an accurate profile be created or used for an artist rendition?

The police declined a release of these records, claiming that it is unsolved and currently under investigation. Ask yourself, does this incident sound like it's an active investigation? When I submitted for the police report in 2020, I was told that the OPP did not have the file because it was never actually investigated by them and was in fact handled in another jurisdiction. I didn't believe them and appealed the file. It turns out they had the file all along. It's brief and heavily redacted, but some progress has been made. In 2016, the details of this discovery were added to CPIC. We can only hope that the right eyes will see this individual's profile and reunite this man with his identity and bring him home.

Provincial Park Bones
Algonquin Provincial Park is a recreational hub for outdoor enthusiasts, particularly those in Ontario's southern reaches. This is a vast woodland whose rocky outcrops, shimmering lakes and abundant wildlife make it a picturesque destination that draws in over 800,000 visitors each year. Portage routes zigzag through the expanse of wilderness that cross a maze of hiking trails, logging roads and other hidden treasures. It would truly take a lifetime to fully explore this outdoor playground.

In the shadow of this giant environment lies many hidden things. In early spring, there is a short window when the maples are still without their leaves. Spotted trout lilies wave in the wind and barren red trilliums yearn to flower. This short period of a week or two gives the wildflowers a chance to bloom, adding splashes of vibrance to the trailside. It is when the foliage is still low that the forest gives up its secrets. On April 19, 1980, while on an outing on the Hardwood Lookout trail, a hiker had spotted a white object some 50 metres back from the path. Beneath the bracken fern, a stark white skull glared like a beacon. The body of a human being had been strewn about.

The man's remains could not be identified but were estimated to have died there between July 1, 1971 and the spring of 1978. That would indicate some considerable decomposition. Authorities guessed his age between 18–29 years old. Based on the skull, it was determined he was Caucasian. The remains were in possession of a folding camp stove, an aluminum camper's pot with a lid, a black down-filled sleeping bag with a nylon outer shell, fragments of a 20-dollar bill and a black wallet with an 8-cent stamp, which was issued between July 1, 1971 and September 1, 1976 — the means of their time of death estimation. The clothing he left behind included low-cut "Greb" brand, size 11 boots; Levi Strauss jeans; a thick, black, knitted sweater; a khaki, green military-style jacket and a belt with a 36-inch waist.

This incident had some significance since I am a regular hiker and camper who enjoys visiting Algonquin park in the early spring.

The skull was missing the lower jawbone and had been sent to a forensic science lab in Toronto. Weeks later, investigators still could not determine the identity of the man. A write-up was printed in the paper that encouraged any and all help from the public. That was in 1980, and still nothing has been learned of this man.

The mystery just kept festering with me. I didn't understand how a man could have met with misadventure on a short trail so close to people and assistance. Knowing that police were desperate to make a positive ID, I reached out to them and requested the case file for more details. My request was denied. I then took the case to the IPC and launched an appeal of this decision, citing a number of reasons.

To be of any help, I needed to see this trail for myself, so instead of waiting around for the results of my appeal, I threw my backpack in my trunk, printed off a map and drove the more than three hours to highway 60, with hopes of adding another piece to this puzzle.

Initially, I missed the turn for the trailhead — it was completely out of sight and tucked behind me to the north. I pulled a U-turn and parked about 20 yards from the sign. I first noticed that I still had cell phone reception there, so if I got into any trouble, I wasn't so isolated. I laced my boots, shouldered my backpack, and filled my nose with the sweet smell of hardwood and earth. I could tell right away that the surrounding forest was rich and healthy, a completely green and humid paradise pulsing with life. I had passed a few young families on the way in, who were likely oblivious to the grim discovery that was made here years earlier. They were blissfully unaware of that glaring white skull that called me to the trail.

As if crossing some security perimeter, I was instantly accosted by insects. I had stumbled into their domain, and they weren't shy about it. Their biting welcome was a way to deter intruders from under the shady canopy I had just entered. To the right of the trail stood numbered trail markers stuck to thick wooden stakes, a friendly reminder that you were still on the path. I was looking for marker five, where the remains were discovered. As I passed each marker, I went through the scenarios of what could have happened to this person. I tried to trace the route I could only imagine that he took, but I was coming at this trail cold. Passing by markers one and two, I could only slow down briefly, as I was not interested in this section of the trail as much. The shade from the maples provided little change in temperature and acted more like a lid for the humid pressure cooker of bugs and blow down.

I passed marker three. As I drew nearer to the site, I couldn't help but feel a bit of heaviness every time I put my foot down. To know that just up ahead a fellow human being met their demise was not a feeling that brought me much comfort. The same giant white pines would have been standing when he passed through the area decades before me. At their 40-metre vantage point, they would have witnessed his every move and at the same time shielded his existence. Perhaps this was the cover he was looking for.

As marker four came into view, I began to get philosophical. I pondered how we knew so little about death still, its existence only held up by pillars of belief. When we go, do we leave something behind? Is there a piece of this man still left in the woods? Does this trail trap his ghost? I listened closely to my surroundings, which was mainly birds and the sawing hum of insects in my ear. At some points, their wings were so loud I felt like I was near heavy machinery.

The post for marker five stood out against a cliff with a near 90-degree drop-off. The bugs were thick here — each breath I was risking getting a mouthful of them. I observed the cliff; there was no clear way up or down. I tried to climb into the gorge, but I realized I was bound to be stuck down there for whatever hours that were left on my watch. I waited for a few hikers to pass before I could properly poke around. The woods were of average thickness on both sides of the rocky path. It would be possible to set up a stealth camp on either side of the trail if one were to hide behind the ridges that the landscape offered. I stood on an island of hemlock and, again, low-growing vegetation, where the wildflowers were no more vibrant here than the rest of the trail. For some reason, this person chose this spot to get off-trail and rest. We can't know why, but maybe because the ridges it offered were adequate cover for an overnight set up.

I tried to imagine this person walking along the trail between the gateway of oak trees. The low leaves of wych elm grabbing at his boots, the crunching gravel pathway … if he even made it that far. Did he reach the lookout point and walk back? I wondered how long he stayed on the trail before ducking into the forest. The cover of darkness made the most sense if one were stealth camping. He must have felt excited and anxious sneaking about in the silence, looking for a spot to settle down out of sight. He left no car in the parking lot, so he was either dropped off by someone or hiked in from somewhere else. If he had already hiked in, he would have been tired. Highway 60 is a long stretch to be walking on.

In the summer, this mystery man would have been shaded by the giant maples that dominate and choke out the light from the young trees that bow beneath. It brings flying insects, mushrooms, and stunted growth all around. If this man ventured out in the colder months when heavy blankets of snow shroud the park in silence, he likely would have found shelter under the towering hemlock in the area. Their groping branches intercept snowfall, giving way to shallow or no snow around their trunks.

It crossed my mind that maybe this person didn't want to be found. Maybe he removed himself from society on purpose, discarded his ID, and told no one where he was going.

An article in the *Huntsville Forester* described the clothes as badly decomposed and oddly laid out beside a tree instead of on the bones, leading investigators to believe that they had been removed before death.

Later in 1995, a lower jawbone was found by a family who was hiking the area, which initiated another search by police. This search brought about additional human remains that were examined by forensic anthropologist Dr. Kathy Gruspier, who concluded that it matched the other bones that were recovered. Despite this, the cause of death is still not known according to Detective Inspector Rob Matthews of the OPP criminal investigations branch.[80] At the time of this writing, very little progress has been made.

The fact that the man had removed his clothes raises suspicions of suicide. The clothes were not described as being torn or tossed about, so an altercation with another person or animal was not a question that was entertained. But if not for suicide, why then remove your clothes? It's possible that he was getting ready for bed and removed his clothes before climbing into his down sleeping bag. Goose and duck down-filled sleeping bags are considerably warmer than synthetic bags, and you wouldn't need to wear layers upon layers to stay warm. Perhaps then, in the middle of the night, he got up to relieve himself and, being without a lantern, got lost trying to retrace his steps. If he was camped out in early spring or late summer, he could have succumbed to the cold overnight temperatures. He could have also heard a noise and went to investigate and, as quoted by Detective Inspector Rob Matthews, "Then something happened during the night."[81] We will probably never really know what that "something" was, but we can still hope that the man's identity will one day be revealed.

With the help of his jaw and other bones, the OPP created a 3D facial reconstruction out of clay in order to spread the likeness of this man from coast to coast. In less than a month, they received 36 fresh tips from the public on this cold case. It was only because this case was publicized that those tips came in. This just goes to show that the public can and will help if they are allowed to. The appeal for public assistance sparked interest in the case and I have witnessed many people conduct their own investigations on their own time and with their own money. The public was working collectively, for the police, to solve this case, which cost law enforcement practically nothing. Here are the 3D models that were created based on the skull fragments found off the trail. I include them here with the hope that someone out there may recognize this man.

While out and about in the spring of 2019, my phone began to ring. On the other end was the mediator that was assigned to me to handle the appeal I had entered with the IPC for this mystery man. The mediator wanted to get an idea of what would be a satisfying resolution to my request. I was hoping for partial access to the file to gain a bit of clarity on the discovery and the search that followed. News articles state that the remains were found near a campsite, but there are no campsites in the area.

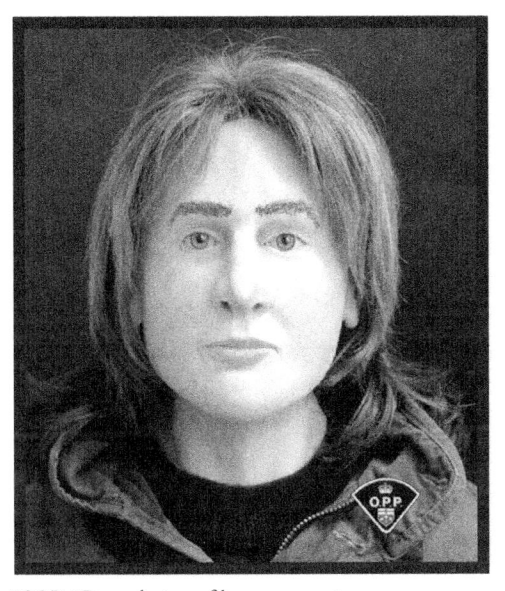

*OPP 3D rendering of human remains

I checked the archives for past campsites and there were none. I reviewed the old maps of the area from the 1970s, and the forest was very similar to how it is today. It's likely that he was not a registered visitor, or the park office would have had his name or alias and reservation details. This meant that he was camping illegally, but it was never hinted at by the media.

I explained my frustrations to the mediator that this case can and will only be solved if the public is involved. It's exasperating when the police refuse to cooperate on such things, taking all, but giving nothing. They continue to thwart their own responsibilities. Simply put, they need to help us, help them.

The appeal went on and on throughout the summer of 2019, when my phone would ring with a response from the other side of the table. It was a frustrating process because the police were just denying requests for more information, but from what we have already learned, they are simultaneously expecting the public to solve mysteries with the bare minimum to work with. I was able to make some headway by getting the police to confirm that this was not a homicide. If no foul play was suspected, then there would be no conflict in releasing information. There would be no future court proceedings in a matter of misadventure.

I was informed that even though the case was not criminal in nature, I would have to pay for a release of all the documents. The fee they were asking was over $1,000 for this case and a second case of human remains found in Washago, Ontario that I had been working on. To give you an idea of the size of the file, I asked to drop the Washago case to better understand the estimate, and the fee was only scaled back a few hundred dollars.

I found myself once again stuck with a bill from the *Freedom of Information Act*. There was no estimate on the number of pages in that report. I told them I'd like to find out what I'd be getting before forking over that amount of money. I was told by the mediator that the Ministry censor would not release a single piece of paper to me for less than $400. In other words, the police were asking the public to solve this case, but they wanted us to pay hefty fees to do so.

I doubt if I will ever get more information on this specific incident. On the other hand, the police have made an effort to spotlight the case in the media by circulating the 3D model for publication.

This is not the only 3D model made from a skull, either. The RCMP has enlisted the help of students from the New York Academy of Art to create facial reconstructions from clay, based on unidentified human skulls. Coroners and medical examiners have submitted 15 skulls (14 from British Columbia and 1 from Nova Scotia) that were recovered between 1972 and 2019 and were in suitable condition for the artists to work from.

In January of 2020, the RCMP released the clay reconstructions on their website and encouraged the public to help to identify the faces. Chief Superintendent Marie-Claude Arsenault of the RCMP commented on the importance of this initiative:

> Every face tells a story and these are 15 individuals who deserve to have their stories told. We started with unidentified remains, then a face, and we are hoping to end each of their stories with a name. We are asking the public to take a close look at the faces and the descriptions and submit a tip if they have any information about any of the

individuals. Any detail, no matter how small it may seem, could be the missing piece of the puzzle.[82]

There are a few factors that make a human skull eligible for such a worthwhile program. The condition of the skull, the likelihood of recognition, and the existence or lack of other information are just some of them.

Facial reconstruction of human remains will go a long way to help close some of these cases, but again, those resolutions will only come from the public. The right person must see those faces. Only then can police continue their investigation, which would involve confirming the identification through DNA or dental records. This will be the first time the RCMP has partnered with the program, which began in 2015. Since its inception, the artistic abilities and visual representation of these reconstructions have led to four confirmations in missing persons cases in the United States.[83]

I hope that the recent push will help solve the mystery of the Algonquin Park man, but we also should consider that he was not a local. It should be shared with our American neighbours and so on. If a person goes missing and there is the possibility that they may be from the United States, then the investigator assigned to the case should post it on NCIC, as stated in the police literature.[84] To test this protocol, I reached out to both the CPIC and NCIC to confirm if the case of the Algonquin Park man was indeed included on their site database. I quickly learned that they wouldn't speak to me because I had no law enforcement credentials.

Further to that, there is literature to expand the investigator's reach beyond North America if need be:

> If appropriate to the circumstances, the investigator should consider contacting the INTERPOL unit at the RCMP to issue an INTERPOL Yellow Notice. Assistance may be obtained from the NCMPUR. The Yellow Notice can make a missing person visible to the international law enforcement community.[85]

All unidentified human remains cases should be kept on the CPIC website until the identity is confirmed by a coroner or forensic anthropologist. Maintaining the database gives international investigators a chance to solve cold or even future cases. Missing people are not always reported right away, and in fact could come years later.

We now have to rely on police opinion and belief before a coroner can confirm a possible match. It's a vetting process rife with errors. It is this disconnect that causes me concern.[86]

DNA technology is relied upon to resolve most of these older cases or where only skeletal remains are recovered.

DNA

For the longest time, I believed in the idea of a DNA database made up of samples taken from unidentified human remains being linked to missing persons cases across the country. This would be the most logical, foolproof and swiftest way to solve two unsolved mysteries at once and eliminate a backlog of cases. You'd be hard-pressed to find others that disagree with this concept, but the startling fact is that this DNA database did not exist until very recently.

Canada's National DNA Data Bank (NDDB) was established in June of 2000 and is operated by the RCMP Forensic Science and Identification Services. Its focus is solely to assist Canadian law enforcement with criminal investigations. It wasn't until December 2014 that the bank was expanded by the RCMP to assist in the investigation of missing persons and unidentified human remains. It then took another four years (March 6, 2018) for the amendments to come into being, meaning for 18 years since the creation of the databank, it was not used as a source for closing these types of cases. Why an amendment was needed to expand the use of the Data Bank is beyond me, and why the idea took 18 years to actualize is another riddle I can't wrap my head around, but we are told that it was due to system upgrades, new staffing and training and the development of new procedures. With no new actual DNA data required to implement the program, I can't understand the lack of urgency here.

Canadian police officials have openly admitted how beneficial such a databank would be:

> Sean Jenkinson and Jim Gurney of the Edmonton Police Service have stated that inclusion of DNA would assist in identification of remains and alert police to homicide cases. A Conservative Saskatchewan MP, Ray Boughen, has twice presented a petition to the federal government to collect the DNA of missing persons.[87]

Judy Peterson fought long and hard for a missing persons databank shortly after the federal government launched the national system. Her daughter, Lindsey Nicholls vanished on Vancouver Island in 1993 and she has been looking for her ever since. Once Peterson learned of the databank, she sent a sample of Lindsey's DNA in to see if the RCMP could find a trace of her among the crime scene DNA they had collected. She was told that DNA profile searches on missing people was not possible.

Peterson's campaign would finally expand Canada's national databank to include DNA from missing persons across the country as well as profiles from unidentified remains. She named the bill *Lindsey's Law* after her daughter. Lindsey was 14 when she vanished on a rural road in Comox Valley, and at the time of this publication has never been found.

Constable Sean Jenkinson went on to say that the database would "...be the first mechanism of its kind, in Canada anyways, it can bring a lot of closure to police agencies, and more importantly, to the families."[88] Prior to this announcement, the police were only able to request DNA samples if evidence of a crime had been committed. Missing persons cases seem to be a lot more complicated, and it's not a crime to go missing.

Canada has fallen short when it comes to incorporating proven, positive practices, and it happened once again with the DNA database. We don't know why that is. According to an article from 2012, a similar data bank was introduced in the United States in 2003; it has reportedly helped solve more than 500 cases.

Pearce touches on the issues and controversies of collecting and storing DNA for future identification in her work, *An Awkward Silence*. Up until recently, this practice was unheard of, even though police officials admitted that the use of DNA samples would be invaluable to solving countless cases.

Without DNA having been extracted from the missing person's belongings or from a living relative, if the remains of the person turn up in another province or country, the family may never be notified. In long-term cases, DNA may be the only way to confirm the identity of a missing person as unidentified remains. This is why missing persons cases and human remains cases are directly linked. Especially when local sources haven't yielded results, DNA profiles would be helpful because they are searchable on a national and international level. Profiles are now stored on the National Missing Persons DNA Program (NMPDP).

Today, the NDDB is split into sections known as indexes, which include: the Relatives of Missing Person Index (RMI), the Missing Persons Index (MPI), the Human Remains Index (HRI), the Victims Index (VI), and the Voluntary Donors Index (VDI). The RCMP are now open to accepting DNA samples from human remains, personal possessions and family members. Now, the DNA bank can compare samples with approximately 500,000 DNA profiles.

Even those without scientific training and education know the power and importance of DNA. The technology is relatively new and keeps changing, but there is no question that it is an asset to unidentified remains cases and will soon be the only way to close some of the older incidents. Because it is a national database, police forces, medical examiners and coroners from across Canada have equal access to the service.

The most important index is the RMI. Any DNA profiles provided by relatives of missing people serve two purposes. They can be used to help confirm the identity of a person whose DNA profile is already in the missing persons index, and they can be used to identify human remains found at a later date if no other DNA samples or relatives are available. Relatives of the long-term missing do not live forever, so without a DNA profile from them, there is no hope to resolve old cases.

According to Pearce, the U.S., UK and Australia have all collected and stored DNA samples to match up with unsolved cases, so why is Canada so late to the table?

That is not to say that DNA has never been used in a missing person or unidentified remains investigation, or that all forces are not going above and beyond. Pearce found that the Vancouver Police Department were able to obtain DNA in the form of pap smear slides to compare with women on the missing persons list. According to her research, the slides were set aside by the BC Cancer Control Agency, but not given to police. They were stored for safe keeping and privacy to ensure they would not be destroyed or lost in varying protocols and retention periods. They were the perfect opportunity to compare DNA directly with found remains. This is a good example of a compromise between protecting privacy but also cooperating to solve a mystery:

> On December 31, 2001 an agreement between Vancouver PD, RCMP and BC cancer control agency allowed the slides of 45 women to be tested for DNA to compare against found human remains.[89]

It's this type of forward thinking and cooperation that will help bring closure to these cases.

It was not long after the national missing persons DNA program was put in place that we started seeing results. In October of 2017, Calgary police reported finding a dead man inside a tent along the Nose Creek Pathway, south of 16th Avenue. His body was determined to be in the tent between five and six months without being noticed, and therefore was too decomposed to make a positive ID using methods like fingerprinting. All that could be done was to gather a DNA profile, put the remains in storage and wait for someone to report their missing loved one. However, not all families are tight-knit and many have estranged relatives, meaning there is no guarantee that they would be reported missing.

Once the DNA Program was put in place a year later, the DNA profile was submitted, and it didn't take long for a match to come back. Finally, the man was identified, two years after his body was recovered. The police were able to close the case on the matter and notify family members.[90] This proves the value of having a program like this in place. Imagine what could have been accomplished if it was in place decades before.

As the NCMPUR illustrates, "DNA testing can be performed even on cases of decomposed, burned or very old remains and may be the only remaining connection to the missing person."[91]

The technology is now at a point where genetic information can be collected from soil. This is known as Environmental DNA. If a body decomposed to the point where it was not recoverable, samples could be taken from the environment to amplify the DNA of the suspected target of interest. The technology has had success in the past but is likely not available to most law enforcement agencies.

If no DNA samples exist and everyone involved has passed on, these long-term cases can never be cleared. The OPP believes that there would still be a chance from the use of dental records to compare to current unidentified remains, however many of these records do not exist for long-term cases, so the chances of them being solved diminish every year.

The quality of dental records is not as meticulous as one might think. If a record does exist, it could be as vague as "filling in upper left first molar," which would not be enough to confirm or exclude the person's identity.

On average, 6-12 unidentified human remains are found and reported in Ontario annually.[92] Many of these individuals are identified over the ensuing months. As for the rest, they are added to the growing total.

There are currently 370 unidentified remains in Canada listed on the RCMP's website — 186 are from Ontario. This number fluctuates with new cases being shuffled on and off the website, and of course more remains are being found each year. It's a frightening number, as each digit is linked to a family who is either looking, hoping, or blissfully unaware of the state of their loved one. But these are only the ones posted online, we know there are over 750 sets of human remains in drawers, boxes, bags and freezers, some never getting publicity. Not only is this a staggering number, but the authorities that should know the exact amount actually do not.[93] Keep in mind, these bags of bones are actually human beings.

Some of these individuals are doomed forever to remain nameless and will go on being identified only as *Bad Teeth Lady*, *Bloated Body* or *Lower Jaw Man*. All these souls play a morbid guessing game with coroners and medical examiners across the country. Each day, another round of "Who Do You Think We Are?"

12

Forbidden Theory

"He had no wish to face whatever lurked in the unknown darkness, just beyond the little circle of light cast by the lamp of science."
— Arthur C. Clarke

Everyone has a theory as to the cause of vanishing people around the world. They range from the mundane to the fantastic. Our minds often race to murder when we think of a cold case, but once I dug deeper into these stories it was clear that there were no facts to support that theory. For homicide to be considered in the previously mentioned stories, there would need to be a group of murderers working together. They would need to operate at a remarkable speed and be able to keep their mouths shut. This would be the only way I could imagine achieving such fantastic disappearances without evidence.

We have also touched on a variety of reasons why people may not be found, such as changes in weather and the challenges of navigating a punishing landscape, but it still does not explain how someone can be there one second and then completely vanish without leaving a trace the next. Is it possible that the dogs were not able to track for other reasons? There may be reason to believe that perhaps these people were no longer in the area last seen.

In the absence of evidence, I believe all theories should be addressed based on what we know. Logically speaking, if we cannot be certain of the facts of a disappearance, then no idea can be confidently eliminated. Theories about how or why people go missing may not lead to solving the mystery, but they do lead to valuable discussions and the brainstorming of new ideas. Since virtually nothing is proven about the disappearances of the men and women I have highlighted earlier, I would be negligent to ignore the theories that have the capability to cause them, no matter how outlandish they may seem. These theories may be too wild for some, but this section was reserved specifically to lay such things on the table.

It's frightening to think that at any moment the ground you walk on could crumble and disappear before your next step. The unthinkable does happen. Sinkholes are a very real geological threat and a theory not often discussed. Sinkholes form in many ways, but most often occur naturally when rain or flood water seeps into ground cavities and collects. There it eats away at corrodible rock, such as limestone or mineral layers like gypsum and anhydrite. The water erodes the subsurface causing fissures, caverns and eventually cave-ins that lead to disaster.

The scariest thing about sinkholes is that many of them appear suddenly and without warning. Somewhere along your commute to work or your favourite walking path may be a gnawing underground trickle, until one day the water gets its way, and you never make it to your destination.

Sinkholes can form at random and could be as little as one foot or as large as acres in diameter. Their depth can be a mere pothole or disappear into a black void of 100 feet or more. There are reports of these random voids opening in the middle of busy city streets and even in people's bedrooms, so why not in the middle of the forest during a hunting trip?

Ontario is not devoid of limestone. It reaches down from the Hudson Bay Lowlands and creeps under well known cities such as Kenora, Thunder Bay, Espanola, and Sudbury.

A sinkhole near North Bay grew so large that it tore into both northbound and southbound lanes, shutting down Highway 11 in April of 2013.

Five kilometres north of Wawa, The Northern Lights Motel received an unplanned renovation when torrential rains caused a sinkhole to grow underneath it. "[The hotel] is gone," said Constable Monique Baker of the Ontario Provincial Police. "It sunk into a sinkhole."[94]

Another uninvited hole opened in a backyard on Gilbert Street, in the community of Hanmer, in June of 2014. The resident noticed the ground give beneath his feet, and when he poked it with a shovel, the earth burped open an unsightly pit. Experts believed the hole was caused by weakened substrate from an old mine. Sinkholes have swallowed people in the past, so it's not a question of "if" they can cause disappearances. The problem with this idea is that sinkholes remain for quite some time after they open, spreading wider instead of shrinking, so any search party would be bound to stumble on them or see them from the air sooner or later.

However, mother nature has amazed us before, so perhaps there is one remarkable way it could cover its tracks. Notable weather events have been known to occur during some disappearances, and that includes heavy rains. There is such a thing as flash floods. If one were to be swallowed up by these yawning traps, who's to say that those torrential rains wouldn't fill the newly formed hole within a matter of hours and voila, a brand-new lake has appeared covering evidence, trees and the victim with it. Not many would question the appearance of a small lake in the middle of the woods, most would assume it had always been there. This is especially true of searchers who have never been to the area.

Mine shafts are the sister theory to sinkholes. While weakened, abandoned mining tunnels have caused cave-ins; they can also pose a danger on their own. Northern Ontario is like Swiss cheese when it comes to groundwork. Places have been drilled by fortune seekers and drilled again. Towns have risen and fallen due to mining rushes and glittering ground veins that tease of bright futures. But these veins eventually dry up or the prospector runs out of funds and is forced to walk away. We're not just talking about large mining operations either. There are private and unregulated dig sites out there, that once abandoned, can be camouflaged by foliage, posing a hazard to those who leave the trail.

A quicksand-like substance covers up to 1.2 million kilometres squared or 12% of Canada's surface.[95] This "quicksand" is known locally as muskeg, a name given by the Cree to low-lying swamps or bogs. It is a soup of water, mosses and partially dead vegetation that cannot fully decay because it remains frozen for a lengthy period of the year. This sucking ground of the northern woods is one of the more natural theories we have yet to touch on. The thought of minding your own business in the woods, walking along to check your traps or stake a mining claim and accidentally stepping into one of these pits is terrifying. These surfaces are scattered where people have gone missing, as I, and some of the newspaper reports, have mentioned earlier.

There is no telling how deep muskeg can reach, but some report it can be as deep as 100 feet and slurps down anything unlucky enough to enter. There's an interesting anecdote in *The Black Soldiers Who Built the Alaska Highway: A History of Four U.S. Army Regiments in the North:* "Unfortunately, until the Corps of Engineers mastered the muskeg, many tractors and other vehicles were simply swallowed up." A demolitionist named Fred Spencer said that he had lost dozens of vehicles in it. Staff Sergeant of the 95th, Otis E. Lee said "I lost two bulldozers, D-7s, D-8s, in muskeg. They were just sinking and I had nothing to yank them out of there. Gurgle, gurgle, gurgle."[96] These diesel giants can weigh anywhere from 31,000 pounds to 66,000 pounds.

Gurgle indeed.

Entire train engines were swallowed in the late 1800s when tracks were laid down through an unstable area of the swampy stuff. A thin layer of soil hides these hazards and was responsible for swallowing a track seven times.[97] Our heaviest and toughest equipment is still no match for nature. If muskeg can swallow moose, tractors and trains, it can surely gobble up people too.

When discussing missing people, one will often hear others say that "people don't just disappear." This statement is not only misleading and uninformed, but it is also not true. People can in fact disappear, and I have named some of those people here. Perhaps the most interesting theory that has yet to be tabled and discussed is the possibility of spontaneous human combustion in the wild. For those unfamiliar, this is the rare phenomenon in which anyone at anytime can burst into flames and be entirely consumed within a short period of time. Cases of spontaneous combustion are well-documented since it involves many facets of investigation, from first responders, medical examiners, fire chiefs, fire marshals, arson investigators, coroners and claims investigators. The phenomenon is controversial in that some medical professionals deem it ridiculous that a person's body can ignite from within, and yet at the same time, are unable to conclude why in fact it continues to happen. Spontaneous combustion is not completely understood, but that doesn't mean it is in anyway supernatural.

Without warning, any person can turn into a raging fireball in the absence of a known, identifiable burn agent. This combustion is reported to be so severe that it has the equivalent to burning at a continued minimum temperature of 3000 degrees Fahrenheit for 12 uninterrupted hours. However, most cases take much less than that time to occur, reducing the victim to ash in minutes. This heat is double what is used in cremation chambers. In some cases, the extremities of the victims have been left behind — for example, a single foot or piece of the head — but it is possible for all traces of the victim to be burnt to a crisp.

The fact that the human body can ignite from within and be consumed more effectively than crematorium conditions for reasons presently unknown to mainstream science, is a cause for concern. The blaze is completely localized to the individual, meaning that any trees, clothing or furniture nearby will not be burnt, singed or otherwise discoloured by the heat or flames. In one such case, a flammable stack of newspapers sat undisturbed beside the remains of one of these victims of combustion. The phenomenon can strike the young and the old, and if it were to happen outdoors in a wilderness setting, it would leave little evidence as to the person having been there. Such a theory can be applied to most of the stories in this book and makes a more convincing argument than sinkholes.

If these people began to combust as they staked claims, hunted, picked berries, and other such activities, then it wouldn't be a surprise that search teams couldn't recover a single trace. The ashes would be scattered like pollen, and before you know it, they would be dust in the wind. There would be no evidence that they had combusted based on their environment. Researchers hypothesize that something occurs with the body's thermogenesis or some malfunction of the hypothalamus gland, which is responsible for controlling the temperature of the body. Spontaneous combustion is just as unnerving as the missing people phenomenon itself. Both have been part of our world since the beginning, and we know very little about them.

Many people I have spoken with tend to believe in what folklore has to say instead of the mainstream scientific community. Perhaps this is due to folklore being around much longer than science, serving as a wise grandfather to our adolescent civilizations. While others may scoff at such beliefs, perhaps it's time we all sit upon its proverbial knee and listen.

The Indigenous peoples of North America share our fears of disappearing and have their own theories, which can be found in pictographs, carvings and ceremonial performances. To them, the deep woods are home to frightening beasts of folklore. Coast Salish bands of the west introduced us to the giant hairy thing we now call Sasquatch. Stories range from docile creatures who trade and protect to spiritual beasts that can traverse other realms. There are stories of them kidnapping women and children for ungodly purposes and killing men effortlessly, as if swatting a bug. The Cree and Ojibway warn us of the Wendigo that stalks the dense borders of the Great Lakes and the impenetrable forests of the north country. This bloodthirsty spirit is rumoured to possess even the most honourable men in times of hardship. Many non-Indigenous now report recent encounters with what matches descriptions of the Wendigo, said to move with the speed of the wind. The Wendigo stems from cautionary tales of greed, isolation, and selfishness, but is it possible that such a creature could exist and be taking people? These legends lack serious study, so we'd never really know.

Indigenous peoples have passed down stories for hundreds of years of horrific creatures that live just out of sight in forbidden groves they dare not go. And those are just the ones we're told about. They whisper of monsters in the North woods with names hard for white men to pronounce, and so they look for validation in carved totems or rock paintings on the sides of cliffs, or in the middle of nowhere. Not far from Lake Nipigon are stories of the Memegwesiwijiw, or "the little people of the mountain." These are small, fairy-like trickster beings that have a reputation to tease and torment. They'd steal fish from the nets of the Ojibway and speed away lightning quick. They are said to possess the ability to move between worlds, and the natural cracks and openings in the cliffs are sometimes regarded as their "doorways." No one would ever know if these hairy creatures took a human being with them to the other side. Pictographs portray their tiny forms doodled in ochre on the rock frames of these doorways. Fairy Point in Missinaibi Lake is a similar site where fairy tricksters dwell and is home to over 100 pictographs. Similar still is the Mannegishi of Cree folklore, who delight in tipping canoes and drowning unsuspecting paddlers. Given the amount of water in Ontario, it's only natural to have a wealth of monsters who lurk beneath the waves. The great horned serpent known as Misiginebig is affiliated with numerous tribes and is said to eat humans. There is also the horrific water panther, Mishibizhiw, which gives many canoeists hesitation before looking over their gunwale into deep water. The

Nebaunaubaequae is a mermaid-like entity that entices travellers ever closer until they meet their watery end.

From the water, we move to the air and into the domain of Pauguk, the death spirit in the form of a flying skeleton. His shrill cries are said to lure people into the darkness to kill them. Pauguk is featured in the story of Hiawatha as a being mankind must fear: "Saw the fiery eyes of Pauguk / Saw the eyes of Death glare at him / Heard his voice call in the darkness…"[98] Haunting spirits and powerful entities are believed to lure people away with deceitful cries for help or mournful weeping.

Back in the West, the Tsonoqua or Dzunuk'wa is a dark-skinned, matted-haired giant, always depicted with pursed lips that send a haunting whistle throughout the forests. She kidnaps people and carries them off into the mountains by way of a woven basket, with the intention to eat them.

The Bakbakwakanooksiewae is a multi-mouthed bird spirit, known to live at the end of the world in the most remote places, who will seek out vulnerable humans for food.

We have lakes and mountains named after these creatures for a reason, many of us forgetting their meaning, but still they remain, sometimes untouched and seldom visited, leaving the monsters to thrive in solitude. Indigenous tribes have totem poles depicting many of the creatures I mentioned, their features carved beneath or above more common animals like the bear, wolf or beaver.

I have heard stories of adults, both fearless and experienced, who have encountered things in the woods that they could not explain. Outdoors folk have reported hearing strange, bone-chilling howls, finding odd footprints or experiencing feelings of dread. They emerge from the woods shaken and overwhelmed with fear at the sight of something unnerving or the sound of something that made their blood run cold. Perhaps they encountered one of these voracious beasts of Indigenous lore or heard the screams of one of their victims in the far-off hills.

Early settlers witnessed some of these mythical creatures as they carved out a new world. Trapper stories were passed down to their children about such nightmarish fiends. Oversized wolf-like prints have been reported along with lightning quick glimpses of upright hairy monsters. The logging camps shared tall tales of mountain devils around the nightly crackle of fire, and Jesuit journals tell us dark stories from the 1660s. Early explorers like Christopher Columbus, Alexander Mackenzie and even Samuel de Champlain left us stories of monsters in their journals. They spoke freely and didn't fear ridicule when they repeated these stories, so I don't know why modern society should. Perhaps they kept these stories in the back of their mind as a safety measure when they hiked through a wild, new world, but at the same time, always having a hand ready to unsheathe their blade. These legends have stuck around for a reason and will continue to snowball as time goes on and we slowly rediscover our past.

The northern forests are dark and dense, not always fit for human feet. In fact, many places have never seen human visitors. The truth is that we still don't know what's out there. In relation to the history of time, we are still toddlers in the universe, and for that reason we should be allowed to explore our world (on hands and knees if need be), tasting and touching what we do not understand without mockery or ridicule. We still have much to learn, and that includes what might be out there. Is it not possible that we have yet to learn about unknown animals some would describe as "monsters"?

There are believers who are adamant that these missing people are being taken by something unusual. For this group, evidence of this "something" is not necessary. The fear of the unknown and of possibility is enough to keep them shut up indoors. Wild theories and speculation have been known to follow missing persons cases. While most police officers and relatives of the missing may not entertain these unconventional ideas, tales of vanishing people have always found themselves on the same shelf beside books of monsters, myths and legends. The reason being that they are all equally mysterious. While they may not be related, the paranormal classifies anything that is not normal, and as we have discussed at length, vanishing without a trace fits into that category.

The Good People or Fae folk have been blamed for mysterious disappearances for hundreds of years. Nearly every culture has tales of the Fae, who go by many names and are said to be quite vengeful. Historical texts repeat anecdotes where they have taken people against their will to the fairy world for long periods of time. These are always wilderness disappearances related to trees or water. I have come upon writings from the 1600s where people vanished at the hands of these woodland sprites. They can shape-shift into pretty much any form they choose, depending on their motives. I have touched upon the global folklore of nature beings in my first book, and so I am aware that they possess the capabilities to appear and disappear at will, with whomever they like. No matter how experienced we get in the wilderness, we can never match the skill of the moose, the bear or The Good People.

Perhaps the most popularized theory as to why people are inexplicably vanishing is the idea that they are carried off by unidentified flying objects. Ontario is not without its UFO sightings. Sudbury and Kenora have both had a high rate of sightings (known as flaps) that made months of newspaper headlines. The activity was prevalent enough that the RCMP and the Department of National Defence took a special interest in it and began keeping tabs on the unexplained lights in the sky. People have returned with stories of being taken aboard unidentified craft and traveling great distances. Their tales are remarkable and surprisingly detailed but are of no benefit to the actual abductee themselves. These people come forward with stories at their own societal peril, and more people are continuing to do so. Perhaps some of these people don't come back and are therefore unable to relate such tales. The life forms that fly saucers from out of our great lakes or into our thermosphere confiscate unsuspecting citizens for who knows what, yet with all our interviews, evidence, testimony, recovered implants, what do we really know about them? More books have been written about the UFO theory than any other, and it has been a phenomenon that has drawn in the brightest brains our planet has to offer.

Both fairy and UFO activity are said to be accompanied by bad weather. You may have noticed that in some mysterious disappearances, a storm (as one example) quickly follows and impedes the search effort. Some theorize that this is a symptom of whatever is causing the disappearances. It's amusing that people on either side of the argument will use the evidence and beliefs of the opposing side to help build up their case. The truth is that we, at the present time, cannot measure what phenomenon weather events are related to or if they are even related at all, but it does provide some stimulating discussion.

If you subscribe to the Flat Earth Theory, then the mystery of disappearances wouldn't be a mystery at all. We've heard the ideas of the world being as flat as a plate, leaving us to walk and sail at our own risk. Samuel Shenton founded the International Flat Earth Research Society in 1956 and had his own theory about disappearing people: "Beyond the edge is a vast ice barrier — from beyond which no man has ever returned."[99] He believed that beyond this barrier could be thousands of people who have been reported missing — literally walking off the edge of the world. Does this theory apply to all disappearances or only those that disappear near the edges? I wonder who or what defines our edges. Could one of them slice through the wilderness of Ontario?

As we delve further into the circulating theories, some barely tethered to our evolved understandings of physics and biology, we must progress with an open mind. I have given a liberal number of words to "natural" explanations, but we have been tiptoeing around an often-disregarded possibility, and so I think we need to come face to face with it here. There is no hiding from the supernatural aspects of human experience, whether they are found at the end of the gravel road or appear before the eyes of Sunday churchgoers. The supernatural hangs over our natural world like a bank of impenetrable fog, of which we cannot grasp its entirety.

Is there something else at work here?

What if there were certain disappearing points connected to other places in our timeline that we never knew were there?

They go by many names, but we are essentially talking about the same anomaly: Portals, Time slips, Window areas, Time traps, Black Holes, Worm Holes, Time Tunnels, Whirlwinds, Stargates, Doorways, Vortices and other Zones of Obscurity. Such ideas are often categorized as fiction, but theoretical physicists say that they exist and are conducting new experiments that may soon expose these hidden aspects of reality. I am not a scientist, so I will not begin to try to explain the possibility of portals and dimensions, but if what I understand is correct, these places could have beings like us (or not) and strange animals and plants. This isn't asking too much of the imagination if you consider our place in the solar system alone, but what if the beings there were not indigenous to that dimension? Do unseen portals exist in our midst and are people accidentally stepping through them?

One might think such theories to be of the crackpot variety, but without a full grasp of our world and its capabilities, we cannot definitively say this. It was always thought that crackpot theories only originated from crackpots, but many of the theories I mention here come from scholars with PhDs. The scientist approaches their hypothesis with an open mind, and so should we. While recovering evidence of a lost civilization off the coast of Bahamas, Dr. Joseph Mason Valentine, renowned explorer, archaeologist and PhD, expressed a theory about where the inhabitants of these ancient cultures could have vanished to: "They are still here, but in a different dimension as a result of a magnetic phenomenon that could have been set up by a UFO."[100] An interesting theory, but to cap it off, he throws a UFO in the mix, as if it wasn't strange enough.

German scientist Dr. Maximillian Hern theorized the idea of holes in our visible world that suck up physical matter and cough it out somewhere else. He published his findings in *"Vershivinden und Seine Theorie"* or *"Disappearance and Theory Thereof."* It was thought that these empty spots of ether appeared at random, lasting only seconds, and would be powerful enough to destroy all physical matter that entered them. In the newspaper *The Christian Union,* Hern is quoted as saying:

> The process cannot proceed gradually, because there is no possible gradation from what is material to what is mere vacuity. These gaps or rents may occur anywhere at any moment and whatever happens to be there when they occur will be snapped up into empty space-which is the invisible world in the twinkling of an eye.[101]

Could this explain some of the mysterious disappearances?

An issue of *Beyond Reality* describes these portals in great detail and includes a few jaw-dropping examples of people who have not just looked at but walked through these "window areas."

On the afternoon of October 14, 1964, Steven R. Miller, a biologist from Baton Rouge, his wife Della, and their three teenage children were visiting the Little Bighorn Battlefield National Monument near Crow Agency, Montana. Just after noon, Miller and his youngest son, Steven Jr., ascended a small hill to gaze out onto what was once a body-strewn battleground. There was no sign of approaching active weather, and the family was treated to a sunny, warm afternoon of sightseeing. Mr. Miller's family was not far behind and they were all witnesses to the event that was about to happen. Without warning, Steven Jr. ran ahead shouting that he could feel the ground move. Before his father could grab him, the young boy ran between two sun-made pillars that had appeared on the field. Other encounters of these pillars are described as two faint vertical lines traced by the suns rays that parallel each other 12 feet apart, with the top joined at a peak. The space between the doorway is said to reflect a bizarre, almost double image, as though the ground and grasses beneath it blended together. It took less than five seconds and Steve Miller Jr. had vanished right before his family, "...as though physically disintegrating into the environment."[102]

Other tourists ran to the spot upon hearing the family's screams. Mr. Miller ran after the boy and disappeared into the pillar formation and out of sight. After 16 minutes, the article states that Miller and his son re-emerged looking horrified. They were shaking, the boy looked sick and their hands and clothing were covered with blood. The details of the case are so shocking that I will let Mr. Miller tell the rest. After he ran into the sun-streamed doorway, the landscape around him completely changed:

> That's when I suddenly became frightened. Behind me was nothing but wide open plain and clear sky for as far as the eye could see. The area my son and I found ourselves in was nothing like the park we had been in just moments before. I called my wife by name, and our children. We both did, but there was no answer. No sound at all in fact, only our echoes piercing the mountains. The stench of death and decay was everywhere. It was real, believe me. It was so bad that my son vomited on the ground.

Miller gives details of the corpses strewn at their feet, which they tripped over as they stepped backward in the direction they came. Miller then describes something like a "whirlwind" that spat them back out (or forwards) to the present day. The report stated that their hands and clothing were blood-stained, and after being sent for analysis, it was determined that the blood did not belong to them. The article supports the claim with sworn testimony from the family, police and witnesses that saw the father and son vanish and return through this strange doorway. Imaginations delight on what could have happened had the doorway completely vanished before their return.

I could not locate any family members for an interview, Miller being such a common name, but if we are to accept this story, it could explain how people can vanish in the blink of an eye. But if these tales of "window areas" are too hard to swallow, perhaps there is more of an argument to be made for teleportation. There is evidence to suggest that teleportation is a natural occurrence in our world, it is only a force of nature yet to be understood. Before electricity was discovered, it would have been considered as woo as witchcraft. Our history is full of other examples of "mystical" discoveries, once laughed at or feared but now as controlled and mundane as a light switch.

Who better to speak of teleportation than author Charles Fort, the man who coined the term in 1931? Just mentioning the word conjures up images of science fiction, and I would agree that the idea is more scientific than supernatural. It's possible that teleportation could be as natural a force as gravity.

There is actually more evidence to support the existence of teleportation than there is to support the existence of a man named Vital Vachon.

Fort believed teleportation was a naturally occurring force in our world and that people, objects and animals could step into the path of this force and be relocated to another point on the planet. He took it one step further, saying that humans may possess the ability to access this force (some already doing so) and use it to travel across vast distances by choice. A teleportation phenomenon would work in one of two ways: either it is orchestrated by someone or something, or there are certain places in our environment that are directly connected to other parts of the world — a short-cut yet undiscovered, a tether between two points on the map.

Are there places humans just shouldn't step? It's frightening to think of human beings walking around unaware of these invisible bear traps that are ready to spring indiscriminately on us at any moment.

One side effect of this type of rapid transit could be amnesia, specifically imposed on those who teleport accidentally. Is it possible that some of these missing people could have been teleported elsewhere and are now living a new life under a different name because they don't remember who they were originally?

Charles Fort did not shy away from events of high strangeness and recorded such events from around the globe in several volumes. He presented his research material plainly, admitting that he, like the rest of us, was left in the dark about such things. He hypothesized that sudden appearances of people, animals and things, were the result of sudden disappearances from other places:

> Little frogs, showers of stones, and falls of water — and they have repeated, indicating durations of transportory currents to persisting appearing points, suggesting the existence of persisting disappearing points somewhere else.[103]

And what comes down had to go up at some point…

Are "disappearing points" and "reappearing points" scattered around the globe? Are there paranormal potholes randomly placed in forests and fields that vacuum people up, only to spit them out somewhere else? Fort could have been right. By tracking and clipping hundreds of newspaper articles, he was starting to see a pattern. He didn't understand what was going on, but he felt that to ignore this phenomenon would be a much worse thing than to entertain a new idea.

Fort shares with us a story from the *Chatham News* (Kent, England), in which a naked man appeared on the street on January 6, 1914. The article stated that the weather was bitterly cold when the man appeared from nowhere. He was running up and down High Street in Chatham and could not communicate any details about who he was or how he got there:

> This naked man of Chatham appeared suddenly. Nobody had seen him on his way to his appearing-point. His clothes were searched for, but could not be found. Nowhere near Chatham was anybody reported missing.[104]

The story is meant to prompt us with the peculiar question: was this naked man of Chatham teleported from somewhere else? There are many cases where people vanish and reappear some time later without memory (a side effect of long distance travel) and this is the perfect example of one.

Upon reading this account, I couldn't help but be reminded of the story mentioned earlier in which clothes were left abandoned at the edge of The Blanche River. When searchers failed to recover a body and no person was reported missing, it begged the question if this man had reappeared somewhere else. Reading this account years later, one's imagination begins to look at this like a missing piece of the puzzle.

In this story, the clothes were found in 1936, and so I would be interested to know if any cities reported the sudden appearance of a naked and confused man on the scene that same year. This idea assumes, of course, that there is no waiting period between the disappearing-point to the appearing-point, but it's possible that re-appearing is not as instantaneous as we might think.

Another incident was printed in the *Hants and Sussex News* on February 25, 1920. The naked body of a man, between 35 and 40, had been found in a plowed field, about a mile from nearby Petersfield, England. His body was intact, and an autopsy could find no wounds, poison or drugs in the man's system. Investigators decided that this was not a homicide. The man did not come from a vehicle because his bare footprints were traced beyond the road and into another field for some distance. He walked for some ways and then dropped dead. At the inquest, the examiners spoke of the man as being "well-nourished, and not a manual worker." His fingernails were clean and trimmed. Other than minor scratches made by bushes and shrubs, the man was unscathed. The cause of death was listed as syncope, a loss of consciousness related to insufficient blood flow to the brain, which was likely caused by exposure.

In an attempt to identify the man, his photograph was circulated by police. It was published throughout the country, but no one came forward. Police at the time searched high and low for his clothing, but those too were never found. Said a report in the *London Daily News*, April 16:

> Although his photograph has been circulated north, east, south, and west, throughout the United Kingdom, the police are still without a clew, and there is no record of any missing person, bearing the slightest resemblance to this man, presumably of education and good standing.[105]

Could some of these unclaimed bodies that we keep finding be from other parts of the world? Is this why local authorities are unable to match them to a name? Perhaps no one in this country, at this time, is actually "missing" these people and would therefore have no reason to come forward. With respect to current cases, that would mean that the person missing was not listed on INTERPOL, or that the details of that person are incorrect.

John Keel provides us with another frightening space-time glitch from his years as a researcher. Keel shares a story from November 1958, in which R.D. Smallridge, a truck driver, was making a routine trip from Hardy, Arkansas to Memphis, Tennessee to deliver eggs — approximately 132 miles. He made a habit of stopping for coffee at a truck stop near Black Rock, Arkansas. When Smallridge left, he checked his watch against the wall clock, showing it was exactly 2:00 a.m. It was

60 miles from the truck stop to his next scheduled appointment in Trumann, Arkansas, where he planned to have another coffee refill. This is where the story takes a weird turn, because Smallridge never remembered reaching the highway. He found himself pulling up to his destination restaurant in Trumann without any lapse of time. Upon entering the establishment, he looked at the clock and was "astounded." It was 2:15 a.m.... As I mentioned, this trip was well-known to Smallridge, and he knew for a fact he did not miss the changing of highways or a state weigh-scale near Jonesboro, Arkansas that would have been required to get to Trumann. He could not remember the drive at all and could not understand how anything could travel that distance in the elapsed time. It's as if he was picked up and plopped down somewhere else. Stories like these are often looped in with alien abduction accounts, even without evidence, but there is no need to make the story out to be anymore fantastic - Smallridge was simply teleported.[106] Stories like these are not rare.

Humans are not the only inhabitants that vanish and reappear in other places either. History has recorded astonishing arrivals of foreign critters that have set paw and claw in strange new habitats.

There is a story of alligators raining down a few times in South Carolina during the 1800s. These stories have stuck with me and act as pillars of strange phenomena, because they were documented and witnessed. Some of the reptiles were even captured for study.

In July 1843, around Charleston, several small alligators were said to fall on Aston Street. *The Aiken Journal* reported that, a Dr. J.L. Smith of Silverton Township, saw something fall to earth in 1877. Upon investigating, he discovered it to be an alligator. Soon, a second specimen appeared, and so on. Dr. Smith located six other reptiles on his property that day, which all seemed to be unharmed from the fall. Another alligator was reported to be found later, on the roof of a barn. They did not crawl there, they fell, so where did they fall from? Florida? Louisiana? Even 5 miles away would still constitute a teleportation, would it not?

For some reason, alligators and crocodiles are one of the most often reported out of place animals. What is it about these reptiles that makes them more prone to travel than any other? In *Mysterious America,* Loren Coleman provides a six-page list of them showing up unannounced, and even notes how many were sighted, captured, found or killed. Sightings were logged from all over the U.S. and in Canada, everywhere from a backyard in Windsor (September 1980) to a vacant lot in Montreal (1973).

Fort gives no shortage of examples in his writings, which is to be expected of the person who invented the idea of teleportation in the first place. No doubt he had skeptics everywhere tapping an incredulous foot. One story cited from the *London Daily Mail* on May 28, 1906, tells the story of a horse that belonged to stable owner J.C. Playfair in Furnace Mill, Lambhurst, Kent, England. One morning, he went to his stable and found horses turned around in their stalls and one of them missing. He searched all the likely places that a horse could be but wasn't able to find it. Then, in desperation, he began searching places where a horse could not be, just in case. A hay room that connected to the stable was the last place searched. Mr. Playfair himself had to squeeze through the entrance, and there he found the horse. There was no possible way that a horse could squeeze into that room, but here it was, laughing in the face of physics. If Mr. Playfair could barely get into the room, how then was the horse able to get in? They knocked a hole in the wall to get to the horse.[107] A fine example of possible teleportation — and one that will never have enough proof for those that can't identify it.

And the list goes on… It seems that no creature is safe. Coleman gives us examples of kangaroos and other creatures going the way of the gator. Fort gives another example from the *New York Sun* on November 12, 1931, involving two witnesses, both being doctors:

> Dr. E.R. Mathers, of Lincoln, Nebraska had seen a strange, small animal in his yard acting queerly. The next day he found the creature dead. The body was taken to doctor I.H. Blake of the University of Nebraska who identified it as that of an African lemur of the galaga group [sic].[108]

The public never learned of its origin, except for its original origin of Africa. There were no follow-up stories of escaped lemurs and no one came forward to claim it. Fort wrote a letter to Dr. Mathers to confirm the story, and it wasn't long until he received a reply from the doctor. All elements of the story were verified, and the lemur was stuffed and on display in the museum of the State University. The following equation is basic math — was there now one less member of the galago group in Africa?

I got in touch with the Nebraska State Museum to find out if they still had this specimen in their collection, but the zoology collections team could not locate any lemurs or lemur-like animals donated from that year. However, I am told that at that time there was a separate Department of Zoology on campus that may have received the specimen instead of the museum, and the specimen could have been lost, traded or discarded at some point. Although I could not track down the actual creature, they were able to confirm the existence of Dr. Blake.

How can the sudden disappearance of animals and humans be explained? We find ourselves in the same predicament: they can't be.

Are they relocated to another appearing point that we have overlooked? Fort had proposed the idea of just such a place, which he called the super Sargasso Sea:

> I think of a region somewhere above Earth surface in which gravitation is an operative and is not governed by the square of the distance — quite as magnetism is negligible at a short distance from a magnet. Theoretically the attraction of a magnet should decrease with the square of the distance but the falling off is found to be almost abrupt at a short distance. I think that things raised from the earth's surface to that region have been held there until shaken down by storms. Derelicts, rubbish, old cargoes from inter-planetary wrecks; things cast out into what is called space by convulsions of other planets, things from the times of the Alexanders, Caesars and Napoleons of Mars and Jupiter and Neptune; things raised by this earth's cyclones: horses and barns and elephants and flies and dodoes, moas, and pterodactyls; leaves from modern trees and leaves of the Carboniferous era — all, however, tending to disintegrate into homogeneous-looking muds or dusts, red or black or yellow — treasure-troves for the palaeontologists and for the archaeologists — accumulations of centuries — cyclones of Egypt, Greece, and Assyria — fishes dried and hard, there a short time: others there long enough to putrefy.[109]

The shaking down of objects, including the colours red, black and yellow, refer to the strange falls of rains we experience from time to time. This would include alligators in South Carolina. His idea of things being shaken down by storms is comparable to things from the deepest seas that are shaken up by storms.

Is there some floating island or plateau where missing people wander and ships and planes pile in a heap like some suspended junk yard?

Keel and Fort have written about disappearances since they began putting pen to paper. Like me, they could not ignore or understand how people can go missing in their day. Now, even more so, it is hard to believe with the advancement of satellite and GPS technology that anyone can go missing; we are always led to believe that there is no place left to hide. On the contrary, all we have left are places to hide.

Since their writings, some of the missing persons cases have been resolved, but there are a few that still linger and hound us with the question of our place in this world. Even some of the reports have gone missing. Fort shares that in 1892, Montreal had a rash of strange disappearances in July and August, but I couldn't even locate these reports. This shows how a lack of information can be detrimental to whether they will be remembered or not. It's also worth noting that Fort didn't leave us much of a paper trail of sources, perhaps because they lacked a thorough investigation by officialdom. His material was cited in the text and some of these original sources are no longer in existence.

As long as at least one of these stubborn mysteries persist, we have no choice but to go on investigating that which we do not understand.

After all of this theorizing, on the heels of facts, speculation and rumour, we cannot ignore the possibility that sometimes people just get lost.

We can either approach the missing phenomenon in one of two ways: either with big, extraordinary ideas or smaller, oversimplified ones. Personally, I have seen the benefit of both, as they lead to horrifying perspectives in which we must humble ourselves. In the spirit of being fair, I will leave you with a hypothesis of each.

This controversial, far-out idea might not even be comprehensible to some, but as I mentioned before, this chapter is about leaving everything on the table. In the grand scheme of things, we are all lucky to exist at all. Statistically speaking, the chances of me and you existing is about 1 in 400,000,000,000,000,000 (that's 400 quadrillion). Perhaps, the existence of some of us was premature, and we were not meant to be born during this time — a simple error or some cosmic glitch, and perhaps this is just the creator using His big eraser to correct it. Fort believed that Earth was like a floating farm in the darkness of space, and we are just the property of something else, some being. Sometimes we are plucked from our comfortable stables and plopped down somewhere else, not unlike Mr. Playfair's horse. It seems that when it's time to go, it's simply time to go.

Are we the citizens of some interstellar game preserve? I can't help but be reminded of Bill McLeod's book, discussed in an earlier chapter. The cover pictures a cow moose running down the centre of the Canadian Pacific Railway tracks and is captioned, "The pregnant cow moose will be safe in the Chapleau Game Preserve if she turns left. If she turns right, she will be fair game."[110] Perhaps like the moose, we cannot comprehend when and how our next step will determine our fate. To turn left or right is a choice, and we can never fully grasp its consequences.

As a final more simplified idea, what if one were to think of the forest as a living, breathing organism. One that, like the rest of us, needs to eat. For centuries, the organism has been thriving on soils enriched by decaying vegetation, animals, and those who do not return — a type of macabre external digestion. To defend itself, the forest generates all those woodland tricksters, feelings of dread, and inclement weather to deter us from treading on through and causing harm.

Scientifically, this idea is known as the Gaia theory and has been tossed around since the 1970s. It was proposed by chemist James E. Lovelock and biologist Lynn Margulis and describes that Earth and all of its biological systems behave like one single entity. Through its biology, this entity keeps the planet's conditions within boundaries that are favourable to life. There is evidence to suggest that you and I are walking on a living intelligence and Lovelock and Margulis do not shy away from pointing it out. Notably, the present conditions of the Earth are near optimal for its most dominant inhabitants and has always been habitable despite major changes. According to science, life has persisted for over 3.8 billion years, even in environments we assume cannot sustain life. The Earth has repeatedly recovered and healed from explosions, tunnelling, hot spewing lava, natural disasters and countless impacts from space. When questioned about how the Gaia hypothesis would fit in with other scientific theories, like Darwinism, Lovelock stated, "It is an extension to it to include the largest living organism in the Solar System, the Earth itself."[111]

To think of such out of the box possibilities may be the next step in understanding some of these wilderness and remote vanishings. At this moment in time, an agreeable cause or theory has not been reached. The explanation may go completely over our heads. It is something out of the *Twilight Zone* and someday when we piece it all together, we will either go completely mad with fear or simply not comprehend the answer once it's revealed to us. In truth, we may not even realize that we have already solved the puzzle long ago. And all the while, what we thought were the leaves rustling in the wind was really just the forest's growling stomach…

13

Leaving No Trace

"People get lost twice: first when they are reported and are being sought, and second when their disappearance ends up piled in a database."
— Horacio Canales

Hikers and campers everywhere are bred to practice the concept of leaving no trace as they venture out in the wilderness. The idea is to pack out whatever you pack in, limiting trash and our impact on the environment. A campsite should appear as if you were never there. It's a concept that I believe in, and I think it is very important for the preservation of our natural world spaces. It is a concept that also contradicts what I have explained in this book. How does this belief stack up to our presence on Earth long-term? If we leave no trace on the planet, it will be like we never existed at all.

I'm sure many started reading this book thinking that it was only about those who have disappeared, and they'd be right, but it is also about those of us that will eventually disappear. The disturbing fact is you don't have to go missing to disappear.

One hundred years from now, it's highly plausible that very few of us will matter. This is a sad reality, and a consequence of mankind's short-term memory. We have a short history, yet still can't remember how we got from here to there or how we discovered this or built that. Those that came before us failed to leave their mark, or it was coded, and we have forgotten how to decipher it. Some ancient civilizations have covered their tracks so well that their societies and cultures have almost completely been erased. Let's not make the same mistake or we may all be lost to history.

As I said from the beginning, time is like an acid that eats away at our existence, and it doesn't matter if you've disappeared into the bush or not. As we have learned, it does not take long for a case to turn cold. It is only through this new perspective that we can take actions to prevent our own disappearances. Now that we know what it's like to go missing, and the actual likelihood of being found and remembered, how can we make sure it doesn't happen to us?

The obvious way is to leave something behind — some legacy that can be passed along. Art, music and literature age well. People still discuss William Shakespeare and he lived well over 400 years ago! I have no doubt that his work and life will be discussed for another 400 years. For the average person, this is not so easy. Many of us are just struggling to provide for our families, let alone create a magnum opus. Some attempt a legacy through the sciences, philanthropy, exploration or discovery. However, not all of us will be remembered for the things that we've done, but we can still be remembered in other ways. For some, having a large family can strengthen the chances of being remembered. The more children you have, the stronger your legacy will be, especially if those children go on to make a notable contribution to society. And hopefully it would be a contribution and not a legacy for abominable reasons, however the latter would unfortunately make them age just as well. Consider the idea that there are dozens of books written on any one serial killer, yet none for their victims. Because of this, serial killers are liable to be remembered well beyond their lifetime.

Our modern culture is one that requires some kind of ending. We have always needed to bury or cremate our dead. This is another reason why we need to have autopsies and death certificates. We do not just throw the dead into a pit or leave them where they're found; we are a society that needs to know. We have always had a need for funerals, no matter how primitive and no matter how simple. An ending is essential to grief and acceptance. Too often there are times when a body is not returned to the family and there is talk of them not having closure. That is a word that gets thrown around a lot, but most people don't stop to think about what it really means. There is no closure when a loved one goes missing, and this word should be avoided.

A more appropriate term is ambiguous loss. Pioneered by psychotherapist Dr. Pauline Boss, an ambiguous loss is one that has no closure or clear understanding. It is unique in the fact that those left behind are unsure if they should grieve yet, creating a complicated inner struggle. Because we do not know for certain if these missing people are dead, we cannot mourn them in the way we normally would. Families and communities are left in a state of suspension — a painful limbo where their grief cannot be experienced in full. We do not know in which tense we should refer to those who have vanished, and so we catch ourselves jumping back and forth from "*He was*" to "*He is.*" Ambiguous loss can be applied to other types of trauma as well, such as when a parent walks out on a family or if a loved one has dementia. Knowing that they are somewhere but not really *there* is a perfect example of this unresolved grief.

When I first learned of the experiment known as Schrödinger's cat in high school, I thought it was just about one of the dumbest ideas I had ever heard. For those who don't know, the experiment is simply the idea of a living cat being put in a box with poison and a radioactive source. The box is then sealed from any observers. If a monitor detects radioactivity, the poison will be released and kill the cat. After a while, the cat is considered both alive and dead at the same time, since there is no way of knowing if the cat has been poisoned or not. It doesn't get much more ambiguous than that.

Looking back at this experiment years later, I saw a direct correlation to the missing person problem. When a person goes missing long-term, there is a punishing sense of ambiguity about their welfare. In our eyes, the person, like the cat, is both alive and dead at the same time. The box, in this case, is the one variable that we do not have. The lack of the box, or where to look, is the obstacle that keeps these people afloat between the living and the dead. When it comes to mysterious vanishings, there is no box to open.

However, experience has shown that there are other ways of healing without this supposed "closure." The importance of memorials is one that has been widely overlooked. We have stone cenotaphs of unknown soldiers, streets named after influential families, churches named after saints but no memorials for missing people. When our loved ones don't come home and remains are not returned, there are no graves for the family to visit, nowhere to celebrate their milestones or to leave flowers. I believe this would be tremendous for healing and could help to preserve the memory of the victims.

Think about the 9/11 memorial and how therapeutic a place like that can be. We still have not identified all the lost souls from that day, but we do have a place where we can mourn them and remember. It's possible for a person to become a place, and in turn hold the energy that this person once had. When we think about the Holocaust memorial sites — the museum in Washington or the Auschwitz-Birkenau State Museum — we can never forget these people because they have a place to be remembered. Since there is no closure when loved ones go missing, a memorial gives not only family but communities a place to visit the loved ones they have lost.

An obvious place to put such missing person markers would be in the place they were last seen. It would not be too arduous a task to put plaques at the edge of the forests where people have gone missing. Those who enter years later will see these markers and wonder about this person's story. It will be a request to keep them in mind as we enjoy our recreational areas. These markers for the missing can be put in discrete places and do not have to be as giant as the 9/11 memorial. Put them at boat launches, the edge of highways, portage trails or fields. After all, there is a chance that these people's remains are still somewhere in the area, so what better place to put a commemorative plaque. Crab Park in Vancouver, British Columbia already has such monuments in place, ranging from benches to boulders. These serve as a torch to be passed down to future visitors who may come to enjoy the park but be unaware of the tragedy that has befallen some members of their community.

Furthermore, we have the capability to immortalize these people in a more integrated way in our communities. We can celebrate these people's lives by naming a street after them in their hometown. I don't think this would be difficult to achieve. Other than the obligatory names of First, Second and Main Street, Maple Street is the most common name in Canada, with 1,138 of those lines running this way and that way on our maps. Perhaps we could swap out just a few Maples for Appleyards. Many of the nearest roads that these people vanish from do not even have proper names anyway. They go by Concession No. 2, County Road 6, RR 21 and other ridiculous names that modern mapping technology can't even locate.

If you've ever driven through the province, you'll quickly notice that the police have commemorated their retired and fallen officers by naming bridges after them, yet no effort has been made for the missing.

Since many of these disappearances occurred in the wilderness, it would be a tribute to see the naming of lakes after these people to make sure that they will always be remembered. The most common name for a lake in Ontario is "Mud." That's right, wet dirt. There are currently 75 lakes named "Mud" in Ontario (897 in the U.S.). Second place goes to Long Lake with 66, and Clear Lake with 45.

In this case, a little variety would go a long way. How many Long Lakes do we need in this province? Can not one of those lakes be a Huggan Lake? Lake Vachon would be much easier to distinguish on a map rather than trying to figure out which of the 66 Long Lakes you're going to be fishing on.

The Ontario Geographic Names Board is responsible for making these decisions, and they have procedures and policies in place for deceased persons and victims of tragedies. According to them, a person must be deceased at least five years before the board will consider a commemorative name proposal. A name will not be used to commemorate the victim of an accident or tragedy unless the individual has contributed to the legacy of the area, the province, or the country. I spoke with the geographic naming board and asked about their long-term missing person policy, who, not surprisingly, admitted that they currently didn't have one. Meaning unless your name is Mud, you've got no chance. However, this could be the next step needed to preserve the rich history we have. Our lakes and forests have stories, but they are not being accurately told.

Why do we continually want to name our lakes after brown-black sludge rather than the people we have lost? If we cannot rename a few of those precious Mud Lakes, then there are many more lakes out there that are crying out to be named. The Geographic Names Board admitted that they "do not know how many lakes are currently unnamed in the province." The Ontario government says it's "essentially impossible" to give an exact number of how many lakes and other geographic landmarks remain unnamed. They guess it is somewhere in the hundreds of thousands.[112]

Until we actively try to solve the missing person problem, explore the missing person phenomenon and take steps to preserve these people with proper memorial sites, we may not be able to really grasp their last moments, and therefore parts of our history.

There are other changes that need to happen if we are ever going to turn the corner on the missing person problem. If we ever want to resolve these cases, the following changes would help:

A) The release of information on cold cases to media and the public in order to advance investigations, especially those where the chances to be solved are low, those that are not assigned to an investigator, and those where the parties involved are deceased.

B) An upheaval of the record retention policies for police agencies that would increase access to historical files with the intention to advance these investigations. All records involving missing or murdered should be kept indefinitely for study, research and the preservation of life.

C) More transparency between police with media and the public. Databases should be accessible to the public, within reason since it is up to the public to close cases.

D) NCMPUR's *Best Practices* should be mandatory procedure across all police jurisdictions. A consistent framework with proper officer training and testing is the only way to seal the leaks in the system.

E) Long-term missing person cases should be prioritized and assigned to a specified long-term investigator. Older cases are not seen as a priority when the investigator has active, recent cases where time is of the essence. This investigator or team of investigators should not have their attention diverted to cases considered not long-term.

F) The front-loading of missing persons investigations without judgement to remove the risk of losing possible leads, tracks, scent trails or other indicators that could bring a swift end to an investigation.

G) Perfect interview and data collection techniques. All missing person files should be accompanied by a recent photograph, a sketch or 3D model immediately.

H) More willingness to collaborate with the public, private investigators and outside investigators, such as retired police officers, when cases go cold.

I) Assistance for families in terms of compensation, therapeutic support and case exposure. Rotating free or discounted billboard space (paid for by the province) for even a limited amount of time would be beneficial to relatives, law enforcement and the public.

J) Next of kin should be made aware, by letter or otherwise, without pressure, of the RMI (Relatives of Missing Person Index), in the event they are not aware that they could help speed up the possibility of a case closure from DNA.

Similar recommendations have been set out in the past, yet not much has changed. Dr. Melina Buckley made similar recommendations in a discussion report prepared for the Missing Women Commission of Inquiry from 2012.

These steps are not meant to enable a morbid curiosity, the intention is to perhaps one day prove what happened to these people, or at the very least prove that they once existed.

I'm puzzled why some of these missing persons cases are still listed as such. When no one is looking and the files no longer exist that would be vital to properly confirm the data, why does it matter? During my dogged search for records, I was met by a number of excuses that attempted to defend the mishandling.

> It is always possible given their age and other circumstances that records that may have existed no longer do. It is unfortunately sometimes the case that older records are more likely to go missing, particularly where there are no associated charges of convictions.[113]

The rationalization that records may become misplaced or destroyed (even by accident) just because they are old is not an acceptable reason. Institutions are not just misplacing case files, they are misplacing records of these people, which in some cases is all there is left of them.

There are plenty of examples where human remains have been found decades after a person has gone missing and they were able to link them to a case, finally reaching a resolution. It seems more cases are being solved every month, many of them 30 years old or older, and that includes the identification of human remains. Forty-four years after the body of "Septic Tank Sam" was found murdered and hidden on an Alberta farm, officials were finally able to confirm his real name. Gordon

Edwin Sanderson was killed in 1977 and was able to be identified through DNA technology.

Police in Toronto were able to solve the murder of Christine Jessop, a cold case from 1984. These resolutions would not be possible without accurate and maintained police files. Without the retention of records and the accuracy of those records, what chance would we really have? A public interest in these cases should not be underestimated either. Showing investigators that the public is thinking about these individuals could spur them on to take another look at the mystery.

Earlier, I mentioned how locations where missing persons were last seen were sometimes difficult to pin down. The coordinates were not precise, names have changed, and maps lack the diminutive data known to locals. We're only talking about cases from the latter half of the last century. We cannot rely on the memory of current and retired investigators alone to solve historical cases.

People need to realize that record-keeping is not foolproof. I have witnessed firsthand the poor state of some archives and collections. I have seen how things are lost, purged or improperly catalogued too many times to count. Birth records, death records, census records, and voter lists don't exist for every person in the most recent of times, and so the farther back we look in history, the chances of a paper trail become less and less likely. Death certificates are not easily obtained. It's a misconception that the next of kin will be in possession of one.

Tragically, we now have instances in which we doubt the existence of a person because they lack just such a paper trail. The belief that they once lived is reliant upon a flimsy, thin government paper tucked away in a place we don't know where to find.

One such case is the disappearance of Mr. Orion Williamson. Many will argue that it never happened; they say there is no proof, but I feel compelled to tell it again in light of any proof that it didn't happen. I will share an abridged version, since while I do not value their doubt, I do value people's time.

In July of 1854, a planter named Williamson was sitting with his wife and child on the veranda of his house. Mr. Williamson tossed away the butt of his cigar and left his seat to tell the overseer in a neighbouring field about a delivery of horses. The field in question was without a single tree, rock or structure that would obstruct a watcher's view. This is important to the story, as you will soon see.

He was seen walking down the gravel path, and even greeting a neighbour in a carriage, Mr. Armour Wren, his son James and the coachman. Mr. Wren's testimony was that soon after greeting the man, Mr. Williamson was seen crossing the field and then in a split second evaporated into nothingness. He was simply walking in the field and then... he wasn't. Mr. Wren's son James was hysterical and repeatedly asked his father a question that we have all been asking for well over 100 years: "What has become of Mr. Williamson?"

Mr. Wren's account of the incident was given under oath in the legal proceedings relating to Williamson's estate. The three men reportedly ran to the spot where Williamson had vanished. There were no holes, cave-ins or wells he could have fallen in, there was only a circle of grass. The group was astonished, as anyone would be, and it's the simplicity of this vanishing that has captivated and haunted many young readers, such as myself. Mr. Wren watched Mrs. Williamson storm down the path, followed by servants, shouting all manner of panic and absurdity. She too had seen the whole thing. They searched the area for two hours, it was said. Mrs. Williamson was hospitalized from the shock. A massive search of more than 300 men and bloodhounds had begun, which focused on the nearby fields and pastures, and had stretched as far as the adjoining countryside. They swept across the field inch by inch, checking the ground with their hands at every foot. When night fell, the searchers pressed on. Nothing of Orion Williamson has ever been found.

This story has been the source for many false retellings, in which the dates, names and places were altered. This has made the original incident a target for skeptics.

More amusing is the fact that some of these altered versions are more widely known than the Williamson case. The copycat stories have been retold hundreds of times in "believe it or not" type books. Explanations ranged from natural to supernatural. The idea of cave-ins was explored but debunked by a geologist who examined the ground. Researchers imagined invisible UFOs stealing people from above and scientists murmured about magnetic fields capable of disintegrating the atomic structure of a human.

The argument made by the skeptic is always the same: they cannot find proof that Mr. Williamson ever existed. They also claim to not find proof of the witnesses — the Wren's and the coachman. While we might not be able to produce birth certificates and census reports, this is not evidence that these people never existed. It's only evidence that we are bad record-keepers — something I have already proven in earlier chapters.

There are a few persistent individuals who believe that stories recorded pre-1900 could not possibly be true unless the characters involved were supported by census records. They argue that anecdotal reports and statements are usually made up and that humans could not be an accurate source of proof. But anyone who has done even a weekend's worth of research will quickly find that census records and archival data are poorly kept. It's often lost, miscatalogued, misspelled, purged, poorly preserved or rife with other human error.

Furthermore, the census records from before the year 1900, are much less meticulous than they are by today's standards. Many people lived without birth certificates, so we would expect some members of society to slip through the cracks.

I still cannot locate every single record of the people I have researched for this book, all of who were born in the 1900s, so why are we surprised when we cannot locate these records from the mid-1800s? In my experience, I have seen newspapers state a person's name incorrectly, when in fact all their life they were called something else. Being born doesn't magically produce a birth certificate and dying doesn't grant you a death certificate. The simple fact is that not everyone receives one. It was not uncommon for people to be born on their homestead and live a lifetime, only to die in the same bed without leaving their property. Many are buried in backyard family plots — what some might view as unofficial cemeteries.

If we cannot rely upon manmade reports and anecdotes, why should we rely on census records that are man-maintained? Proof is subjective and varies between individuals, so if I can provide one reader with proof of a story, there is no guarantee that others would accept it. How can we identify proof, with all of us watering it down to our own standards? The real question is when you see proof of something fantastic, will you even recognize it?

Mr. Williamson never had a first name until Jay Robert Nash revealed it to us in his 1978 book. His write-up of the incident was more detailed than any other telling of the story, and it was clear that he had done a bit more digging. In his summary of the story, he emphatically stated that Orion Williamson "was no figment of the imagination but a real, live resident of Selma, Alabama — until, of course, he slipped into eternal mystery."[114]

There is one obvious reason for not being able to locate more records of the Wrens or the Williamsons to corroborate the story, that reason being the people in this story could have had their names changed. After all, people like to get on with their lives without being badgered. Ironically, the skeptic mind is always too credulous to expect that every minute detail of a person's life would be documented for them to scrutinize years later on a Google search. It's not reality. If this story were simply a lie, it would be quite easy to trace, just like the false retellings of the Williamson case were easy to sniff out. A lie starts somewhere and with someone, and yet the truth seems to come from nowhere.

It would be a travesty to make an argument against the existence of a person, only to find out later that they did exist. How strongly would the skeptics go to convince us that these lives are so insignificant that they were made up? If that were you or a family member 100 years from now, I'm sure you would not appreciate being "debunked." All this because they couldn't get their hands on your death certificate.

The missing people I have covered in this book are at risk of just such ambiguity. Imagine 50 years from now if people were discussing the cases of Lingman, Michaud, Weeden and Newcombe as myths just because they couldn't verify all the facts. Make no mistake, we are not far off from this point. It's hard to believe that one day people could doubt if a tragic disappearance were true, but if it could happen to Williamson, it could happen to all of us.

Until we can prove that such stories as Mr. Williamson's are 100% false, we cannot say that a human's life has been the figment of our imagination.

During my work at the Archives of Ontario, I had somewhat of a breakthrough. I was becoming frustrated with the lack of search results I was getting through certain keywords. Then I remembered just how poorly the details were on some records I was able to obtain, and it got me thinking. On a hunch, I began to search through a list of keywords that I purposely spelled incorrectly. The logic behind this was to eliminate possible data entry error for some of these old records. After all, they are done by human hands and some of the records can be harder to read. I could not assume that every archivist knew the context of every record they entered into the database, and so they wouldn't know the difference. Since I knew what I was looking for, it gave me another vantage point.

My hunch paid off instantly. In my first attempt I got a hit. I was surprised by the lack of information on the KRNO mining records, and so I entered the spelling incorrectly and bingo! I was able to find a 15-page geological report for the company that otherwise would have been left hidden. The spelling error was not on the original record, but instead on the listing of the record on the Archives of Ontario website. Because of one single letter, this made the record unsearchable. This just goes to show you how important it is to be accurate, but the more unsettling response had yet to come. I was pleased that I had found the error and reported it to their feedback team, but to my surprise they didn't seem to think it was an issue. They would not fix a typo in their search database that was clearly preventing results. Keep in mind, this would have no effect on the original document, as it did not have the error. They refused to update their records to correct the spelling of the search listing. I was flabbergasted. That day I learned that it doesn't take much to stay hidden.

During my research, there was one incident I referred to as "The Killarney 12." This was another one of those "flash in a pan" type of stories that often catch my attention. While scrolling through databases, I came across the microfilm article from the *Sudbury Star*. The article was printed on September 15, 1977, with a headline that would tug at anyone's curiosity: "Twelve Missing in Killarney Park."

The article described a situation where a group of 12 people had come up from Michigan State as part of a wilderness education course. They entered the Three Narrows Lake area on Monday, September 12 to practice bushwhacking. It appears they missed their exit date because the papers did not report them missing until Friday, stating that they had not been heard of for two days. When the coordinator of the course had not heard back from their group, they contacted the authorities.

I was keen to find out more. Not only was it dramatic, but how was it possible for 12 people to go missing, especially with an outdoor education and presumably an instructor, in a Provincial Park? Killarney Park is a 645-square-kilometre wilderness with dozens of lakes to provide a challenging search, but it is nowhere near the largest park in the province. Stack Killarney up against parks like Quetico and Algonquin and the park looks downright dinky. But I could not find a resolution as to the whereabouts of this group. Like my other attempts at requesting information, I hit that all-too familiar roadblock. I requested records from the Ministry of Environment, Conservation and Parks — the most logical place to start, I figured. However, when I heard back, they complained about a split between two ministries, which could have sent the case files in a multitude of unmapped directions. *Here we go again,* I thought. The request was passed through the Ministry of Environment and Parks, the Ministry of Natural Resources and Forestry (MNRF) and The Ontario Provincial Police because of the use of their helicopters and resources during the search. All departments came up empty handed; the files were gone. I learned that the retention period on such things was only 10 years and after that they would be shipped and donated to God only knows where...

On June 11 of 2019, I received an unexpected call from a rather helpful agent in the FOIA department at the Ministry of the Environment. He too was surprised that the files seemed to have vanished and that none of the ministries could present them. Going forward, he suggested two things: first, I should try contacting the OPP Museum, and the second was that I should check with the Archives of Ontario. I took his suggestions and ran with them, but I quickly found a dead-end with the OPP Museum, and a search of the archives turned up nothing. I could not fathom how such a story could completely vanish, especially since a fair amount of money would have been spent on the search. Then, on a hunch, I decided I would start at the very beginning. I often do this when I reach a dead-end, thinking I must have missed something.

I went back to the microfilm of the *Sudbury Star*, where I originally found the paper, and again I searched. There, mislabeled and misdated, was the resolution to my story. Here is the excerpt:

> *Lost Students Emerge Safely*
> The 12 Michigan students who hadn't been heard from for four days in Killarney Provincial Park walked out of the bush shortly before noon Thursday. The group was participating in an outdoor education course. The lost students came out of the bush at George Lake where they joined the rest of their party of 38. The OPP helicopter was on the way to the scene when the group was reported found.[115]

The story was labeled something completely irrelevant and therefore made it impossible to locate in a database. Here the 12 students made it out safely and had been living out a life somewhere.

In this case, the mystery was solved long ago but the evidence was forgotten, and it resulted in a wild goose chase and exposed the incompetence of several agencies. They did not know where to look for the record, or who would have been responsible for it. As far as the police and park officials were concerned, the remains of these people were still out there and I almost had them sending in the dogs. This is a perfect example of how poor spelling and grammar can have you killed. It's alarming to me, that we are just one typo away from being forgotten.

Oh well, no harm done, just some research time wasted, but much can be learned from this. We have a surprisingly short memory for being such a young country. Perhaps it's more shocking that the authorities did not even remember if the case was solved or not. They didn't keep a record of it at all, and the final clue was found mislabeled in the archives. It may not make an exciting story, but the Killarney 12 serve as a reminder that we need to carefully catalogue our history or another unfortunate few might be doomed to repeat it.

Newspapers cannot be relied upon for accuracy either. Another example of this was found when newspapers from the United States were writing about young Geraldine. They mistakenly printed that George Warren, Mrs. Warren's husband, had also gone missing. The error was copied and pasted in other newspapers around North America, without first being verified.

As they have done in the past, if successful, books tend to outlive people. As the family members of the lost people pass away, we can hope that the names of their loved ones will be preserved in writing forever. Even if what has been written here fails to incite any legislative change, at the very least the names of these missing individuals will live in this text, spelled correctly, with the record as straight as I could get it.

You don't have to be an intrepid explorer to vanish off the face of the earth. One doesn't have to have a dangerous job or live in the far reaches of the globe. The phenomenon is indifferent; it seems we are all up for grabs.

Missing people are the ghosts of our society. They are translucent, living between the known and the unknown and left to haunt the rest of us. It's unclear if they haunt us knowingly for some purpose or if it is only due to our guilt and grief that they remain here. Is it our duty to bring these lost souls to rest or do we refuse to accept the fact that some mysteries cannot be solved?

There have always been unexplained disappearances and there always will be. Our country and history are founded on mystery and so we must accept that it is only natural that it permeates our future. Trailblazers and early explorers are no closer to being found than they were hundreds of years ago. No one can say for certain what really happened to Henry Hudson as he sailed out of the bay of the new world and into the zone of obscurity. Such disappearances have been on written record for centuries and will remain unsolved — a thought that should be unsettling to us all.

Our names, like bones scattered in the forest, become brittle with age. If we do not take steps, we will fade into the wind. If no-one cuts the grass in the graveyard, it won't take long for it to turn into an unrecognizable forest, fertilized by forgotten friends and neighbours. Which names will we be able to remember and how many have we already lost?

You only live as long as the last person who remembers you.

Our willingness to absorb this fact will profoundly heighten what we have explored.

The fear of going missing was a real and justifiable thing at the beginning of this journey, but now we have a broadened perspective of the dreadful picture. There is one conclusion, which I regret will not bring much comfort — there is something far worse than disappearing, and that is being forgotten.

Afterword

Funny thing — I originally intended to write this book focusing on the paranormal aspects of missing persons cases. However, through my research and discovery I found that these vanishings were just as mysterious and frightening on their own and a paranormal approach wasn't even necessary. I have included some paranormal aspects, but I may look at the paranormal a bit differently than most. I consider the paranormal to be quite normal — it is just something that we do not yet understand, and only becomes normal once science tells us it has. My thinking is: why wait until then? In the spirit of "anything is possible" and the fact that no single theory is stronger than the other, both being without evidence, I did include some yet-to-be-understood phenomenon.

The intention of this book is to bring about awareness and hopefully change the systems we have in place to help those who've been forgotten and those who have been left behind. My depiction of some of the police practices and individuals may come off as harsh, but those were based on the facts I uncovered, not my opinion. If they look bad, it's likely because they are.

I was impressed with the relentless and exhaustive efforts that many of the responding officers put into searching for some of these individuals. I would have loved to meet and shake the hands of men like Ken Wilson, William Hayes and Bob King.

So many nights of sleep were lost to me wondering about vanishing people, what their final thoughts were and what really happened to them. This is a subject you can really lose yourself in and some days it would be all I would think about no matter how hard I tried to take a break from the research. When you spend enough time with these cases, they start to linger in your mind. It is a very surreal and dreamlike feeling to become so attached to a person who you have no connection to. I believe that after spending years learning about these individuals I too may be suffering from some version of ambiguous loss.

Throughout the course of this project, I wondered if getting these people out of my head and down on paper would allow me to heal and get some sleep. However, it doesn't look like I am completely cured of this curse. Try as I might, there always seems to be a faded face or sketch that flashes before me in bed, or a name that scrolls across my closing eyelids. I have no way of knowing if these hauntings will subside.

Sander Lingman was about my age when he disappeared, and it gave me a new perspective on his story — a perspective that frightened and touched me in a way that I can't describe. Sander was still a young man with his whole life ahead of him, which had the potential to be a prosperous one. He would never marry or feel the joy of having children of his own. This could have easily happened to me. I could be out there lost and missing in the bush. That's where power comes from: perspective, and I did everything I could to find out more information about Sander. I had quite a few nightmares about Sander and imagined being in his position. I saw myself on Gripp Lake almost nightly, far away from any roads, camping by my lonesome. The same vision occurred to me night after night: the pale slick of moonlight, the rubbing together of looming pines and the drone of the insects. Once there, I faced another sleepless night.

I have spent so much time on the mysterious vanishing of Sander Lingman that I feel like he was a personal friend of mine. It's odd, after you spend so much time pouring over snippets of a person's life and speaking with his family members and friends, you start to build a relationship with him in your head. I wish I could talk with him; I wish I could ask him not only what happened that day, but what he was thinking, what he wanted out of life and what he hoped to accomplish one day. I sometimes wonder if he would disapprove of me telling his story, a thought that is followed by hesitation and doubt. But then I think of it from his perspective, if it were me lost in the woods, I would not be satisfied with the work that had been done in the 60 years since my vanishing. This was a complex case to research. At no time during the process was it ever easy, but I have tried my best for him.

I have spent years of my life on the story of young Geraldine Huggan, a little five-year-old girl that I have never met. To an outsider, it might be a bit extreme or obsessive, but to me it had become an absolute priority to get this story down on paper. I rehashed the story in my first book, perhaps with a more mystical angle, but that in no way should affect its credibility, because we still don't know what happened. At the time of that writing, I had exhausted every single avenue of research and I thought it would be my only chance to get it down on paper. Little did I know that a year later I would be fortunate enough to track down more information on the case. Those interviews and additional material I uncovered needed to come to light, and so I felt the story was worth a retelling. I decided to tell all versions of the story, broken up in sections for the reader's benefit. I did this rather than omitting any detail or opinion that might later be an important part of the historical record. It has been a hair-pulling, heartbreaking hunt for the truth, and I treated her story as if she was a relative of mine. It's very odd to look at this from a broadened perspective.

This is also what I tried to do when telling the story of May Appleyard. I had considerable trouble tracking down people to interview, until I was discovered by some family members and neighbours in the spring of 2021. Until then, no one seemed to be working the case or even discussing it. I couldn't understand why, and at that point the theories and information were scarce. Once I connected with those that were involved, they confirmed what I had heard so far and would be responsible for adding some key details skipped by earlier retellings of this story.

There was a point when I had so many people messaging me with information that it was overwhelming. Other times I would have people contact me with information and then break off all communication without notice. I could not judge which stories were more factual than the others, because none of them were accompanied by proof. I included the versions that were most prominent and those I could cross reference with police information and other records I came upon. The good thing about all this digging I did and the interest it brought to her disappearance was that rumours have circled that police have reopened the case as of 2020.

One of my police sources told me that detachment property vaults are audited frequently, and it is not uncommon for items to be destroyed. This could explain what happened to the skull found in the swamp, along with other historical missing persons cases that FOI agents are unable to locate.

Merle Newcombe's name was added to his parents' tombstone in the new Protestant Cemetery in Chapleau. To make things more confusing it was spelled "Merl." I thought it was strange to carve the name of a person on the stone who is not buried in the plot, but perhaps it helps the family by giving them a place to remember. Funny enough, the plot is right next to where Bill McLeod's grandparents and aunt Lera are buried.

After all was said and done, after all my efforts, I wondered if what I am doing here would be of any help or use to anyone. My original plan for this book was to visit each of these forgotten locations and report back with my findings. However, I quickly learned that this would have been impossible. Not only would it be extremely difficult and expensive, but I also learned that many of the locations were not accurately listed.

The wilderness is a comforting place for me, despite all its hazards and spooky legends passed over the campfire. Each time I paddle backcountry lakes or bushwhack through the overgrowth, I feel embodied with the spirit of the woodsman, the logger and the prospector. It is probably the reason why I feel so close to these stories. I think about those that have come through before and have been absorbed into the boundless landscape. I am careful of my actions and gauge risks from the perspective of a potential missing person. I do not want to end up as some name on a forum with a barely accurate blurb to describe me. As insurance, I now leave a trail of breadcrumbs in the event I do not return. Setting out on each trip, it is hard not to be reminded of these individuals because of the simple fact that they are still out there. Their memory haunts the Northwoods. Sometimes their stories overwhelm my mind. My heart beats against my ribs with a little more vigour, knowing this is how the day started for so many others that have disappeared. Even though I remain on my toes, I am always accompanied by that haunting feeling of vanishing. A careful scan of the shoreline and a brave glance down into the shadowy waters is now an instinctive necessity. The fear comes in whispers, intermingled with the ancient, creaking pines, between each paddle stroke.

Stroke.

You're going to die out here.

Stroke.

They'll never find you.

Stroke.

Your bones will sink.

Stroke.

How long until they forget?

Tim Marczenko

Appendix A

Additional information recovered from the Sander Lingman file

The adjudication process for my investigation into Sander Lingman began on January 11, 2022. I had now been working on the case for over five years and had gotten virtually nowhere with numerous requests for information into the police files. After I was denied because, "the OPP have confirmed that no records exist" in 2020, I had no choice but to escalate the matter to the adjudication process because of the very serious implications that came with this decision.

First off, I knew for a fact that there was records on this incident created and stored by the Ontario Provincial Police. After being in touch with next-of-kin, she confirmed that she had received correspondence from the OPP about the case. I am also in possession of the physical letter of the assigned investigator, whose name is signed at the bottom. Police would not have been able to cross reference or record any data if they did not have files or records of the incident. Furthermore, I also had notes books detailing the investigation of W.J. Hayes. This journal would have been transcribed into a formal police report and in some form or another been filed. I also had written confirmation from the OPP and confirmation from Detective Sergeant St. Onge, over the phone that a police file does exist, the Lingman profile is also listed on the *Canadas Missing* website.

The response from the FOI office came on February 8 in a letter which stated that they had discovered "a significant number of additional responsive records..."[116] It turns out that their initial search was not thorough and after five long years, I was able to get my hands on the police report. Although it was heavily redacted, the papers showed that the Lingman story did not end in 1960. Hayes included details of the return visits by family members in 1961. FOI sensors continued to make a mess of things by redacting information that they had no right to. In the months that followed, I would have to call them out on a number of violations within the *Act* and request a redisclosure of the records after they had corrected these errors.

Perhaps the most startling detail in the police report happened a decade later. In the summer on 1970, alleged human remains were found in the Gripp Lake area. The dates on the document conflict from June 22 to July 5. Someone had stumbled on the remains of something and reported it to police. It was investigated by Constable Patrick John Maguire who indicated that seven photographs of the site were taken. The descriptions of the photographs tell a story on their own and upon reading through the list, the burning question echoed in my head: *Were these the remains of Sander Lingman?*

- Location of found axe
- Location of found hat
- General location of above articles
- Location of bones foreground fire charred wood
- Bones at location
- Bones at location
- General scene of tote road where bones located

I know of no other missing people in the Gripp Lake area, however no specific coordinates of the discovery were noted, so we cannot know for sure if these bones are related or where they were in relation to Lingman's last known location. The items that stuck out were the found hat and the proximity to the tote road. Was this the hat that Bourdignon was referring to? Likely not, as this was 1970 and Bourdignon was approached by police much later about the discovery of a hat. But who knows, perhaps it was sitting it a locker until recently. If the found hat was a ballcap then this could be a significant find. I thought if I could locate these photographs, I would be able to help identify them based on the hat. This is where the disclosed police report really goes off the rails...

What followed was a frantic search by police officers for any information they could find on this mysterious photographic report from 1970. It turns out that no follow up reports regarding an investigation into the bones could be located or any indication that it was investigated at the time. Is it possible that Officer Maguire was unaware that there was an unresolved missing persons case in that exact area? From what I could conclude, police had not actually looked into the alleged human remains until 2009, nearly 40 years after their discovery, but at that point, the report and the photographs had vanished along with any indication of where the bones were.

Detective Constable Tyler Sturgeon was assigned to review the Lingman file in 2009 and did everything in his power to locate the missing report. He reached out to neighbouring detachments as well as the Criminal Investigations Branch, Office of the Chief Coroner and even the Archives of Ontario. His journey sounded very much like my own in that he could not find a single trace of them. I picked up where he left off and began my own hunt, after all, I knew firsthand that a simple archival search was not foolproof. I also noticed that Officer Maguire's name was spelled wrong during the search done by Sturgeon so this would have had an effect on the results.

I conducted a thorough search of the database with all relative keywords and proper spellings, but instead of specific dates I requested to see every single photograph taken with a police agency owned camera in the summer of 1970.

Believe it or not, there are actually zero police photographs from that year in the archives database. My next step was to check with the Thunder Bay Police service, as I had reason to believe that the lost report was shipped to them and never returned. Unfortunately, an agent from their *Freedom of Information* office confirmed that they didn't have the records either.

Once again, because of retention periods, indiscriminate audits or poor file management, we have allowed a chance to learn the truth slip through our fingers. Could the case of Sander Lingman have been solved long ago? Even if it were his remains, because his profile contains no physical description and there was no DNA collected and stored for just such a discovery, the Forensic Pathologists would not have much to go on. If these remains were not Lingman's, they may belong to another one of our hundreds of missing people. A very rare opportunity to collect DNA and measurements from these bones is now gone.

On the other hand, we mustn't get too far ahead of ourselves. Keep in mind the report was labeled as "alleged human remains." Perhaps the file was not kept because police confirmed that they were not human and so destroyed the photographs and remains. Lingman also had a day bag and compass with him, but neither item was listed to have been recovered at the site so there is still a chance that this discovery is unrelated. However, it is troubling that this puzzling page is included in the Lingman file. The fact that we don't know if it is related either way is the curse that we continue to face with each passing decade.

When the Missing Person Registry was established in Canada in 1986, a number of cold cases were shuffled on and off of CPIC based on their profiles. OPP Detachment Commanders were notified by superior officers that now was the time, "…to review the case files to see if there is any useful purpose in maintaining your entry."[117] The thinking behind this was that since many of the older cases were alleged drownings, there was no point in keeping these files. It was at this point that the Lingman file was reviewed again and a response issued:

> The Crime Report on file does not contain enough information to allow for a Profile Data report to be added to the CPIC entry. As this matter is 26 years old and no further evidence has come to light as to the missing person, I feel the matter can be closed and the case file destroyed. Lingman has been removed from CPIC and the Identification Section of #16 District advised.[118]

This is further proof that police investigations are based on opinion rather than official protocols or practices. Lingman was suspected to have drowned, but there was no evidence whatsoever to support this theory. As a side note, if police believe that Lingman drowned, why was I continually denied the file based on reasons that it was a criminal case? Another contradiction. There seems to be very little emphasis on solving old cases.

Thankfully, in 2013 members of the Missing Persons Unidentified Bodies Unit made a push to re-add Sander Lingman to CPIC so that other police agencies, including the RCMP would have access to it. But it wasn't as easy as that. CPIC administration denied the Lingman entry because of the lack of information on him, specifically his birthdate, which leads us back to the importance of detailed and comprehensive victim profiles. Officer Sturgeon and others eventually found a way to get Lingman re-added to the database.

There were numerous other inaccuracies that I came across during the adjudication process, which at the time of this writing, is ongoing.

Appendix B

Missing Manitoban Children resolved by hunches, dreams and premonitions

In 1934, three-year-old Florence Spence went missing from Central Manitoba. Officials believed there was no way that she could have survived by herself in the dropping temperatures at night. As days passed, RCMP were out hunting a bear that potentially could have eaten her. After initial search efforts were abandoned for the girl, a man identified as M. Blair had a dream. His premonition showed exactly where Florence would be found alive. Blair, a diamond-drill setter, did not return to work the next day and instead followed his hunch, which told him that she would be found 3 miles west of her home in an isolated spot. His coworkers were reported to laugh at his premonition. Blair set off that morning and within 40 minutes had a groggy Florence in his arms. He found her almost naked, semi-conscious between two rocks — exactly where he had dreamed.

She immediately asked for water. He gave her some from a small pool nearby, then carefully lifted and carried her one mile out of the forest to the nearest hospital. Florence should have been dead, but by a miracle she was found alive — alone in the bush without food, water, shoes or shelter and in the realm of wild animals. Her body had taken a beating due to the lack of these basic necessities, but she recovered. If Blair never had the dream or decided not to act on it, Florence would have never been found alive. The newspaper of the time was not remiss in observing the impossibility of her survival: "...The incident will go down in the history of the north as the impossible, actually happening."[119]

Maybe the hunch that Harry Hawes mentioned was a dream, and if so, wouldn't be so far-fetched. He may have wanted to avoid ridicule, which leads to some unfortunate questions. Florence Spence was meant to be found, but we will never know why. If Harry Hawes acted on his hunch faster, would he have found Geraldine Huggan alive? Did the delay of finding the float plane cause him to reach her too late? Was Huggan supposed to survive and live a full life? I only repeat these unknowable questions here because they are the thoughts that pop into my head as I lay awake at night.

. . .

The second story also took place in 1934, on May 3. Numerous Manitoba newspapers tell a story of Mrs. T.H. Vigfusson's disappearance. Seventy-year-old Mrs. Vigfusson and her 35-year-old son drove their buggy from their home in Weedy Point, Manitoba to Steep Rock, approximately 12 miles. After a shopping trip that afternoon, they started back to Weedy Point, but being a rural and undeveloped settlement, the road was treacherous, and their buggy shafts broke. They returned to Steep Rock and arrived just before midnight. Mrs. Vigfusson expressed concern for her husband being alone at home throughout the night. Her husband who was sick and blind, was not used to being abandoned in the house and would worry if his wife did not return. Mrs. Vigfusson was stubbornly determined to make it home that night and asked the store owner, F.E. Snidal, to give her a ride home in his car. Mr. Snidal was unprepared for the ask, seeing that it was midnight and he had just returned from a trip, but he couldn't refuse the elderly woman. They set off down the rough, potholed, dirt road until they were about a mile and a half from Weedy Point. Glancing at his gas gauge, Mr. Snidal realized that he was running out of fuel and would never make it to Weedy Point and back to his home. Concerned he'd be stranded; he stopped the car. There was a discussion between Mrs. Vigfusson and Mr. Snidal about what to do, until the old woman said she would walk the rest of the way. Being familiar with the road, she shared no fear or hesitation about the idea. This was the last time she was seen. Due to the isolation of these villages, news of the woman's disappearance was not known until Saturday evening, nearly two full days after her visit to Steep Rock. RCMP and searchers descended upon the bush once dawn broke on Sunday morning.

The terrain was a challenge and searchers were unable to find a trace of the woman. On Monday, 55 men participated in a daylight to dark search that produced nothing but frustration and a stubborn mystery. On Tuesday, 70 men looked under leaf and limb only to return at dusk empty handed. As searchers walked the wooded shoreline, they found what may have been a single footprint. It led rescuers to speculate that she may have attempted to cross the softened ice only to have fallen into the frigid waters.

Mr. Vigfusson told of a dream or vision he had early Friday morning where he saw his wife come to him, asking for help. As he moved towards her, she faded away. As if that wasn't odd enough, only a few hours later, the missing woman's son had a dream about where his mother would be found. The dream he described was a collection of kaleidoscope imagery and messages that grew and transformed within his head. The words eventually became clear and commanded him to "Go to the beach, there is a letter there for you."[120] When he awoke, he rushed down to the beach that ran along Lake Manitoba, to the exact spot that was shown to him in his dream. There his mother's body was found. There was no indication of foul play, and it was reported that all her money was accounted for. Lake Manitoba would have been more than twice the distance from her destination. How could a woman walking on a flat road that she had walked on for decades make this miscalculation and pass her home?

. . .

I am not the only one who saw the connection between lost children, dreams and hunches. The next story was retold by newspapers during the search for Geraldine and has been printed in many journals over the past century. The account took place exactly 80 years before the disappearance of Geraldine. What has now become somewhat of a Manitoba legend seemed to be a factual account that was corroborated by a handful of citizens - including an Archbishop.

On July 3, 1873, a young boy named Billy Service wandered from his family's house in Bird's Hill, north of Winnipeg, to pick strawberries. When he did not return by nightfall, his parents and neighbours searched the surrounding property until dark. At dawn, concerned townsfolk from nearby Springfield, Kildonan, Sunnyside and Winnipeg joined the search, some of them riding on horseback. Among the searchers was the entire staff of the *Manitoba Free Press*, which was the paper that first covered the story (this is oddly similar to Bob Metcalfe of *The Winnipeg Tribune*, who would search for Geraldine and write daily articles on their progress). The only trace of the boy reported to be found were footprints that zigzagged through a wet area in the direction of Petite Pointe des Chênes to the south. Billy's father offered a reward of $200 for the recovery of his son, dead or alive.

The boy was lost for 10 days in the wilderness. According to Archbishop Samuel Matheson, a local identified as Mrs. Fidler had a dream that the young boy would be found alive hiding inside a badger hole. She convinced her husband, Peter Fidler to go out to a specific spot and continue to search. (Some retellings say the boy's mother had the dream) Fidler went out and found the boy exactly where his wife's dream had indicated. Billy Service was found alive and well, 8 miles from his home, living in a badger's den. He had survived on swamp water and strawberries. His clothes were torn and he suffered a number of scratches from the badgers that lived there. The story goes on about his intrusion into the badger's home and how eventually they shared the space, which was in fact an abandoned wolf den, large enough for both. Here we have another story of a missing child that was located with the aid of a dream. The story told by Fidler even has some resemblance to the journal of Harry Hawes. Like Hawes, Fidler was "guided" to the location and while there he witnessed bird activity that made him curious and would eventually lead him in the direction of the den. While he paused and debated his next move, he boiled his tea.

What are we to make of these odd dreams and hunches that lead searchers to lost loved ones? Why Manitoba? It is likely that there are other stories like these that may have been overlooked.

We have to seriously start to question if there is some supernatural element involved in some of these missing persons cases. Whether they are responsible for the disappearance or only possess knowledge of it we cannot definitively say, but I think going forward I will keep an open mind about the matter since after so much time has passed, we still don't have the answers.

Appendix C

Poem for Geraldine Huggan

As a final farewell and tribute, I wanted to include a poem written by Franklin Johnson, an Icelandic poet who lived on a farm in Arborg, Manitoba. In the Icelandic newspaper it was printed, Johnson describes that he, "felt compelled to try to describe the beginning and eventual ending of this terrible ordeal as I saw it in my mind's eye." So, after a very long winded and thorough exam, I will end the saga of Geraldine here, with a poem I wish I had written.

> Lured by the lilting strains of nature
> Lightly skipped in tune to the breeze
> Here some mammoths of mystic stature
> Mingling with the smaller trees.
> Here perhaps some fragrant flowers
> Forth emerging after showers
> Or perhaps a flutt'ring fledgling
> From his nest so gently edging.
>
> But the joys she found were fleeting
> As forth the time of day had sped
> Now she heard life's heartless greeting
> From her the joys of life are fled
> The bitter pangs of burning hunger
> Brought despair and agony wrung her
> Relentless realistic terror
> Wrought by one small childish error.
>
> Lost and lonely through the forest
> Long she wandered day to day
> Drank the cup and drained the sorest
> Dregs that any human may.
> Cold and clammy nights of weeping
> Cramped her body ee'n in sleeping
> Ah' little heap of huddled sorrow
> Hath the dawn a brighter morrow?
>
> Will the dawning's dimpled scions
> Dim the years with brighter clime?
> Years for her though only ions
> On the faded sands of time

Tim Marczenko

Oh lost and forlorn little child
Locked within the clutching wild
For you there no brighter dawn
While breath and life would carry on.

Here she spied a sprawling out clearing
Spread beneath the summer skies
Her lagging feet at last were nearing
The land where sweet oblivion lies
Myriad mists of the wild surround her
Mirages on the lakes astound her
Warping thoughts in wivern fears
Her withered cheeks now streaked with tears.

Plodding in tragedy's wanton wake
Worn and tattered bruised and sore
On the shore by Long named Lake
She lay to rest forever more
None to hear her plaintive pleading
Passive cries for help entreating
Cold and stolid stoic violence
Stifled all her cries in silence.

Merciful lotus-like lethargy
Limpidly creeping oe'r her mind
Lullabies winging from tree to tree
Her tragedies, all are left behind
And her little life has fluttered
Long before she could have uttered
Thoughts - akin to human harshness
Forever hibernate in darkness.

Fluttered from this world of sorrow
Far into the bright unknown
Where ne'er is seen a misty morrow
Where meek and kindly thoughts are sown.

Into the fragrant fertile lands
The future smiles on distant strands
Where endless love and hope abide
Unhampered by the darkest night.
(Johnson, 1994)

Gone Cold

Endnotes

[1] RCMP, Updated March 16, 2018. Accessed January 22, 2021, https://www.rcmp-grc.gc.ca/en/questions-and-answers.
[2] Public Safety and Emergency Preparedness Canada, "DNA Missing Persons Index (MPI), A Public Consultation Paper" (March 2005). www.psepc-sppcc.gc.ca/publications/Policing/mpi/index.
[3] NCMPUR interview, personal correspondence with author, December 18, 2020.
[4] OPP interview, personal correspondence with author, July 20, 2020.
[5] Tim Marczenko, *Disembodied Voices: True Accounts of Hidden Beings* (Pennsylvania: Schiffer Publishing, 2020).
[6] Chris Oke, "What the dog smelled: The science and mystery of cadaver dogs," CBC News, July 23, 2016. https://www.cbc.ca/news/science/cadaver-dogs-science-training-1.3654993.
[7] Kim Cooper, OVSARDA interview, personal correspondence, November 3, 2021.
[8] Glavaš, V., Pintar, A., "Human Remains Detection Dogs as a New Prospecting Method in Archaeology," *J Archaeol Method Theory* 26 (2019): 1106–1124. https://doi.org/10.1007/s10816-018-9406-y.
[9] William D. Haglund and Marcella H. Sorg, *Forensic Taphonomy: The Postmortem Fate of Human Remains* (CRC Press LLC, 1997).
[10] OPP interview, personal correspondence with author, July 20, 2020.
[11] OPP interview, personal correspondence with author, July 20, 2020.
[12] *Freedom of Information and Protection of Privacy Act*, R.S.O. 1990, c. F.3..
[13] Ibid.
[14] Dr. John B. Alexander, *UFOs Myths, Conspiracies, And Realities* (New York: St. Martin's Press, 2011).
[15] Dr. Melina Buckley," Policies and Practices in the Investigation of Missing Persons and Suspected Multiple Homicides," A Policy Discussion Report Prepared for the Missing Women Commission of Inquiry, March 2012.
[16] *Best Practices*, NCMPUR, v. 2.0, s. 4.7.9, June 14, 2017.
[17] Alberta, *Missing Persons Act*, 2011, c. M-18.5 (2)(a-j).
[18] *An Act to amend The Missing Persons and Presumption of Death Act* (Bill No. 106), 2017, (2)(a-j). https://publications.saskatchewan.ca/#/products/89001.
[19] Manitoba, *Missing Persons Act*, 2012, 4(2)(a-j). https://web2.gov.mb.ca/bills/40-1/b004e.php#Explanatory%20Note.
[20] British Columbia, *Missing Persons Act* (SBC 2014) c. 2., 9 (a-n). http://www.bclaws.ca/civix/document/id/complete/statreg/14002_01.
[21] Canada, *Missing Persons Act*, 2018, S.O. 2018, c. 3, , 1–9. https://www.ontario.ca/laws/statute/18m03.
[22] "New Missing Person act gives Ontario police more power to investigate," CBC News, June 6, 2019. https://bit.ly/3nKUp2K.
[23] NCMPUR, 7.
[24] Buckley, 8.
[25] NCMPUR, 7.
[26] Maryanne Pearce, "An Awkward Silence: Missing and Murdered Vulnerable Women and The Canadian Justice System," 2013.

[27] "Pickton revelations," CBC News, August 5, 2010, video. https://www.cbc.ca/news/canada/pickton-revelations-1.1783995.
[28] "Amanda Sophia Bartlett," Missing & Murdered: The Unsolved Cases of Indigenous Women & Girls, CBC News. https://www.cbc.ca/missingandmurdered/mmiw/profiles/amanda-sophia-bartlett.
[29] Robert Cribb, "Child abduction and murder data paint chilling new portrait," *Toronto Star* (Toronto, ON), May 25, 2016. https://www.thestar.com/news/world/2016/05/25/child-abduction-and-murder-data-paint-chilling-new-portrait.html; Bruce A. Arrigo, *The SAGE Encyclopedia of Surveillance, Security, and Privacy* (New York: SAGE Publications, 2016).
[30] NCMPUR, 12.
[31] Greenwood, Peter W. and Joan R. Petersilia, *The Criminal Investigation Process: Volume I: Summary and Policy Implications* (Santa Monica, CA: RAND Corporation, 1975). https://www.rand.org/pubs/reports/R1776.html.
[32] Greenwood and Petersilia, 14
[33] Curtis Rush, Stephanie Findlay and Liam Casey. "Suitcase murder: Dad, stepmom charged in 1994 slaying of 17-year-old Toronto girl," *Toronto Star* (Toronto, ON), March 21, 2012. https://www.thestar.com/news/crime/2012/03/21/suitcase_murder_dad_stepmom_charged_in_1994_slaying_of_17yearold_toronto_girl.html.
[34] NCMPUR, 27.
[35] *Best Practices*, NCMPUR, v. 2.0, s. 3.5.9, Jun. 14, 2017.
[36] Wilson, B.C. Geology of the Lingman Lake area, District of Kenora, Patricia portion (1987); Ontario Geological Survey, Report 244, 42.
[37] Albert E. Allin, M.D., Regional Laboratory report, November 9, 1960.
[38] W.J. Hayes, Ontario Provincial Police Report, November 10, 1960.
[39] *Report of The Honourable Mr. Justice Wilfred D. Roach As A Commissioner Appointed Under the Public Inquires Act. Royal Commission on Crime in Ontario* (Toronto, 1963).
[40] Stephen Schneider, *ICED: The Story of Organized Crime in Canada* (Toronto: John Wiley & Sons, Ltd., 2009).
[41] Canada. *Official Report of Debates* (Hansard) Legislative Assembly of Ontario, 1961–62.https://archive.org/stream/v1hansard196162ontauoft/v1hansard196162ontauoftdjvu.txt.
[42] Thomas R. Hart, Provincial Geologist, Technical Report on the Marshall Lake Property, June 7, 2016
[43] E.G. Pye, Mineral Deposits of the Big Duck Lake Area District of Thunder Bay (1961); Ontario Geological Survey, Department of Mines, p. 78.
[44] *Best Practices*, NCMPUR, v. 2.0, s. 4.7.9, June 6, 2017.
[45] Ibid.
[46] *Sander Lingman v. J. & H. Koski*, Appeal from Decision of Mining Recorder, K.K – Letters, Archives of Ontario, RG 1-321, September 15, 1955.
[47] "Fruitless search for little girl," *The Brandon Daily Sun* (Winnipeg, MB), July 9, 1953.
[48] "Footprints found," *The Winnipeg Tribune* (Winnipeg, MB), July 13, 1953.
[49] "Tangled underbrush forces search party to go slowly," *Winnipeg Free Press* (Winnipeg, MB), July 9, 1953.

[50] "Posse scours Ontario bush for city child lost 3 days," *Winnipeg Free Press* (Winnipeg, MB), July 7, 1953.
[51] "Fruitless search for missing girl in stifling swamp land," *The Brandon Daily Sun* (Winnipeg, MB), July 11, 1953.
[52] "Indians read child's fate from clothing, hair found," *Winnipeg Free Press* (Winnipeg, MB), July 16, 1953.
[53] "Child Hunt," *The Winnipeg Tribune* (Winnipeg, MB), July 15, 1953.
[54] "Little girl devoured by wild animal," *The Lethbridge Herald* (Lethbridge, AB), July 16, 1953.
[55] "Tragedy," *The Winnipeg Tribune* (Winnipeg, MB), July 16, 1953.
[56] Deb Cantrell, personal correspondence with author, June 15, 2020.
[57] Debbie Huggan, personal correspondence with author, October 10, 2019.
[58] Correspondence with Winnipeg Police Service, September 11, 2019. Response taken from the author's FOIA request.
[59] In Memoriams, *The Winnipeg Tribune* (Winnipeg, MB), July 10, 1954.
[60] "Woman, 54, on second bush hunt," *Winnipeg Free Press* (Winnipeg, MB), July 9, 1953.
[61] Patricia Gendreau, personal correspondence with author, July 2020.
[62] "Still No Trace of Lost Hunters Near Chapleau," *Sudbury Star* (Sudbury, ON), November 6, 1959.
[63] William E. McLeod, *The Chapleau Game Preserve: History, Murder, and Other Tales* (North Bay, ON: Beatty Printing, 2004).
[64] W. McLeod, 171.
[65] Bob King, *OPP Day Journal B438802* (1960)
[66] B. King, (1960)
[67] Her Majesty the Queen v. Sidney Arthur Appleyard [1988] S. 218 (1) (2)
[68] Jo-Anne Appleyard, personal correspondence with author, April 28, 2021.
[69] Gary Alexander, personal correspondence with author, January 12, 2022.
[70] Newstead family, personal correspondence with author, April 27, 2021.
[71] "Dr. Charles Smith: The man behind the public inquiry," *CBC News*, December 8, 2009. https://www.cbc.ca/news/canada/dr-charles-smith-the-man-behind-the-public-inquiry-1.864004
[72] Inquiry into pediatric forensic pathology in Ontario. In the matter of the Public Inquiries Act, R.S.O. 1990, c. P. 41. Closing argument of Dr. Charles Smith https://www.attorneygeneral.jus.gov.on.ca/inquiries/goudge/submissions/pdf/Submission_Dr.Charles_Smith.pdf
[73] "Emsdale area man charged with murder," *The Huntsville Forester* (Huntsville, ON), September 14, 1988.
[74] "Jury acquits man of murder," *Parry Sound Beacon Star* (Parry Sound, ON), May 29, 1990.
[75] Ibid.
[76] *Her Majesty The Queen against Sidney Arthur Appleyard*, December 2, 1988.
[77] "Locate Body Of Missing Man," *Huntsville Forester* (Huntsville, ON), November 1, 1962.
[78] "Autopsy to be done on body of Ajax man," *Toronto Star* (Toronto, ON), September 12, 1988.

[79] "Seek Identity Of Body Found In Lake," *The Porcupine Advance* (Timmins, ON), May 4, 1939.
[80] Roland Cilliers, "COLD CASE: A dead man on an Algonquin trail," *Huntsville Forester* (Huntsville, ON), September 10, 2017. https://www.muskokaregion.com/news-story/7520680-cold-case-a-dead-man-on-an-algonquin-trail/.
[81] Lauren Pelley, "Do you know this man? OPP hope forensic art will crack decades-old case," *CBC News* (Toronto, ON), July 26, 2017. https://www.cbc.ca/news/canada/toronto/opp-forensics-1.4222770
[82] "RCMP seeks public's help in identifying reconstructed faces," RCMP News Release, (Ottawa, Ontario), Jan. 13, 2020. http://www.rcmp-grc.gc.ca/en/news/2020/rcmp-seeks-publics-help-identifying-reconstructed-faces.
[83] Poland, Travis, "RCMP teams up with art school to identify human remains," January 31, 2020. www.rcmp-grc.gc.ca/en/gazette/rcmp-teams-art-school-identify-human-remains?fe&fe.
[84] *Best Practices*, NCMPUR, v. 2.0, s. 3.6.10, June 14, 2017.
[85] Ibid., s. 3.8.4.
[86] Ibid., s. 4.6.8.
[87] Pearce, Maryanne, "An Awkward Silence: Missing and Murdered Vulnerable Women and The Canadian Justice System," 2013.
[88] Patricia Kozicka, "Mother of missing man on crusade for national DNA data bank," Global News, Posted Mar. 1, 2012. https://globalnews.ca/news/218080/mother-of-missing-man-on-crusade-for-national-dna-bank/.
[89] Pearce, 578.
[90] Melissa Gilligan, "Man found dead in Calgary the first to be identified using National Missing Persons DNA Program," Global News, November 26, 2019. https://www.msn.com/en-ca/news/canada/man-found-dead-in-calgary-the-first-to-be-identified-using-national-missing-persons-dna-program/ar-BBXmzS6?ocid=sf&fbclid=IwAR3mbn8-W0g6nGEnD93K-hZmN_d30TfDbCB5ieiZNzs4_4pdIfpHntAYOdE.
[91] NCMPUR, 6.
[92] Office of the Chief Coroner interview, personal correspondence with author, April 12, 2022.
[93] Paglinawan, Denise, "RCMP unveil 15 reconstructed faces from decades old remains and seek public's help in identifying deceased," January 15, 2020. https://nationalpost.com/news/canada/rcmp-unveil-15-reconstructed-faces-from-decades-old-remains-and-seek-publics-help-in-identifying-deceased.
[94] Brian Kelly, "Surreal flooding cuts off Wawa, Ont," *Toronto Sun* (Toronto, ON). October 26, 2012.
[95] Terasmae, J., "Muskeg," *The Canadian Encyclopedia. Historica Canada*, Posted February 7, 2006. https://www.thecanadianencyclopedia.ca/en/article/muskeg.
[96] John Virtue, *The Black Soldiers Who Built the Alaska Highway: A History of Four U.S. Army Regiments in the North, 1942–1943* (North Carolina: McFarland & Company, Inc, 2012).
[97] Louise Hall Tharpe, *Company of Adventurers* (Boston: Little, Brown and Company, 1946)

[98] Henry Wadsworth Longfellow, *The Song of Hiawatha*. (Boston: Ticknor and Fields, 1855).
[99] "Many Walk Off Edge: His World Is Plate-Shaped," *The Globe and Mail* (Toronto, ON), June 6, 1960.
[100] Richard Winer, *The Devil's Triangle* (New York, NY: Banton Books, Inc. 1974).
[101] Henry Ward Beecher, *The Christian Union*, vol. 33., (New York: J.B. Ford & Company, 1886).
[102] Richard Schwartzberg, "Portholes Through Time and Space," *Beyond Reality*, August 1979.
[103] Charles Fort, *The Book of the Damned: The Collected Works of Charles Fort* (New York: TarcherPerigee, 2008).
[104] Ibid.
[105] Ibid.
[106] John Keel, *Operation Trojan Horse*.
[107] C. Fort, 915.
[108] C. Fort, 900
[109] C. Fort, 90.
[110] William E. McLeod, *The Chapleau Game Preserve: History, Murder, and Other Tales* (North Bay, ON: Beatty Printing, 2004).
[111] Martin Rice, Ann Henderson-Sellers, *The Future of the World's Climate*, 2nd ed. (Elsevier, 2012).
[112] Haydn Watters, "Hundreds of thousands of Ontario's islands, lakes, beaches don't have names. Here's why," CBC News (Sudbury, ON), December 4, 2020.
[113] Author appeal, personal correspondence Legal Services Branch, 2022.
[114] Jay Robert Nash, *Among The Missing* (New York: Simon and Schuster, 1978).
[115] "*Lost Students Emerge Safely*," *Sudbury Star* (Sudbury, ON), September 16, 1977.
[116] Author appeal, personal correspondence Legal Services Branch, 2022
[117] District Communications Supervisor memorandum to Detachment Commanders, September 8, 1986.
[118] Detachment Commander of Nakina OPP, memo to the superintendent #16 District Headquarters, September 17, 1986.
[119] "Survival of Child, Missing five days, Modern Miracle," *The Winnipeg Evening Tribune* (Winnipeg, MB), August 13, 1934.
[120] "Dreams Solves Mystery Tragedy," *Winnipeg Free Press* (Winnipeg, MB), May 12, 1934.

Bibliography

Alexander, Dr. John B. *UFOs Myths, Conspiracies, And Realities*. New York: St. Martin's Press, 2011.

Beecher, Henry Ward. *The Christian Union*, vol. 33. New York: *J.B. Ford & Company*, 1886.

Best Practices. NCMPUR. v. 2.0, s. 3.2.5. June 14, 2017.

Buckley, Dr. Melina. *Policies and Practices in the Investigation of Missing Persons and Suspected Multiple Homicides: A Policy Discussion Report Prepared for the Missing Women Commission of Inquiry* (March 2012).

Fort, Charles. *The Book of the Damned: The Collected Works of Charles Fort*. New York: TarcherPerigee, May 01, 2008.

Freedom of Information and Protection of Privacy Act. R.S.O. 1990, c. F.3. Consolidation Period: January 1, 2016 to the e-Laws currency date. Last amendment: 2015, c. 20, Sched. 13.

Glavaš, Vedrana and Andrea Pintar. "Human Remains Detection Dogs as a New Prospecting Method in Archaeology." *J Archaeol Method Theory* 26 (2019): 1106–1124. https://doi.org/10.1007/s10816-018-9406-y.

Government of Canada. "DNA Missing Persons Index (MPI), A Public Consultation Paper." Public Safety and Emergency Preparedness Canada. March 2005. www.psepc-sppcc.gc.ca/publications/Policing/mpi/index.data.

Greenwood, Peter W. and Joan R. Petersilia. *The Criminal Investigation Process: Volume I: Summary and Policy Implications*. Santa Monica, CA: RAND Corporation, 1975. https://www.rand.org/pubs/reports/R1776.html.

Haglund, William D. and Marcella H. Sorg. *Forensic Taphonomy: The Postmortem Fate of Human Remains*. CRC Press LLC, 1997.

Johnson, Franklin. "Geraldine Huggan." Winnipeg, MB: *Lögberg-Heimskringla*, June 3, 1994.

Keel, John. *Operation Trojan Horse*. United Kingdom: Abacus, 1970.

Kelly, Brian. "Surreal flooding cuts off Wawa, Ont." *Toronto Sun* (Toronto, ON), October 26, 2012.

Marczenko, Tim. *Disembodied Voices: True Accounts of Hidden Beings*. Pennsylvania: Schiffer Publishing, 2020.

McLeod, William E. *The Chapleau Game Preserve: History, Murder, and Other Tales.* North Bay, ON: Beatty Printing, 2004.

RCMP. "Missing Persons. National Missing Persons DNA Program." https://www.rcmp-grc.gc.ca/en/questions-and-answers.

Rice, Martin and Ann Henderson-Sellers. *The Future of the World's Climate*, 2nd ed. Amsterdam: Elsevier, 2012.

Roach, Wilfred D. *Report of The Honourable Mr. Justice Wilfred D. Roach As A Commissioner Appointed Under the Public Inquires Act.* Toronto, ON: Royal Commission on Crime, 1963.

Nash, Robert Jay. *Among The Missing.* New York: Simon and Schuster, 1978.

Oke, Chris. "What the dog smelled: The science and mystery of cadaver dogs." *CBC News*, July 23, 2016. https://www.cbc.ca/news/science/cadaver-dogs-science-training-1.3654993.

"Pentagon's UFO Program / Encounters & Research." Interview by George Knapp. Coast to Coast AM, Premier Radio Network, May 26, 2019.

Schneider, Stephen. *ICED: The Story of Organized Crime in Canada.* Toronto: John Wiley & Sons, Ltd., 2009.

Terasmae, J., "Muskeg." In *The Canadian Encyclopedia Historica Canada.* February 7, 2006. https://www.thecanadianencyclopedia.ca/en/article/muskeg.

Virtue, John. *The Black Soldiers Who Built the Alaska Highway: A History of Four U.S. Army Regiments in the North, 1942–1943.* North Carolina: McFarland & Company, Inc, Nov. 27, 2012.

Watters, Haydn. "Hundreds of thousands of Ontario's islands, lakes, beaches don't have names. Here's why." *CBC News* (Sudbury, ON), Dec 4, 2020.

Winer, Richard. *The Devil's Triangle.* New York, NY: Banton Books, Inc., 1974.

"Lost Students Emerge Safely." *Sudbury Star* (Sudbury, ON), September 16, 1977.

"Many Walk Off Edge: His World Is Plate-Shaped." *The Globe and Mail* (Toronto, ON), June 6, 1960.

"New Missing Person act gives Ontario police more power to investigate." *CBC News*, June 6, 2019. https://www.cbc.ca/news/canada/kitchener-waterloo/ontario-missing-persons-act-maureen-trask-

1.5164532?__vfz=medium%3Dsharebar&fbclid=IwAR0qPv3A9GLxXthynXfSMi9zz3L0bidY4HWrnBn450zoYYXFfhfZdXRwC4

Thank you for supporting writers.
If you enjoyed this book, please leave a review.

Printed in Great Britain
by Amazon